Wall Street People

Volume 2

True Stories of the Great Barons of Finance

Charles D. Ellis

with

James R. Vertin

JOHN WILEY & SONS, INC.

Published by John Wiley & Sons, Inc., Hoboken, New Jersey.
Published simultaneously in Canada.

For general information on our other products and services, or technical support, please contact our Customer Care Department within the United States at 800-762-2974, outside the United States at 317-572-3993 or fax 317-572-4002.

Wiley also publishes its books in a variety of electronic formats. Some content that appears in print may not be available in electronic books.

For more information about Wiley products, visit our web site at www.wiley.com.

ISBN 0-471-27428-3

Printed in the United States of America.
10 9 8 7 6 5 4 3 2 1

Introduction

ADAM SMITH

What is the fascination of financial markets? They concentrate an enormous pool of natural talent in a small area, whether the area is taken geographically or by computer. The talent is attracted because the rewards are so magnificently and irrationally outsized. Markets have elements of a game—rules, beginnings, endings, the score is kept by numbers. While numbers can be translated into cash, they are deceptive, because numbers suggest science, reason, rationality, precision. That is illusory. For all the quantitative and academic studies done—and they must number now in the tens of thousands—certainty eludes us. It is always just over the horizon, no matter how we move toward it. The most computer-skilled experts have come to the most cataclysmic of ends.

Markets represent not only economic and business fundamentals but also complex human emotions. Some writers have suggested that markets are organic entities, with growth and decay embedded in their DNA. It is perhaps no accident that recently, for the first time, a Nobel prize in economics went to a psychologist, Daniel Kahneman, who calculated how much people fear to lose against what they hope to gain. Leverage is a word used in markets; the leverage of the crowd nature of markets is television, through which tens of millions of people can watch the players. Markets have giddy feelings and sweet moments; they also have passages of thunder, tragedy, and grief. You could say they are the opera of business.

Here, in this book, are some of the players on this stage. There is a dashing figure of the Italian Renaissance, there are nineteenth-century robber barons, an American president, railroad builders, swindlers of heroic proportions, and statesmen.

We start with Warren Buffett, who began as a simple down-home investor working from his bedroom, and who has become an icon, very much with us, and quoted in the media all the time. He is not the leadoff hitter in our batting order merely because he made billions through investing. (Buffett loves baseball metaphors.) He is here because, like Babe Ruth pointing his bat at the center field bleachers, he told us what he was going to do a generation ago and did exactly that. His gift for metaphor makes his wisdom comprehensible to multitudes of Americans. His folksy, Will Rogers persona has become very much part of the American scene and by consistently repeating his commonsense, middle American approach, he taught us to remember, through both manias and depressions, who we really are.

• • •

Who's Warren Buffett?

ADAM SMITH

The handwritten letter was from "La Champouse." 42 Avenue de Marseille, Aix-en-Provence. Benjamin Graham was living in the South of France, retired, with his lady friend, and translating Greek and Latin classics. That was a favorite avocation. The prescript of *Security Analysis*, the forbidding black bible of security analysts, is from Horace: *many shall be restored that are now fallen and many shall fall that are now in honor.*

I hadn't known him, but I had written some sentences about him in *The Money Game*. Graham, I had written, "was the dean of our profession, if security analysis can be said to be a profession. The reason that Graham is the undisputed dean is that before him there was no profession and after him they began to call it that."

Graham liked being called the Dean. He corrected a sentence in my book in Greek that no one had checked, and one or two other references. He said he had something in mind to discuss, when he came to New York.

Shortly after, he did appear in New York, to see a publisher about his translation of Aeschylus and to see his grandchildren. I asked him what he thought of the market. *Hoc etiam transbit*, he said, "this too shall pass."

Graham said he wanted me to work on the next edition of *The Intelligent Investor*, the popular version of his textbook. "There are only two people I would ask to do this," he said. "You are one, and Warren Buffett is the other."

"Who's Warren Buffett?" I asked. A natural question. This was 1970, and Warren Buffett wasn't known outside of Omaha, Nebraska, or Ben Graham's circle of friends.

Today, Warren is so well known that when newspapers mention him they sometimes need no phrase in apposition to identify him, or if they do, they say simply, "the investor." There are full-length biographies of Buffett on the shelves. He is indeed "the investor," one of the best in history. Investing has made him the second richest person in the country, behind his bridge buddy Bill Gates.

Even in 1970, Warren had an outstanding investment record with an unfashionable technique. He started an investment partnership in 1956 with $105,000 from friends and relatives. When he terminated that partnership in 1969, it had $105 million and had compounded at 31 percent. Warren's performance fee meant he was worth about $25 million. He ended the partnership because he said he couldn't understand the stock market anymore.

I was not the right author to work on the next edition of *The Intelligent Investor*. I was an acolyte of Sam Stedman (not the mutual fund nor the bridge conventions) by way of Phil Fisher. Stedman's investment philosophy, loosely called "growth," said you should find a couple of rapidly growing companies whose growth rates were secure. The companies would have a competitive advantage because of their patent protection or impregnable market positions; they would have three years of earning visibility; and you would buy them at less than their growth rates, because their prices would seem high compared to the average stock and they paid no dividends.

The machine that addicted us to growth investing was the Xerox 914. It was the first machine to copy plain paper, and I can remember writing that some day people would use the word "Xerox" as a verb. That seemed radical at the time. Xerox was a ten-bagger, and, once you have a ten-bagger, everything else seemed tame. The Xerox crowd even got to play the game again, with Rank Xerox in the United Kingdom and Fuji Xerox in Japan.

We all went to Dunhill on 57th Street and had suits tailored where the four buttons on the sleeves had real buttonholes. We did not think much about Ben Graham. Charming as he was, he had written, in 1949, that he could not buy IBM because its price precluded the "margin of safety which we consider essential to a true investment."

At Graham's urging, I had several conversations with Warren, and then I flew to Omaha to meet him, even though I still didn't think I was right for the job. We had a steak dinner. We had a bacon, eggs, and potatoes breakfast. We got along famously. Warren was, and is, cheerful and funny. He has a gift of metaphor that is irresistible. And, as everybody now knows, he is very smart.

Warren didn't look like the Xerox crowd. While he wore a suit and a tie, his wrists emerged from the sleeves, revealing an indifference to tailoring. (Today, as our senior financial statesman, he is dressed impeccably, but without, I suspect, intense interest in the process.) To a member of the Xerox crowd then, he looked like he had fallen off the turnip truck.

I went to Warren's house on Farnam Street, which he had bought for $31,500 in 1958. It was a rambling, comfortable house. He had added a racquetball court to it.

How, I wanted to know, could he operate from Omaha? In New York, the portfolio managers were all trading stories at breakfast, lunch, and dinner.

"Omaha gives me perspective," Warren said. He showed me a write-up from a Wall Street firm that said, "securities must be studied on a minute-by-minute program."

"Wow!" Warren said. "This sort of stuff makes me feel guilty when I go out for a Pepsi."

I couldn't interest Warren in the truffle hunt for the next Xerox. Our growth crowd was sniffing everywhere, talking to vendors, customers, competitors, the Phil Fisher geometry. Not that Warren didn't do research his own way.

For example, Warren noticed that the bonds of the Indiana Turnpike were selling in the 70s, while the nearly identical bonds of the Illinois

Turnpike sold in the 90s. The casual word among the bond crowd was that the maintenance allowance wasn't high enough behind the Indiana bonds.

Warren got into his car and drove the length of the Indiana Turnpike. Then he went to Indianapolis and turned the pages of the maintenance reports of the highway department. He thought the Indiana Turnpike didn't need that much work, and bought the bonds. This closed the gap with the bonds of the Illinois Turnpike. Not exactly the next Xerox.

Warren showed me the principles he had written on a lined, yellow legal pad and framed: (a) our investments will be chosen on the basis of value, not popularity; (b) our investments will attempt to reduce the risk of permanent capital loss (not short-term quotation loss) to a minimum; (c) my wife, children, and I will have virtually our entire net worth in the partnership.

Warren had ended his partnership, so I couldn't have bought into it anyway. The partnership had bought shares in an old New England textile company, Berkshire Hathaway, and that stock was traded in the "pink sheets." I looked up Berkshire. It seemed to be a failing New England textile company.

"Berkshire is hardly going to be as profitable as Xerox in a hypertense market," Warren wrote to his investors, "but it is a very comfortable thing to own. We will not go into a business where technology which is way over my head is crucial to the decision." Berkshire's attraction was that it had $18 in net working capital, and Buffett's investors had paid $13.

I didn't buy Berkshire Hathaway. At the end of my stay, I said I didn't want to work on Ben Graham's book. Warren said he didn't either. We wrote a note to Ben saying his book didn't really need any improvements.

The little story about Ben and Warren went into my book *Supermoney*. Random House gave a party to launch the book. Warren came to the party and had a good time. We have the pictures. My hair is embarrassingly long, and Warren's haircut looks, well, mid-American. We kept in touch.

"Who's Warren Buffett?" the people at the Washington Post Company asked when Warren bought a stake. They ordered 50 copies of *Supermoney*.

I tried the Washington Post idea on my Wall Street friends. They couldn't see it.

"Big city newspapers are dead," they said. "The trucks can't get through the streets. Labor problems are terrible. People get their news from television." And anyway, it wasn't the next Xerox.

In 1976, Rupert Murdoch's News Corp. launched an unfriendly takeover of The New York Magazine Company. I had been one of its founders, with 5-cent stock. We had spent eight years building a unique property. We not only had *New York Magazine*, but also the *Village Voice* and a California magazine called *New West*. Now Murdoch had bought 50.1 percent of the stock.

I called up Warren and whined.

"You want it back?" he asked.

I got very attentive. He sent me News Corp.'s annual report. It was full of British and Australian accounting terminology. I didn't get it.

"News Corp. has a market cap of only $50 million," Warren said. "For $27 million, you could have two big newspapers in Australia, 73 weekly newspapers in Britain, two televisions stations, 20 percent of Ansett Airlines, and you'd have your magazine back."

"How do we do it?" I asked.

"What is this *we*, kemosabe?" Warren said, using a term from our radio days with "The Lone Ranger." "You want your magazine back, I'm telling you how to do it."

"But Murdoch controls News Corp." I said.

"You didn't read carefully," Warren said. "Look at footnote 14. Clarendon has 40 percent. The rest is Australian institutions. Clarendon is Murdoch and his four sisters. I figure it would take one sister and the float and a year in Australia, and guess which one of us is going to spend the year in Australia?"

I didn't go, and we didn't get the property back either. I should have bought News Corp. Murdoch sold our magazines for many times what he had paid in the raid.

When we launched the weekly Adam Smith television show, we took it to Omaha right away. It was the first television Warren had done, and for a long time, the only television. It didn't take much to get Warren to use his baseball metaphors.

"When I look at the managers who run my companies, I feel like Miller Huggins looking at his lineup of the 1927 Yankees." (Those were the Yankees, of course, with Babe Ruth and Lou Gehrig.)

Or this one: "In the stock market, it's as if you are the batter and the market is the pitcher. The market has to keep pitching, but in this game there are no called strikes. The market can throw you a hundred different pitches every day, but you don't have to swing until you get a fat pitch."

"So, you might not swing for six months?"

"You might not swing for two years. That's the beauty of Berkshire not being on Wall Street—nobody's at the fence behind me calling out: 'Swing, you bum!'"

Warren continued this theme in our subsequent television interviews.

"You have said: 'They could close the New York Stock Exchange for two years, and I wouldn't care.' But you are considered an investment guru. So how do you reconcile this?"

"Whether the New York Stock Exchange is open or not has nothing to do with whether the *Washington Post* is getting more valuable. The New York Stock Exchange is closed on weekends and I don't break out in hives. When I look at a company, the last thing I look at is the price. You don't ask what your house is worth three times a day, do you? Every stock is a business. You have to ask, what is its value as a business?"

Warren once sent me the collected annual reports of National Mutual Life Assurance, when Lord Keynes was the chairman of that company in Britain. "This guy knows how to write a chairman's report," Warren scribbled.

Warren's own chairman's letters for Berkshire Hathaway became even more famous than those of Keynes. They were teaching instruments. They carefully spelled out not only the businesses, but also the accounting procedures, and a very plain vanilla evaluation of the scene.

The annual meeting of Berkshire in Omaha draws more than ten thousand people, and Buffett and his vice chairman Charlie Munger answer questions for hours, questions on all sorts of subjects. It is a unique seminar. This year, Warren told me, attendance will hit a new record, up perhaps 205 percent from the previous peak. No matter whether Berkshire has had a really good year or not, when you leave Omaha after this Woodstock of capitalism, you feel more light hearted.

During the dot-com bubble, Buffett kept his cool. He said that if he were teaching an investment course, he would ask: "How do you value a dot-com?" If the student answered anything at all, Buffett said: "He would get an F."

Warren has never wavered either from the warm and folksy persona or from his sound, shirtsleeves wisdom. He is a powerful intellect, but he is also *bien dans sa peau*—"comfortable in his skin"—which mobilizes him and helps to keep him from second-guessing his perceptions.

Corporate and institutional icons have fallen and others are under suspicion. "Growth" companies that once were accorded reverence are now said to "smooth" their earnings. A prominent accounting firm whose name was an imprimatur has lost its credibility. Many have fallen that had been in honor, as Horace wrote.

But Buffett is still Buffett: still in the same house on Farnam and still in the same office in Kiewit Plaza as when I first went to discuss the Ben Graham project. Warren was counted on by the government to right the wrongs at Salomon. He takes to print pieces in the Op Ed pages of the *Washington Post* on important issues. Recently, his chairman's letter found him in high moral dudgeon. "Charlie and I," he wrote referring to his vice chairman, Charles Munger, "are disgusted by the situation so common in the last few years, in which shareholders have suffered billions in losses while the CEOs, promoters, and other higher-ups who fathered these disasters have walked away with extraordinary wealth . . . to their shame, these business leaders view shareholders as patsies, not partners."

"Who's Warren Buffett?" He's more than "the investor." The five-hour seminars at the annual meetings, the flow of common sense on the issues, his willingness to act on his convictions, have made him one of our great national teachers, articulating and exemplifying what we used to take for granted in America: the voice within each of us that knows right . . . if only we listen.

Contents

(By Order of Appearance)

Contents

(In Alphabetical Order)

CONTENTS

WALL STREET PERSONALITIES

August S. Belmont

GREGORY HUNTER

August Schöenberg Belmont was a protégé of the Rothschilds, who
trained him in his native Germany. On coming to America in 1837,
he represented their U.S. interests, developed his own successful firm
in Wall Street, and was a social leader in New York City. He was also
the *de facto* head of the Democratic Party from 1860 to 1884, served
as a U.S. diplomat abroad, and played a key role in blocking both European recognition and financing for the Confederacy during our
Civil War. Racing's Belmont Stakes are a memorial to his interest in
breeding fast horses.

Belmont was born on December 8, 1813, in the village of Alzey in the
Rhenish Palatinate region of Germany. His father, Simon Belmont, was a
community leader who served as president of the local synagogue for many
years. . . .

Tragedy came early to young Belmont's life. His mother died when he
was seven, followed one month later by the death of his brother. Less than
a year later, Belmont went to Frankfurt, 40 miles to the north, to live with
his grandmother, Gertrude, and her husband, Hajun Hanau, who had connections with the Rothschilds.

In Frankfurt, Belmont attended a Jewish school. . . . In 1828, his father
had to remove him because the tuition payments had fallen so far in arrears.

After he left school, Belmont's relatives convinced their Frankfurt
friends, the Rothschilds, to train the boy for a business career. His association with the Rothschilds thus began in 1828, when he was fifteen. . . .
The Rothschilds first made Belmont an apprentice at their Frankfurt
branch. Clearly learning the business from the bottom up, he began by
sweeping floors, polishing furniture, and running errands. Young Belmont
was neat and punctual; he worked industriously at whatever tasks the
Rothschilds gave him. He also showed drive and initiative, rising daily at
five o'clock to have a private tutor instruct him in French, English, com-
position, and arithmetic.

The Rothschilds recognized Belmont's talents and hard work and, after
a few years, advanced him through the ranks. In 1832, they gave Belmont
a confidential clerkship and in 1834 made him secretary and traveling

From *The Encyclopedia of American Business History & Biography: Banking and Finance to
1913*, edited by Larry E. Schweikart. Copyright © 1990 by Bruccoli Clark Layman, Inc.,
and Facts On File, Inc. Reprinted by permission of Facts On File, Inc.

companion to one of the partners. The latter responsibility significantly broadened his horizons, as he traveled to Paris, Naples, and the Vatican. While in Italy, Belmont learned to speak Italian and spent much of his leisure time in art galleries. That led to a lifelong interest in and support of the arts.

The turning point in Belmont's life and career came in 1837. Because of the instability of the Spanish Empire, the Rothschilds decided that they needed a reliable agent in Havana to watch over their interests. Belmont accepted the assignment and sailed for Havana via New York City. He reached New York on May 14 and walked into the midst of a financial crisis: the Panic of 1837 had begun just one week before; all New York City banks had suspended specie payments.

The New York commercial community was hard hit by the financial downturn and resulting panic, with many businesses failing. Among the businesses affected was the Rothschilds' American agent, J.L. and S.I. Joseph & Company, which failed on March 17, leaving liabilities of $7 million.

Belmont therefore faced a dilemma. While he had instructions from the Rothschilds to go to Cuba, it was obvious that the Rothschild interests in the United States were at great risk. Because of the slow communications with Europe, it would take several months to receive new instructions from the partners. Belmont concluded that the situation required immediate action, and he decided to delay his Cuban departure: he stayed in New York to look after the Rothschilds' concerns.

Belmont established a firm, August Belmont & Company, and rented a room at 78 Wall Street. When the Rothschilds learned of his actions, they approved and appointed Belmont's company their new American agent. The Rothschilds gave him a $10,000 annual salary, a princely sum in the then-depressed city.

Because of its powerful international connection, Belmont's firm quickly became a success. Within three years, Belmont amassed a personal fortune of more than $100,000, making him one of the richest men in New York City. From 1837 to 1842 he sorted out the complicated Rothschild interests in the United States. He served as their disbursing agent and dividend collector even after the immediate crisis passed, and his affiliation with the Rothschilds extended to the close of the century.

August Belmont & Company also became a power in its own right. Belmont was involved in foreign exchange, commercial and private loans, acceptance of deposits, and the handling of commercial paper. By the time of the Mexican War, Belmont's firm had sufficient resources to underwrite a large portion of the loans made to the U.S. Treasury. . . .

Belmont and his wife originally lived at 72 Fifth Avenue. In the 1850s, Belmont purchased and renovated a mansion at 109 Fifth Avenue, on the corner of 18th Street. According to all accounts the house was magnificent.

The picture gallery Belmont had built was the first in New York City to include skylights. The house also had the first private ballroom in the city. The Belmonts frequently hosted and entertained guests in their mansion. Belmont won acclaim as one of the first gourmets in America, and the fine food and drink at his house constituted a source of much conversation in social circles.

As a change of pace, Belmont bought a 1,200-acre farm on Long Island a few years later. Called the Nursery Farm, it was located in Babylon and was virtually a self-contained community.

The farm had a 24-room mansion; a 30-acre lake; fields and silos for corn, hay, wheat, and rye; pastures for cows and horses; and even a bowling alley. The pride of the farm, however, was its stables, where Belmont hoped to raise the best racehorses in America. So that Belmont could watch his equine investments, the farm had a private one-mile-long racetrack complete with grandstands. Belmont emerged as one of the most influential figures in American horse racing during the second half of the nineteenth century. He served as president of the American Jockey Club and helped transform racing from a casual pastime into a professional sport.

Belmont's family connections led to his involvement with politics. In 1851, John Slidell, Belmont's wife's uncle, tried to secure the upcoming Democratic presidential nomination for his friend, Secretary of State James Buchanan of Pennsylvania. In order to win the nomination, it became clear that Buchanan needed to win New York State. At Slidell's urging, Belmont agreed to head Buchanan's New York campaign. Despite Belmont's hard work, Buchanan lost the 1852 nomination to Franklin Pierce.

In a show of party unity, Belmont worked for Pierce's election. . . .

With the victory in hand, Belmont began his own campaign to secure a diplomatic appointment. He reminded the Pierce administration about this active role in the election and stressed his experience in international finance. Belmont hoped to secure the position in Naples, a city he had come to love while working for the Rothschilds. Because of the various political demands on Pierce, Belmont did not receive the Naples post. Rather, the President appointed Belmont chargé d'affaires at The Hague. . . .

Although in Europe, Belmont closely followed American politics. As the 1856 presidential election approached, he promoted Buchanan for the Democratic nomination. Buchanan eventually defeated Pierce, marking the first time in American history that an elected president desirous of another term failed to secure renomination.

When Buchanan won the general election, Belmont angled for an appointment to a more prestigious diplomatic post. In particular Belmont wanted to serve in Madrid, for that would give him the opportunity to pursue a long-standing plan of his for the United States' acquisition of Cuba. Despite Belmont's long association with Buchanan, the new administration ultimately offered him nothing more than a reappointment to his current position at The Hague. When Belmont learned of this, he resigned and returned to the United States. Belmont's furniture, artwork, wine cellar, and personal belongings required 250 crates to ship home.

Belmont returned to a city in the midst of another panic. Many businesses had failed; unemployment and crime had risen. During that crisis, Belmont contributed generously to several charities. He also did something to try to raise the spirit of the city: he arranged a public exhibition of his art collection. This was a first in New York City and was well received in the press. Ever the art patron, Belmont eventually installed a large art gallery in his Fifty Avenue mansion.

Upon his return, Belmont reclaimed his place at the head of the New York social scene. He brought his chef back with him from Europe, raising dinner parties to a new pinnacle. Belmont typically seated up to 200 people at gold place settings. Each guest had a personal footman to serve and remove plates. He also used his private ballroom for lavish parties that lasted until dawn. The cost of all this socializing was high: Belmont's monthly wine bill alone exceeded $20,000.

Charles D. Barney

Charles D. Barney was a son-in-law of Jay Cooke and a Civil War veteran who lived to celebrate his 101st birthday. His name is one of the few founders' names that are still carried by the firms they started—in this case, more than a century ago. He died in 1945.

PHILADELPHIA, Oct. 24—Charles D. Barney, formerly one of this city's most distinguished financiers and one of the country's oldest Civil War veterans, died last night in his home in nearby Elkins Park after a long illness. His age was 101.

He was born in Sandusky, Ohio, where his father was a grain merchant. His mother was the former Elizabeth Caldwell Dennis, a member of an old New York family. Mr. Barney was attending college in Ann Arbor, Michigan, when his elder brother, Henry, was killed in the Civil War. After two more years of study he persuaded his mother to permit him to enlist. . . .

After the war, he returned to Sandusky and worked as a clerk and bookkeeper in the Second National Bank, but he quit after two years and came to Philadelphia. . . .

From *New York Times*, October 25, 1945.

About the same time he renewed his acquaintance with Laura E. Cooke, daughter of Jay Cooke, the financier, who maintained offices here but who returned annually to Sandusky. Mr. Barney became affiliated with the banking house of Jay Cooke & Co. in 1867—and a year later married Mr. Cooke's daughter. . . .

The Cooke bank failed in 1873 and a year later, with Jay Cooke Jr., Mr. Barney founded the brokerage and banking house of Charles D. Barney & Co., which soon became internationally known and was one of the leaders in the stock and bond business in Wall Street.

Finance alone, however, did not occupy all of Mr. Barney's time. He was an amateur musician, actor, and devout churchman. He taught Sunday School in St. Paul's Episcopal Church, where he was rector's warden. . . .

Mr. Barney retired in 1906 at the age of 62, but retained his directorships in many organizations until a few years ago. . . .

He said his greatest ambition was realized when he celebrated his one hundredth [birthday].

Ferdinand Eberstadt

Ferdinand Eberstadt graduated from Princeton, served in France, got a "war degree" in law from Columbia, joined Dillon, Read & Co., quit when they wouldn't pay him what he considered his due, and set up his own firm in 1931. Sometimes "Ferd," sometimes "Eber," he was always a dreadful golfer. After a 12 on the first hole at Ausable, he said to his caddie, "You know, I believe I'm the worst player in this Club." "Oh no," said the caddie, "there's a far worse player than you, sir." "Who?" "Mr. Eberstadt."

By late 1933, most of the water was wrung out of the fabric of finance. The reorganization business of F. Eberstadt & Co. was ebbing fast, and Ferd returned to the problem of creating an investment business. "Most new firms in Wall Street," said Eberstadt, "were formed by successful salesmen." If you were prudent and careful—and knew the right people—you could get on the big syndicate lists. If not, you had to take any list you could get, for the Wall Street syndicates operate on the backscratching principle, and there was no profit for them in scratching a new back. So Ferd had to scratch for himself. . . . He decided to look for business among

Excerpted from *Fortune Magazine*, April 1939, pp. 74–75 & 136–142. Reprinted by permission of Time Inc.

the smaller companies that Wall Street in general was ignoring—namely those earning from $250,000 up.

Just where hindsight laps foresight in a man's career is difficult to determine; the fact is that Eberstadt moved into this field and, once there, found it the right place for him to be. Indeed, he landed right next to a nice proposition. One of the officials of Square D Co., manufacturing electric-control equipment in Detroit, had been caught in the panic. He had put up 16,000 shares of Square D stock as bank collateral and because there was no market for it, the bank threatened to clean him out. Eberstadt learned of this from a Princeton classmate. The block, consisting of 8,000 preferred and 8,000 common, was offered to him for $40,000. He looked up the company, and when he saw that it was earning nearly a dollar a share, he took up the offer. In March 1934, he tested the market and offered the preferred at $8; it went very well, but the common at $3 was sticky. So he put Square D on the shelf for a year. In early 1935, when the market turned up, he dusted off the common and got rid of some at $15, and, early in 1936, still more at $50. The common was later split three for one and even this sold for almost $50. At present levels, the original 16,000 shares would be worth over $900,000. What Mr. Eberstadt made on the Square D deal is his own secret, but his outright profit probably ran close to $500,000—and the firm still has some shares left.

• • •

This little operation was important to Mr. Eberstadt on several counts. It introduced F. Eberstadt & Co. as a dealer in the securities of a medium-sized company; it brought an inordinate profit for a new firm; and it was so spectacular that it left tongues hanging out in Wall Street. But the really important byproduct was to put him in intimate touch with the problems gathering around the small, closely held corporation. The Square D Co. had asked Eberstadt to draft a financial plan, and he was working on this when the first shocks of New Deal reform came. In 1934, the maximum federal estate-tax rate was hiked from 45 to 60 percent and, a year later, to 70. Meanwhile, in many states the death duties were also increased.

To Eberstadt, sitting on the inside of a closely held corporation, the effect of these duties upon families and groups controlling smaller enterprises was obvious; where no current market existed for such holdings, a forced sale might be necessary to provide cash to meet the higher death duties. Thinking back, Eberstadt chuckles and quotes what Max Schmeling said when he first saw Joe Louis fight: "I sink I see somesing.". . .

These operations fall into what might be called special situations; they embrace a fairly limited field. Yet, besides keeping his young firm going, the experience helped Mr. Eberstadt down the road; specifically, it introduced him to the little blue chips. The . . . [following are] characteristics . . . that attract Eberstadt: "sound earnings record, compact management, a strong position in their fields, and an instinct for research." There is another reason why he likes to do business with them. Through the hullabaloo in Washington, Eberstadt saw that the political attacks aimed at the big corporations scarcely touched the little businessman. Instead of haunting Washington, he was staying home and attending to business.

The more Eberstadt studied these small companies, the more convinced he was that here was a chance for an investment banker willing to look beyond the Big Board. Many of them would need financing in the recovery years ahead; and by distributing and listing their securities on the big exchanges he could give them access to the money market. So far as the total possibilities are measurable, Eberstadt had succeeded only in wedging a foot in the door. The new-money financing that he has thus far done for smaller corporations totals . . . $17,000,000.

• • •

To F. Eberstadt & Co., as to every Wall Street investment house, making money is no quotidian [commonplace] routine. It is a long, painstaking task involving two operations: (1) buying an issue, which means getting the issue under contract, preparing it for the SEC, pricing it right, and timing the offering to best advantage, marketwise; and (2) selling it, which means moving the issue into the hands of investors. Because his firm is young and a majority of his clients are not in the habit of making periodic trips to the capital market, Mr. Eberstadt has to spend much more time buying an issue than selling it.

• • •

Mr. Eberstadt likes to think of his firm as a meeting place for smaller corporations in need of new capital and investors with idle funds—and he always emphasizes the new capital. The *quodlibet* here is obvious. For example, Square D, Cleveland Graphite Bronze, Norwich Pharmacal, in fact most of his issues, have been of a special nature: distributing for the account of families or groups, not for the company. However, the emphasis is properly placed in the case of James Talcott, Heller, and Victor Chemical. Here he performed a constructive act in strengthening independents in their separate fields and he is in an excellent position to do more of this sort of financing in the future.

But another real need, capital for *new* enterprises, Ferdinand Eberstadt won't touch—under his own name. He may broker an issue of this sort, but F. Eberstadt & Co. will not underwrite it. Ferd likes nothing better than to discover a new piece of research to pass on to his financial clientele. He will help an established company to raise capital to develop a new product. But further he will not go. The promoter of a new enterprise, however promising, will have to look elsewhere. Eberstadt feels safer with a sure thing.

The quicker you realize this, the sooner you can place Ferdinand Eberstadt in his proper perspective. Filling an economic need, per se, is not his business, and in this he is no different from anyone else on Wall Street except that he is shrewder than most. Fundamentally, Ferd is an opportunist—a word that in Wall Street simply means someone who finds a good thing, times it right, and carries it through. And for further proof of his opportunism consider Chemical Fund, an investment trust of the management type that he brought out in July 1938.

When offerings started to dwindle toward the close of 1937, Eberstadt looked for something to fill the gap. Now, underwriting serves two functions: supplying capital to industry and supplying investments for idle funds. The first side having disappeared, Eberstadt determined to concentrate on the second; and in the absence of capital offerings, shares in an investment trust were just about the only thing that might be apt to tempt investors. Wall Street, however, was littered with investment trusts of almost every kind, and to launch another one with any success would obviously require something special with a new sales appeal.

Victor Chemical had given Eberstadt a good look at the chemical industry, and he liked what he saw. He liked it even better after he and his aides scanned the rest of the industrial horizon. The industry's depression record was good, its future looked firm, especially to a man hipped on research; and he resolved to build his investment trust around chemistry. With characteristic caution, Eberstadt studied innumerable companies, interviewed scores of chemical experts. "I asked them who was the best consultant in the field. They all named themselves first and Arthur Little second." Arthur D. Little, Inc. is a great chemical consulting firm of Boston, now controlled by the Massachusetts Institute of Technology. Mr. Eberstadt persuaded the firm to act as adviser. "I'm no engineer, and if somebody is going to invent a new process that might knock my holdings apart, I want to be well warned." On the strength of this contract, he formed Chemical Fund last July, with $100,000 capital he and his friends put up for 10,000 shares.

Being an open-end trust Chemical Fund has a distant ceiling, of which the limits are roughly set by an authorized capital of 2,500,000 shares of stock. So far, sales of the Fund have averaged around 1,200 shares a day. . . .

Wall Street is a place of hero-worshipers. The big money-makers always have a following—so long as they leave scraps of profits along the way. Wall Street is also a place where prestige comes second only to profits. To an established investment house the fact of having its name on an underwriting list is almost as necessary to its pride as the cut is to its till. To Eberstadt, playing a lone hand, Wall Street's touchiness is of little consequence. His attitude toward the backscratching ritual of the syndicates is summed up in his own words, "Why should I take them in as participants? As dealers, yes—if they can sell." To an old-line house nothing could rankle more.

On Wall Street you will hear some hard things said about Eberstadt. You will hear it said that he doesn't share underwriting profits and also that he drives what even the Street considers a shrewd bargain, and that he is overly cautious in protecting himself on an issue. The last gripe has to do specifically with the "market-out" clause, a clause allowing the underwriter to pull out if the market looks sour. To protect himself, Eberstadt has insisted upon a market-out clause in almost every contract. Ordinarily this requires a commitment within a few days after the effective date of registration, but on occasion he has extended this privilege over months. In other words he gives himself plenty of time before he decides to go "on the hook."

The fact, however, is that Eberstadt, on practically all of his issues, has gone firm within a day or two of the SEC's clearance. Nevertheless, the hedge is always there, as it is in practically all current underwriting contracts. But it is the liberal period of grace that Eberstadt allows himself before he goes on the hook that raises eyebrows on the Street—that, and his occasional practice of not even contracting for an issue but taking it only on option. To all this Ferd answers, "I don't want to stick anyone else and I damn well don't want to get stuck myself."

Charles Hayden

Charles Hayden was perhaps better known to the public for the planetariums he endowed than as the senior partner of Hayden, Stone & Co. A man who believed that time was a bankable asset, he was active across a broad range of business, public, and cultural involvements, including the financing of most of the New York City area's transit lines.

Charles Hayden, senior partner of Hayden, Stone & Co., bankers, died at 10 o'clock last night in his apartment at the Hotel Savoy-Plaza. He was 66 years old. . . .

Mr. Hayden was an officer and director in 58 corporations, banks, mines and railroads, comprising some of the outstanding utilities and industrial concerns of the country.

• • •

From *The New York Times*.

Rated as one of the most powerful figures in the financial world, and senior partner of the banking firm of Hayden, Stone & Co. . . which was founded in 1892, Mr. Hayden was never publicized to the extent that many other big business men of the day figure in the news.

In 1934 he took rank as one of the city's most distinguished benefactors when he donated $150,000 for the apparatus of the planetarium at the American Museum of Natural History, which bears his name.

• • •

In the few brief biographical sketches that have appeared in recent years of Mr. Hayden, he is described as a rich boy who worked his way up in the brokerage business, starting as a broker's clerk at 21 at $3 a week. He was famous as a fast worker, phenomenally active, and it was a matter of comment in Wall Street that the rising men in his organization took on many of the characteristics of their employer, moving on the jump, talking in quick, clipped sentences and making decisions in a flash.

Mr. Hayden was quoted as saying once that "time is money to a business man, but they don't seem to know it. They pinch pennies and throw away thousands of dollars' worth of time. And they rob other men of thousands of dollars' worth of their time.". . .

In 1892 with a companion clerk, Galen L. Stone, he organized the banking firm of Hayden, Stone & Co., opening an office at 87 Milk Street, Boston, which prospered from the outset. The New York office was opened in 1906.

He became a member of the corporation of the Massachusetts Institute of Technology, and was a member of the Massachusetts State militia for 14 years, rising from a private to paymaster-general.

• • •

Mr. Hayden was chairman of the Research Association of the Massachusetts Institute of Technology, which was formed in 1935 by a group of leaders and organizations in business and industry. When his gift for the purchase of the "artificial heaven" in the planetarium was announced, F. Trubee Davison, president of the American Museum of Natural History, made public a statement by Mr. Hayden, in which he said:

"I believe that the planetarium is not only an interesting and instructive thing, but that it should give more lively and sincere appreciation of the magnitude of the universe and of the belief that there must be a very much greater power than man which is responsible for wonderful things which are daily occurring in the universe. I hope that the planetarium will give many people that view of life."

• • •

Mr. Hayden was listed in James W. Gerard's directory of the men who rule the United States as one of those "who are too busy to hold political office, but who determine who shall hold such office." He exerted his influence over copper mines, railroads, express companies, airplanes, automobiles, public utilities, oil fields, chemical companies and many other industries.

He helped finance most of the transit lines here and was a director in the leading companies in this field. Unification of the city's rapid transit system came within the realm of possibility in February 1935, as the result of a "memorandum of understanding" signed by Samuel Seabury and A. A. Berle Jr., negotiators for the city, and Mr. Hayden, representative of the B.M.T.

• • •

Mr. Hayden was a bachelor and his brother is his only survivor. While devoting so much time to his multiple business connections and to charitable and welfare enterprises, he found time to take part in various social and sports affairs. He was rated in a recent book on reminiscences of Fifth Avenue as one of the 75 persons in New York society invited to all important functions.

Earlier in his life he was fond of steeplechasing and had a stable of thoroughbred horses. Devoted to outdoor sports, he was said to have worked over them as hard as he worked in his office, directing big business. . . . He was also a notable player of bridge. . . .

Among many other corporation posts he held Mr. Hayden was chairman of the board of the Chicago, Rock Island & Pacific Railway and the International Nickel Company; chairman of the executive committee of the Cuba Cane Sugar Corporation; chairman of the finance committee of the Kennecott, Utah, Nevada and Ray Copper companies; a member of the executive committee of the American Locomotive Company, International Cement Corporation, Mack Trucks, Inc., Equitable Trust Company and the New York Trust Company.

Edward A. Pierce

ROBERT COLE

Edward A. Pierce, one of Wall Street's most respected leaders, built an innovative firm that became an important predecessor to the present Merrill Lynch. He led the reformation of the New York Stock Exchange in the 1930s and was 100 years old when he died in 1974.

Edward Allen Pierce, the last living original member of Merrill Lynch, Pierce, Fenner & Smith, Inc., the country's largest brokerage house, died here yesterday in his home. He had turned 100 last August 31.

In 1901, at the age of 27, Mr. Pierce gave up what was then the handsome salary of $100 a week, as manager of a lumber business, to become a $20-a-week clerk on Wall Street.

By good fortune, he picked A. H. Housman & Co., one of the most eminent houses in Wall Street, remembered even today as the firm where J. P. Morgan had kept an account.

By the time he reached the age of 47 he was managing partner of the company. By 1927, as a tribute to his stature in the industry, the firm's name was changed to E. A. Pierce & Co. It was merged with Merrill Lynch & Co. in 1940.

Under his guidance the firm that bore his name became the first to bring stock ticker service from one coast to the other. Soon after World War II he convinced WRUL, the shortwave station, to bring stock quotations to Europe and Latin America.

• • •

Mr. Pierce's name was associated with dozens of important ventures of the times and he was often mentioned as a candidate for top government posts, including chairman of the Securities and Exchange Commission, the industry's chief regulatory body. He was one of the earliest and most prominent supporters of strong federal regulation of stockbrokers.

• • •

Mr. Pierce, who was born in 1874 in Orrington [Maine], once told an interviewer that . . . [some] of the fondest memories of his youth were the Fourth of July strawberry festivals in Maine.

From Robert Cole, *New York Times*, December 17, 1974.

"We young fellows would start ringing the church bell about 11 o'clock at night," he recalled, "and we wouldn't let up 'til morning." By that time the church would serve strawberry shortcake—topped with whipped cream—and served with piping hot coffee. "You gulped down as much as you could," he recalled.

Company records show that he attended Bowdoin College for a while. He dropped out, he once remarked, because it was the start of the deer season.

In 1956 Bowdoin conferred on him an honorary Doctor of Laws degree, pointing to the "sagacity of his New England heritage." Four years later Brown University gave him another degree and spoke of his "Yankee judgment."

Asked once why he had left a "big" job in the lumber business to start over on Wall Street, Mr. Pierce is said to have replied:

"Because the financial world fascinated me and seemed to offer more of a challenge in those far-off days."

• • •

In 1909, Mr. Pierce married Luella Van Hoosear, now 102 years old. They had no children.

Dwight Morrow

HAROLD NICOLSON

Dwight Morrow was so enjoyed and esteemed by others that the senior partner of the law firm he left to join J.P. Morgan & Co. said, "My love of the law went with him." After a productive career as a leading Morgan partner he committed himself to public service, was a magnificently successful ambassador to Mexico and a Senator from New Jersey. Only in his late 50s when he died, he was considered a Presidential possibility. This vignette is from his Morgan days.

One day in the spring of 1917, Dwight Morrow and Mr. Thomas Cochran . . . of J.P. Morgan & Co., had to attend a board meeting up town. They agreed that after the meeting they would lunch together at the Plaza Hotel. As they walked away from the meeting Cochran observed that Morrow was in one of his moods of abstraction. He kept edging

Excerpt from *Dwight Morrow*, Copyright 1935 and renewed 1962 by Harold Nicolson, reprinted by permission of Harcourt, Inc.

Cochran off the sidewalk, and when Cochran crossed to his other side, he started, in complete oblivion of his presence, edging him against the shop windows of Fifth Avenue. They entered the Plaza Hotel; they were shown to a table; Cochran ordered luncheon; even when the food was set before him Morrow remained in a trance. Cochran decided to watch just how long this trance would continue. He ate his own meal in silence, motioning to the waiter from time to time to remove from Morrow's place the dishes which accumulated untouched before him. Suddenly, while Cochran was lighting his cigar, Morrow emerged from his stupor. He struck the table with his hand. "That's done it!" he exclaimed. "What," Cochran asked him, "has done what?" "I've mutualized the Equitable! Now, Tom, let's go out somewhere and get something to eat!"

The ingenuity of the scheme which had then occurred to him was such as to be almost incomprehensible to any layman. Its main outlines were as follows: The [Equitable Life Assurance] Society was to transform itself into a mutual life insurance corporation and to purchase from General du Pont the shares that he held. The price of these shares was to be paid in half-annual installments running from November 1, 1917, to May 1, 1937, out of the interest received by the Society upon a mortgage of $20,500,000 given to the Society by the Equitable Office Building Corporation. This involved the surrender to General du Pont of the 9 percent of the dividends of the Equitable Building Corporation hitherto held by the Equitable Life Assurance Society. It also entailed an extension agreement under which the previous mortgage bond of 1913 was altered so that the mortgage should be paid off, not by November 1935 as previously stipulated, but by May 1974.

The minor adjustments necessitated by this device were of the utmost intricacy; yet, even when these had been agreed to, there remained the problem of how to induce General du Pont to part with his holdings at what would certainly represent a heavy loss. To this day it remains a mystery how Morrow was able to secure his consent. The persuasiveness with which he appealed to his sense of public duty was reenforced by their persistence with which, month after month, he drove him into acquiescence. At such moments Morrow was perfectly capable of adopting third degree methods and wearing down his opponent by actual physical exhaustion. And, as always happened with Morrow's victories, the vanquished felt delighted at their own defeat. When, in July of 1917, the Equitable was finally mutualized and the stock handed over to three trustees for the benefit of policyholders, Mr. George Baker drove down to Morgan's office and asked to see Dwight Morrow. He went up to him, took him by the lapels of his coat, and scrutinized him with a penetrating stare. "I just wanted," he explained, "to look at you."

• • •

The mutualization of the Equitable was generally recognized as being one of the most brilliant successes in financial and legal adjustment ever achieved. A less dramatic, more prolonged, but no less complicated problem was that of the Interborough Rapid Transit Company. It must at least be mentioned since it absorbed a great proportion of Morrow's time and energy between the years 1919 and 1927. In the end he became so involved and interested in the New York subway and transit systems that they almost came to represent for him what the "roads of Cephalonia" had represented for Napier. The unification of the whole system was one of his most persistent dreams.

It was Dwight Morrow's custom . . . to approach a problem cautiously and to study it in all its bearings before reaching a decision. Another characteristic was the persistence with which he pursued a problem during the course of several years. Yet when faced with a crisis, he could work with lightning rapidity and dispatch. A good illustration of his more rapid method is furnished by the rescue of Mr. William C. Durant, founder and president of General Motors.

Mr. Durant was an ingenious but haphazard man. He combined breathless energy, great manufacturing ability, and unbounded self-confidence with a reckless disregard for accountancy and a merry contempt for the old-fashioned methods of more stable financiers. For some weeks, during the fall of 1920, rumors had been circulating that Mr. Durant was in difficulties. It was not, however, until 2 P.M. of Thursday, November 18, that Mr. Durant himself became aware that these difficulties called for urgent solution. On that day, at that hour, he telephoned to 23 Wall Street demanding assistance. Dwight Morrow, accompanied by Mr. Cochran and Mr. Whitney . . . proceeded to the offices of General Motors where they found Mr. Pierre du Pont and Mr. John J. Raskob. It was disclosed to them that the situation was a most serious one, involving brokers' loans for $25,000,000 and that calls for additional margin of a most pressing character had been sent to Mr. Durant and would have to be honored immediately. Morrow took the situation under his control. He asked Mr. Durant to sit down at once and prepare a full statement of his assets and obligations, this statement to be ready not later than 9:30 P.M. that night. At 10 P.M., he returned, accompanied by Mr. Pierre du Pont. Already a broker had ensconced himself in the anteroom demanding checks. The ensuing discussion lasted all night. The following agreement was eventually secured. The du Pont interests were to form a security holding company to purchase 2,500,000 shares of General Motors stock from Mr. Durant. The capital of this new company was to be supplied by a subscription to preferred stock of $7,000,000 by the du Pont interests and a loan of $20,000,000 one year 8 percent notes on the part of J.P. Morgan & Co. A memorandum of agreement was initialed at a quarter to six in the morning. During the whole of the following Friday, Saturday, and Sunday, Dwight Morrow worked upon the contracts and other details. By the opening of the Stock Exchange on Monday morning, all arrangements had been completed and Mr. Durant's brokers began delivering General Motors stock to J.P. Morgan & Co. against payment.

"Yes," Morrow remarked to his partners when the crisis was over, "Yes, Durant thanks us humbly now for saving his life, but within a week he will be cursing us for something else."

Otto H. Kahn

JOHN KOBLER

Otto Kahn was second only to Jacob Schiff at Kuhn, Loeb and was banker to Harriman. A vain, fastidious man, he was not only a devoted patron of the opera, but also a demonic golfer. Once, he nearly stood for Parliament.

The situation had elements of a Feydeau farce. The scene was the senior partners' room of Kuhn, Loeb & Co., the nation's second most powerful private bankers after J. P. Morgan. Some 60 feet long and 40 feet wide, the room took up nearly all of the second floor of the firm's 22-story headquarters on the corner of William and Pine streets. Each of the four senior partners received his clients at a desk in a corner of the oblong expanse, out in the open, visible to everybody in the room, with a small office behind for negotiations requiring greater privacy. The southwest corner belonged to Jerome Hanauer, the northwest to Mortimer Schiff, the southeast to Felix Warburg, and the northeast to the commander in chief of the firm, Otto Hermann Kahn, who had prepared the master coup that would excite Wall Street and the entire railroad industry.

By Kahn's choice it took place on a Saturday morning in April of 1928 . . . for Saturday was the quietest, least crowded time of the workweek, and so he opted for a Saturday convenient to the principals in his scheme.

The challenge Otto Kahn faced was to conciliate two warring railroad magnates, Leonor Fresnel Loree and William Wallace Atterbury, presidents,

Excerpted from John Kobler, *Otto the Magnificent*, 1989, pp. 3–5 & 27–30 & 41 & 83. Published by John Scribner & Sons.

respectively, of the Delaware & Hudson and the Pennsylvania, both burly six-footers in their sixties. Loree's nose was disfigured by a skin disease.

At the time there existed four major Eastern railroad systems running between New York and Chicago—the Pennsylvania, the New York Central, the Baltimore & Ohio, and the New York, Chicago & St. Louis. Loree, whom ill-informed Wall Streeters dismissed as "a big man with a jerkwater road," proposed to create a fifth system in competition with the four. To that end he added to his holdings enough shares of the Lehigh Valley, the Wabash, the Western Maryland, and the Chicago & St. Louis to obtain control of those lines. Atterbury vigorously opposed the five-system plan. He threatened to file a protest with the Interstate Commerce Commission and to take other dire measures against the interloper. What distressed Kuhn, Loeb was that both adversaries were long-standing clients. They could not allow themselves to side against either. Otto Kahn, his colleagues agreed, had the technical and economic ken, the diplomacy, the knack for mediation, and the personal charm to restore peace between the two railroad titans.

Shortly before 10 A.M., the hour fixed by Kahn, Loree went from his headquarters at 32 Nassau Street to Kuhn, Loeb, only a few steps away. Kahn, welcoming him warmly, walked him into his oak-paneled little office, asked him to wait a few minutes, and left, closing the door behind him. Shortly after 10, again in accordance with Kahn's design, Atterbury arrived from the Pennsylvania Station building and was shown into Mortimer Schiff's office. Neither Loree nor Atterbury was as yet aware of the other's presence. Kahn, a David between two Goliaths, now began moving from one to the other and back again, feeling each man out for any signs of a concession, striving to persuade each to yield a little, and in the end to renounce a destructive competition in favor of a lucrative alliance.

Kahn cut an appealing figure. Small, light-brown-eyed and ruddy-cheeked, his normal expression a gentle smile, he walked with a springy step, his spine erect, his stride soldierly, a carriage that he himself ascribed to his training as a young cavalryman in his native Germany. A slight Germanic accent lingered in his speech, mingled with the broad vowels and clipped consonants of upper-class England, where he had lived for three years. His hair was silvery white, and his mustache waxed to fine points. He wore pearl-gray spats, and the vests beneath his impeccably tailored jackets were trimmed with white piping. Spruce as a Savile Row dandy, a fresh rose in his lapel, he was one of New York's best-dressed men. Lewis Strauss, a later Kuhn, Loeb partner and chairman of the Atomic Energy Commission, described Kahn as "the Lorenzo de Medici of his day . . . with an air of detachment from anything as plebeian as money."

The Loree-Atterbury conflict was not Kahn's only concern that Saturday morning. In Jerome Hanauer's office smoldering like Vesuvius, the Metropolitan Opera's bulky, irascible general manager, Giulio Gatti-Casazza, waited to confront Kahn, the president and chairman of the board of the Met, with a repetition of complaints. The stage was too short and shallow, the scenery warehouse too far from the theater. There were no rehearsal rooms for ballet, chorus, and orchestra, and too many seats in the side sections provided only a partial view. Felix Warburg's office was fragrant with the presence of a soprano whose identity and purpose the discretion of Kahn's colleagues has obscured. Thus, pulled in four directions, Kahn exercised his wizardry as a conciliator, a mediator, and an expositor of crystalline lucidity.

Gatti-Casazza left placated by the renewal of Kahn's promise to build him a new opera house. The smile illuminating the face of the departing soprano indicated that whatever she wanted she got.

There remained the contending railroad tycoons. At a moment when Kahn considered the psychological climate propitious, he brought them together. The three men now reexamined every facet of the issue. Was there to be the five-system network that Loree's ambition hankered for, or Atterbury's four systems? Toward 1 P.M., three hours after they had entered Kuhn, Loeb, a spectacular solution seemed likely. Subject to the agreement of his board, Atterbury offered to buy Loree's holdings for $102 million. There would be no fifth system. Diplomacy had prevailed. It was one of Otto Kahn's greatest achievements.

• • •

"A promising chap," the National City Bank's James Stillman had once observed of Kahn, who was collecting a lot of fine paintings, "if only he will forget that art nonsense."

The young Kahn's considerable revenue flowed from two main sources. Every December, Kuhn, Loeb . . . distributed the annual profits among the partners. What percentage each partner received depended on seniority, the volume of business he had engendered, and other considerations. Kahn eventually got 14 percent. Railroad reorganizations in the Harriman mode and railroad securities yielded the fattest returns. When Kuhn, Loeb assembled and managed a security-purchase syndicate, it customarily charged a fee of one percent. During their first nine years the securities they underwrote totaled approximately $821 million. Kahn's second major source of capital was Wall Street, where, as an astute investor, he repeatedly realized a killing. Thus, his means, together with Addie Kahn's inheritance, enabled the couple to live grandly. But he was never, as the press persistently misreported, "one of the richest men in America." It is difficult to estimate how much his fortune amounted to at any given period because he spent money as fast as he made it, sometimes faster. "I must atone for my wealth," he said on several occasions. "I will reward the country of my adoption for the great benefits I have gathered." In all probability his liquid assets never topped $50 million, a paltry sum in those halcyon days before federal taxation when compared to the royal wealth of a Rockefeller, a Carnegie, or a Morgan. It was more than enough, however, to maintain a town house just off Fifth Avenue at 8 East Sixty-eighth Street.

On February 5, 1905, while the Kahn family was at the New York house, a faulty flue and an overheated furnace started a fire near Mrs. Kahn's boudoir at Cedar Court [the Kahn's country place]. . . . The blaze engulfed art objects, paintings, and an Egyptian rug woven at a cost of $100,000 to cover a living room 75 feet square. The total damage came to $750,000.

On the site of the incinerated house Kahn built a Palladian villa harmonizing with the architecture of the surviving structure, and he further embellished the grounds. Together with what his father-in-law had laid out there were now horse trails, an 18-hole golf course, a squash court, a croquet court, a tennis court, greenhouses, sunken gardens, a pond on which swans floated amid exotic water plants, a 40-acre deer park, and a wooden roller-skating rink that meandered through woods where the deer grazed. The estate, according to one of the gardeners, "showed people what God could have done if he'd had the money.". . .

• • •

Men in Kahn's business milieu tended to regard the opera world as effete, no place for a serious financier. Colleagues warned him against involving himself in operatic or theatrical activities lest he alienate people important to his business. No reputable banker, they insisted, should associate himself with such frivolous doings.

He consulted Harriman, who, to his amazement, told him: "You just go ahead and do your art job, but don't dabble in it. Make it one of your serious occupations. As long as you do not let it interfere with your other work, with your business duties and ambitions and thoughts, it will do you no harm. On the contrary, it will exercise your imagination and diversify your activities. It ought to make a better businessman out of you."

• • •

He was as fastidious a dresser, and as vain of his person, as a matinee idol. His clothes closets contained, among a vast collection of ensembles, eight identical pinstripe business suits, and he would stand before them lost in contemplation before choosing the one he would wear to work that morning.

At musical or theatrical first nights, on or off Broadway, no matter how unpretentious the performance, he would emerge from one of his Rolls-Royces in full fig, a satin-lined cape draped over evening dress, wearing a silk top hat and swinging an ebony cane with a silver ball for a handle.

Saturday morning was devoted to golf on his own 18-hole course. . . . If he invited others to join him, the time customarily fixed was 10. Should they fail to appear within three minutes after the hour, he was likely to tee off without them. A bit of a duffer, who hated to lose at any game, he would, if he hit too often into a bunker, have it removed, and if he shot too wide of a green, he would order the green repositioned.

• • •

By the fall of 1912, Kahn was so nearly sure of entering British politics that he began hunting for London real estate. The first property that seized his fancy was 2 Carlton House Terrace, a showplace of 28 rooms with a price tag of $500,000. The owner, one of the world's wealthiest women, was formerly married to an American millionaire, Marshall Field Jr., and also formerly to a Scottish multimillionaire, Maldwin Drummond. Kahn cabled Mrs. Drummond, expressing interest in the estate, then changed his mind. He preferred to take a year's lease for $20,000 (and later to buy for a million dollars) the Earl of Londesborough's Regency mansion, St. Dunstan's Lodge, standing amid twelve and a half acres at the center of Regent's Park, London's second largest private residence after Buckingham Palace. . . .

Mrs. Drummond, meanwhile, having mistaken Kahn's cable as a firm offer, accused him of bad faith. Incensed, he showed a copy of the cable to his attorneys, who assured him that it implied no such agreement. Thus armored in the conviction of rectitude, he made a typically Kahnian gesture. With St. Dunstan's already on his hands, he bought 2 Carlton House Terrace, never occupied it, and resold it at a loss. "I would much rather be burdened with a house I cannot use," he said, "than rest under the imputation of attempting to evade a moral commitment."

André Meyer

CARY REICH

André Meyer built Lazard Frères into one of the most effective and profitable investment banking firms in America. He also developed an extraordinary network of contacts, acquaintances, and relationships with the nation's financial, political, and social powers and made a large fortune as an investor before he died at 81 in 1979. This excerpt tells us how Meyer, improbably, takes over in New York years after being forced to leave France by the Nazis.

In many ways, André Meyer was not a nice man.

He was greedy, vindictive, domineering, and often quite sadistic. His constant browbeating and temper tantrums made life unbearable for his business associates and his family. No matter how wealthy he became— and he became *very* wealthy— he could not stop plotting and scheming to build an even bigger fortune. He would allow nothing and no one to get in his way. Once, a Lazard colleague gave some investors the right of first refusal on a deal, after they had given Lazard first-refusal rights on one of *their* transactions. After all, this Lazard partner explained, it was a two-way street. Meyer was furious. "Where is it written there is a two-way street?" he demanded.

"He could be brutal, and he *enjoyed* being brutal," says his old friend Andrea Wilson, who worked for Meyer as a securities analyst. "When he was through with somebody, when he wanted to get rid of you, it was something to behold." But Wilson readily recognized what others only grudgingly acknowledged: that Meyer could not have come as far as he did—specifically, from obscure lower-middle-class origins—by relying solely on gentility and charm. "For him to break through to the extent that he did, and to achieve the position that he did, that took something," she says.

What it took was the ruthlessness of the totally self-made man, writ large. And leaving aside his methods and his personality, there can be little doubt that André Meyer did accomplish great things. "What Horowitz is to the piano," said a friend, "what Picasso was to painting, André Meyer was to banking.". . .

Excerpt from Cary Reich, *Financier*, William Morrow and Company. 1985, Chapters 2, 4, pp. 18–19, 36–42.

The son of a struggling Paris printing salesman, Meyer left school in 1914, when he was sixteen years old, to become a messenger on the Paris Bourse. By the time he reached thirty, he was a partner in the eminent private banking firm of Lazard Frères. By the age of forty, he had helped save the foundering auto giant Citroën, had founded France's first consumer finance company, and was awarded the Legion of Honor.

• • •

When the Meyers arrived in New York, their first stop was a luxury hotel, the Stanhope. Then, after a short stay, they moved on to another luxury hotel, the Delmonico. After a brief while, they moved on to another, then another, before finally settling into one of the poshest of them all, the Carlyle. "We were in all sorts of hotels," remembers Philippe Meyer. "Some were too big, some were too small."

The Meyers' life as well-heeled nomads had more to do with André's state of mind than with the family's living requirements. During those initial months in the United States he was uncertain and unstable, alternating between his natural restlessness to *do* things and an acute torpor that prevented him from doing *anything*. For days on end he would lie on his hotel suite soft in his pajamas, mired in depressed contemplation of his plight. "It was all a great shock for him—Nazism, the war, France's defeat," says Philippe. "On the personal side, he had been a great, great success, and suddenly everything collapsed, and he had to start all over again. And he didn't know if he had the strength or the courage to do it."

Suddenly, he was adrift in a world whose language he barely knew; whose ways were strange and unfathomable; whose movers and shakers were, for the most part, merely names to him, nothing more. The sureness and self-confidence with which he had cut such a quick, broad swatch through the French banking world were now denied him; in their place were the fumbling and groping of someone stumbling across a darkened room. His mastery of the Bourse and his hard-won roster of Paris contacts were of little use to him now.

It was not that he and his family were starving. He had discreetly transferred enough of his wealth to accounts outside of France in the months before the war to assure them of a comfortable existence. But for André Meyer, to be denied his métier was virtually to be deprived of life itself.

He lay on the sofa awhile longer. And then he steeled himself and went to work.

Not at Lazard, though; the New York firm was an entity that functioned independently of Paris, and while he was welcome to hang his hat there, he didn't really fit. Instead, he rented an office of his own in the same Wall Street-area office building that housed Lazard, 120 Broadway.

He would be on the thirty-second floor, while Lazard was down on the ground floor and the fifth. . . .

From his perch, Meyer gradually began to master the workings of American business and American banking. He was far enough away from Lazard to be totally detached from its activities—yet close enough to watch what was happening. And watch he did.

Lazard Frères New York was then run by Frank Altschul. Few men could have brought to the job a more impressive pedigree.

Altschul's father, Charles, was the eighth employee hired by Lazard Frères and spent his entire business life there, rising to one of the highest positions in the San Francisco bank. Upon moving to New York in 1901, when Frank was fourteen, the Altschul's became members in good standing of the "Our Crowd" network of German-Jewish banking families. In the best Our Crowd tradition, the Altschuls soon became securely intertwined by marriage with another prominent banking family, the Lehmans; Frank's sister Edith became the wife of Herbert Lehman, the future governor of New York, and Frank himself married Herbert Lehman's niece, Helen Lehman Goodhart. After graduating from Yale in 1908, Frank joined his father at Lazard in New York; and when Charles Altschul stepped down as a partner in 1916, Frank took his place.

Frank soon rose to be one of Wall Street's grand dukes, both in style and influence. In the 1930s, he served on the governing board of the New York Stock Exchange and became a director of the Rockefeller family bank, the Chase National. During the 1920s, while André Meyer was speculating on the rise and fall of the French franc, Altschul was advising the French government on how to steady the currency and was awarded a Legion of Honor. One of the world's most prominent rare-book collectors, Altschul set up his own small printing plant, Overbrook Press, at his 450-acre Connecticut estate to turn out exquisitely printed and illustrated limited editions. And, faithfully each fall, Altschul would ride to hounds in the Fairfield and Westchester hunts. . . .

The Lazard that Frank Altschul ran was every bit the epitome of the old-line, prewar Wall Street firm. It did a little of this and a little of that. . . . The partners still worked at rolltop desks in a big old-fashioned partners' room. In one corner, behind a battery of four telephones on his mahogany desk, sat Altschul, the smoke of his pipe lazily floating past the rare prints hanging on the walls.

The firm's business took a turn for the worse with the outbreak of the Second World War. Bond underwritings were few and far between. . . . But Altschul and the four other partners weren't panicking. Business had been good before, and it would be good again. All it took was a little time and a little patience, and everything would be as it was.

• • •

In the meantime, Altschul was doing his best to help the émigré partner who arrived on his doorstep in the summer of 1940.

Virtually from the moment the Meyers stepped off their clipper, Altschul had been in the wings offering aid, advice, and companionship. He helped them find a hotel. He suggested private schools for the children. He invited them to spend their weekends at his Connecticut estate. . . .

Then, in 1942, Frank Altschul found himself with another uprooted Paris partner on his hands: Pierre David-Weill, newly arrived in New York. The urbane, aristocratic crown prince of Lazard Paris, however, needed far less handholding than Meyer, having long since acclimated himself to American ways and customs; from 1926 through 1939 he had visited the United States at least one or two months a year. David-Weill's attitude toward Meyer at this point was an ambivalent one. . . . With his air of jaunty, moneyed self-assurance, David-Weill had far more in common with Altschul than he did with his old partner. And, indeed, David-Weill and Altschul soon became fast friends.

In view of all this, Meyer definitely seemed to be the odd man out. Yet, unaccountably, he was starting to show signs of his old bounciness. To some of his new friends—chiefly fellow French émigrés—he was positively cocky, with the ebullience of someone bursting to tell them a wondrous secret. To a few, he confided what it was: "In one year," he told these friends, "I will be the boss."

Coming from someone so out of place, someone who barely spoke English, it was a rather bizarre prophecy. But that is exactly what happened. In the December 16, 1943, *New York Times* appeared this announcement:

ALTSCHUL RETIRING
FROM LAZARD FIRM

WILL QUIT DEC. 31—PARIS HOUSE
RESIDENTS AND 2 OTHERS TO
BE ADMITTED THEN

Frank Altschul will retire from partnership in Lazard Frères & Co., investment bankers here, on Dec. 31, the firm announced yesterday. He will continue as a member of the New York Stock Exchange and will remain president of the General American Investors Company, Inc.

Pierre David-Weill and André Meyer of the Paris firm of Lazard Frères et Cie., residents in New York for several years, will be admitted as resident partners of the New York firm. The French firm also will continue as a partner in the house here.

Frank Altschul, in essence, was sent packing—with General American Investors bestowed upon him in the manner of a going-away present.

How did Meyer and David-Weill do it? How did they manage to unseat a man who had been a dominant force in the New York firm for over 35 years, whose family had been a part of Lazard almost from the beginning, whose power and connections in the financial world and in New York society were so formidable?

The short answer is that while he ran Lazard New York, Frank Altschul never actually had voting control of it. That power had always remained in the hands of the David-Weill family—as the sole blood relations of the Lazards still in the banking empire in the early forties—and to a lesser extent in the hands of the other partners in the French house, including Meyer, who were given shareholdings by the David-Weills over the years. . . .

Meyer, it was now clear, had simply been biding his time during those first three years, watching and waiting in his aerie for the right moment to strike. And when he felt he knew enough, he did what he had had the power to do all along, secure in the knowledge that David-Weill would back him up. Because for David-Weill, too, the demands of the times—namely, the need to secure a beachhead for himself in the only major nation unscarred by the war—outstripped the demands of friendship. And given the choice, David-Weill preferred to hitch his family's fortune to André Meyer rather than to Frank Altschul. David-Weill and Meyer would share control of the New York house, but from the outset David-Weill let Meyer dominate its affairs.

The man they displaced, meanwhile, went on to successfully run General American Investors until his retirement in 1961, while continuing his rare-book collecting and publishing and his myriad philanthropic activities. But he never forgave André Meyer. "To the best of my knowledge," says someone who knew both Meyer and Altschul, "André and Frank never spoke to each other again.". . .

If André Meyer felt any remorse over the turn of events, he never revealed it. As far as he was concerned, Lazard was simply not big enough for both him and Frank Altschul.

George Ames, a young assistant in Lazard's corporate underwriting department, had quit the firm in 1942 to join the navy. When he came back in 1946 to pick up where he had left off, he was amazed by what he found. The old rolltop desks were gone. The old partners' room was gone. And the old partners were gone, too.

And running the firm was the awkward, mysterious Frenchman from the thirty-second floor.

What André Meyer had in mind, from the start, was the total gutting and rebuilding of Lazard Frères. Lazard's mix of business—which was typical for a firm of its size—he regarded as an unstructured, unprofitable hodgepodge. And Lazard's partners and staff, as far as he was concerned, were largely a bunch of lazy mediocrities. In both areas, he wasted no time forcing through major upheavals.

By 1945, all the old partners had been dismissed. By 1948, the firm had shut down its Boston, Philadelphia, and Chicago offices, and had become, once again, a one-office house. . . .

The branches were anathema to Meyer on two counts: first, they built up overhead, and he intended to run as bare-bones an operation as he possibly could. Second, they were largely in the retail stockbrokerage business, which meant they dealt with the general public. André Meyer did not want Lazard to deal with the general public. He wanted the New York firm to be what the French firm was: a very private, very elite house whose customers were corporations, financial institutions, and a few wealthy friends of the proprietor. Exclusivity, even a certain snobbishness, were to be encouraged. . . .

But at the same time, Meyer was acutely conscious of his own shortcomings. He knew few of the powerhouses of corporate America, few of the bankers who made the financial system tick. To gain the sort of clientele he sought, he needed someone who could open the right doors, and who was as well known and respected in America as he had been in France. Fortunately, he found such a person almost immediately. His name was George Murnane.

By the time he joined forces with André Meyer, Murnane was already something of a legend in the investment-banking business. As one of the top partners in Lee, Higginson & Company, he had gained a reputation as a superb deal-maker whose determination and grittiness were second to none. . . .

Murnane's string of successes, however, was abruptly cut short by the troubles that dogged his firm. Lee, Higginson had been the leading bankers for Swedish match king Ivar Kreuger, and when Kreuger's empire collapsed after his suicide in 1932, Lee, Higginson was buried in the rubble. Virtually wiped out, Murnane started from scratch again in a partnership with a French financier, Jean Monnet. Their firm, Monnet & Murnane, thrived, thanks to both men's extensive international connections. But when another world war loomed, Monnet quit to work on building up the Allied defensive forces, and Murnane was on his own again. He was not someone who enjoyed being a lone wolf. And so, when Meyer asked him in the fall of 1944 if he was interested in helping rejuvenate Lazard, Murnane leaped at the opportunity.

He brought with him, as Meyer knew he would, a network of contacts that was the envy of almost every investment banker in America. He was a director of Allied Chemical & Dye and American Steel Foundries, and was the main American adviser for Belgium's great industrial dynasties, the

Solvays and the Boëls. What's more, he was the key investment banker for many of America's leading glass companies. His prestige was such that wherever he went, this business followed. So Lazard suddenly fell into a block of clients it had never had before—and Meyer had his instant entrée to corporate America.

Murnane, in fact, was the only other individual at Lazard, other than Pierre David-Weill, whom Meyer could or would accept as a peer. He needed George Murnane, a lot more than Murnane needed him. . . .

Still, there were limits to what even a Murnane could do for Meyer. Lazard also required someone who could serve as a liaison to Wall Street, particularly to the syndicate managers, the tightly knit group of brokerage-house executives who controlled the allocation and flow of new stock and bond issues. Theirs was a world of patrician after-hours camaraderie, a world whose inner circle was closed to foreigners, and for that matter to anyone who hadn't gone to a select handful of Ivy League schools. The only way Meyer could gain access to it was to hire one of *them*.

After making some discreet inquiries around the Street, Meyer came up with just the man he was looking for: Edwin Herzog, late of Shields & Company and the United States Army Air Corps. Still in uniform, his discharge papers in his pocket, he met with Meyer and Murnane at Meyer's summerhouse in Ossining, New York, in 1945. Outwardly gregarious but inwardly flinty, Herzog seemed perfectly suited for the demands of the job. Meyer told him he could take charge not only of syndication, but of securities sales and trading. His first task, Herzog recalls, was to "clean out a lot of the deadwood that was sitting here, trading and pretending to be bond dealers."

As logical as the acquisitions of Murnane and Herzog were, in view of Meyer's own limitations, Meyer's other key personnel move must have seemed to Lazard-watchers eminently *illogical*. That was to bring on board, as a partner involved in investment strategy, Albert Joseph Hettinger, Jr. The lanky, quiet, pipe-puffing Hettinger was a rather unlikely soul to be spending his time in the hurly-burly of Wall Street, let alone in the company of the hustling, impatient André Meyer. A former Harvard Business School professor, Hettinger had ambled into the securities business in the mid-1920s and, in 1935, found a position at General American Investors. When Meyer offered him a partnership upon taking over Lazard, Hettinger was still what he had been for most of his career: a scholarly, often absentminded, and slow-moving observer of the securities markets.

But Meyer saw something in Hettinger that eluded nearly all his contemporaries: that behind the philosophical facade was a man with a unique gift for ferreting out investment opportunities. It was a talent that Meyer cherished. The hiring of Hettinger, in fact, said more about the direction in which Meyer was moving than anything else he did during those first few years at the helm.

By the mid-forties, the term "investment banking" had evolved into a classic misnomer, since most of its practitioners were neither investors nor bankers. Banking in the traditional sense—the gathering of deposits and the making of loans—had been ruled off limits for these firms by the Glass-Steagall Act. And investing of the sort done by such hallowed figures as Jacob Schiff and J. Pierpont Morgan at the turn of the century— putting one's own and one's bank's money into potentially lucrative new ventures—was virtually an extinct art form.

The role investment bankers now played was almost strictly that of financial intermediaries. They would advise companies on financing strategy, and when the time came for the companies to raise money in the market, the investment bankers would underwrite the stock or bond issues. Investment-banking underwriters did not really keep the stocks and bonds on their own books; they would purchase the issue from the company and then resell it to institutions such as pension funds or insurance companies, or to individual investors, at a spread, or commission.

That, in a nutshell, was what Lazard New York did before Meyer came along. And as his hiring of Murnane and Herzog showed, it was a business he still very much wanted to pursue.

But with the Second World War drawing to a close and America girding itself for recovery, the people Meyer closeted himself with most weren't Murnane and Herzog, but Al Hettinger and Fred Wilson, the young man Meyer had also just brought over from General American Investors. Hettinger and Wilson weren't corporate advisers or new-issue specialists. They were securities analysts, men who specialized in finding intriguing investment opportunities.

The message was clear. André Meyer didn't want Lazard to be only an investment banker. He wanted Lazard to be an *investor*.

Meyer could see a postwar boom coming, and he wanted to be in on it— not just as an intermediary but as a principal. . . .

He didn't have to wait long. In April 1946, the U.S. Supreme Court upheld the Securities and Exchange Commission's power to break up the giant public-utility holding companies. The decision sent the stock prices of such holding companies as Electric Bond & Share into a tailspin. Meyer, Hettinger, and Wilson concluded that the inherent values of the holding-company shares—even assuming forced breakups—were well in excess of what the shares were selling at. So they bought and bought and bought— for Lazard and for themselves. . . .

When utilities were broken up, the Lazard partners' perceptions were proven correct. The liquidation values of the shares were far above what the market had foreseen. "It was about the easiest money I've ever made," says Wilson. "It's still hard to believe, it was so easy."

André Meyer had had his first taste of the opportunities the post-war economy offered. It only whetted his appetite for more.

At Lazard, other changes were afoot.

Each year, in the old days, the firm would have a big, raucous Christmas party. In 1944, Meyer attended his first one and was flabbergasted by the amount of alcohol that was consumed.

The next year, there was no whiskey at the party, only champagne. And even that . . . "was measured out with some care."

It was now, truly, André Meyer's Lazard Frères.

Robert Lehman

STEPHEN BIRMINGHAM

Bobby Lehman allegedly kept the titans of Lehman Brothers—at the firm's peak of power—under his control by encouraging them to war among themselves. That way, they would feel a protective need and be too tired to disobey him. He eventually assembled a great house—and a great art collection—but had not built a great firm.

Robert Lehman, Philip's son and the present head of Lehman Brothers, . . . has been called "the last of the imperiously rich men" and "the aristocrat of the autocrats." Robert Lehman's power in the money market is . . . vast . . . , and the phrase, "Bobby wants to speak to you," stikes terror in the breast of all at 1 South William Street. His office in the building is small—many junior partners have larger space—but it gives him a psychological advantage. "When you go into that little office, you really feel crowded out by him," says one man. He himself, also slight of stature, seems to fill the room.

Lehman, however, in recent years has turned his attention increasingly to his art collection. Started by his father, who bought paintings more for an investment than out of a love of beauty, the Lehman Collection has been so enormously added to by Robert that it is now the largest, and possibly the finest, private art collection in America. . . . The collection—guided by Robert Lehman's straightforward philosophy, which is, "If I see something I like, I buy it"—hangs in the offices of Lehman Brothers downtown, and also on the walls of Robert Lehman's 18-room Park Avenue apartment. But the bulk of it is contained in the late Philip Lehman's

From *"Our Crowd": The Great Jewish Families of New York* by Stephen Birmingham. Copyright © 1967 by Stephen Birmingham. Copyright renewed © 1995 by Stephen Birmingham. Reprinted by permission of Brandt & Hochman Literary Agents, Inc.

town house in Fifty-fourth Street, which his son maintains as a private museum and which outsiders—art scholars only—may see by appointment. Here, heavily guarded, behind gold doors and in rooms covered with deep Persian rugs and hung with gold-fringed red plush, are most of the old masters, the Gothic tapestries, the Renaissance furniture, the Italian majolica, and the other *objets d'art*. Often at night the collector himself visits the house, sometimes with his curator, sometimes alone, and prowls the great, silent rooms like a solitary Croesus contemplating all that he has amassed.

It was once supposed that Robert Lehman, being a banker, would buy art more with an eye to the dollar than with discrimination or taste. There is a concentration, in the collection, on Sienese primitives, which are painted with a great deal of gold leaf, and Lehman's public-relations man, Benjamin Sonnenberg, once commented, "What other kind of paintings would a banker buy than Sienese, with all that gold in them?" At the same time, when some 300 items from the Lehman Collection were sent for exhibit at the Orangerie of the Louvre in Paris in the summer of 1956, one French critic wrote; "We would like the purchases of our museums to be inspired by a taste as severe as that of which M. Robert Lehman today gives us dazzling evidence." The exhibition was the talk of Paris, waiting lines formed outside the Orangerie, and over 17 thousand people saw the show in the first two weeks alone—statistics which gratified the banker in Robert Lehman.

Today Bobby Lehman is 74, and the collection continues to grow. Its total value is now impossible to calculate, and, inheritance taxes being what they are, it is unlikely that Lehman's son or any of his other heirs will be able to maintain the Lehman Collection intact and in the family.[1] The future of the town house in Fifty-fourth Street is uncertain, and the subject of much speculation in the art world. Benjamin Sonnenberg, however, has an answer. He says of his friend and client, "To begin with, Bobby isn't *going* to die. He's firmly convinced he's immortal. And furthermore, if he should turn out to be wrong, being a Lehman he'll figure out some way to take it all with him."

Robert Lehman himself is quite aware that his death and the disposition of his collection are often discussed,* and he is able to view his situation with a certain humor. Not long ago he visited the Sterling and Francine Clark Institute in Williamstown, Massachusetts, where twin tombs for the museum's founders flank the entrance to the building that houses *their* art collection. Starting up the museum's steps, he paused to gaze solemnly at the marble plaques bearing the names of Mr. and Mrs. Clark. He whispered softly, "What a way to go!"

---

[1] The collection is now separately and handsomely on display at the Metropolitan Museum of Art in New York.

Edwin Lefèvre

EDWIN LEFÈVRE

Edwin Lefèvre was a self-styled "Stock Operator" from the early 1900s, who had been "in the speculative game" since he was 14. He wrote with charm and insight. Mr. Johnson said that reading Lefèvre's *Reminiscences of a Stock Operator* stimulated him to leave the life of a Boston lawyer to take over the Fidelity funds. Readers will sense this same feeling of fascination.

The recognition of our own mistakes should not benefit us any more than the study of our successes. But there is a natural tendency in all men to avoid punishment. When you associate certain mistakes with a licking, you do not hanker for a second dose, and, of course, all stock-market mistakes wound you in two tender spots—your pocketbook and your vanity. But I will tell you something curious: A stock speculator sometimes makes mistakes and knows that he is making them. And after he makes them he will ask himself why he made them; and after thinking over it cold-bloodedly a long time after the pain of punishment is over he may learn how he came to make them, and when, and at what particular point of his trade; but not why. And then he simply calls himself names and lets it go at that.

Of course, if a man is both wise and lucky, he will not make the same mistake twice. But he will make any one of the ten thousand brothers or cousins of the original. The Mistake family is so large that there is always one of them around when you want to see what you can do in the fool-play line.

To tell you about the first of my million-dollar mistakes I shall have to go back to this time when I first became a millionaire, right after the big break of October 1907. As far as my trading went, having a million merely meant more reserves. Money does not give a trader more comfort, because, rich or poor, he can make mistakes and it is never comfortable to be wrong. And when a millionaire is right his money is merely one of his several servants. Losing money is the least of my troubles. A loss never bothers me after I take it. I forget it overnight. But being wrong—not taking the loss—that is what does the damage to the pocketbook and to the soul. You remember Dickson G. Watts' story about the man who was so nervous that a friend asked him what was the matter.

"I can't sleep," answered the nervous one.

"Why not?" asked the friend.

"I am carrying so much cotton that I can't sleep thinking about it. It is wearing me out. What can I do?"

"Sell down to the sleeping point," answered the friend.

As a rule a man adapts himself to conditions so quickly that he loses the perspective. He does not feel the difference much—that is, he does not vividly remember how it felt not to be a millionaire. He only remembers that there were things he could not do that he can do now. It does not take a reasonably young and normal man very long to lose the habit of being poor. It requires a little longer to forget that he used to be rich. I suppose that is because money creates needs or encourages their multiplication. I mean that after a man makes money in the stock market he very quickly loses the habit of not spending. But after he loses his money it takes him a long time to lose the habit of spending.

After I took in my shorts and went long in October 1907, I decided to take it easy for a while. I bought a yacht and planned to go off on a cruise in southern waters. I am crazy about fishing and I was due to have the time of my life. I looked forward to it and expected to go any day. But I did not. The market wouldn't let me.

I always have traded in commodities as well as in stocks. I began as a youngster in the bucket shops. I studied those markets for years, though perhaps not so assiduously as the stock market. As a matter of fact, I would rather play commodities than stocks. There is no question about their greater legitimacy, as it were. It partakes more of the nature of a commercial venture than trading in stocks does. A man can approach it as he might any mercantile problem. It may be possible to use fictitious arguments for or against a certain trend in a commodity market; but success will be only temporary, for in the end the facts are bound to prevail, so that a trader gets dividends on study and observation, as he does in a regular business. He can watch and weigh conditions and he knows as much about it as anyone else. He need not guard against inside cliques. Dividends are not unexpectedly passed or increased overnight in the cotton market or in wheat or corn. In the long run commodity prices are governed but by one law—the economic law of demand and supply. The business of the trader in commodities is simply to get facts about the demand and the supply, present and prospective. He does not indulge in guesses about a dozen things as he does in stocks. It always appealed to me.

Of course the same things happen in all speculative markets. The message of the tape is the same. That will be perfectly plain to anyone who will take the trouble to think. He will find if he asks himself questions and considers conditions, that the answers will supply themselves directly. But people never take the trouble to ask questions, leave alone seeking answers. The average American is from Missouri everywhere and at all times except when he goes to the brokers' offices and looks at the tape, whether it is stocks or commodities. The one game of all games that really requires study before making a play is the one he goes into without his usual highly intelligent preliminary and precautionary doubts. He will risk half his fortune in the stock market with less reflection than he devotes to the selection of a medium-priced automobile.

This matter of tape reading is not so complicated as it appears. Of course you need experience. But it is even more important to keep certain fundamentals in mind. To read the tape is not to have your fortune told. The tape does not tell you how much you will surely be worth next Thursday at 1:35 P.M. The object of reading the tape is to ascertain, first, how and, next, when to trade—that is, whether it is wiser to buy than to sell. It works exactly the same for stocks as for cotton or wheat or corn or oats.

You watch the market—that is, the course of prices as recorded by the tape—with one object: to determine the direction—that is, the price tendency. Prices, we know, will move either up or down according to the resistance they encounter. For purposes of easy explanation we will say that prices, like everything else, move along the line of least resistance. They will do whatever comes easiest, therefore they will go up if there is less resistance to an advance than to a decline; and vice versa.

Nobody should be puzzled as to whether a market is a bull or a bear market after it fairly starts. The trend is evident to a man who has an open mind and reasonably clear sight, for it is never wise for a speculator to fit his facts to his theories. Such a man will, or ought to, know whether it is a bull or a bear market, and if he knows that he knows whether to buy or to sell. It is therefore at the very inception of the movement that a man needs to know whether to buy or to sell.

Let us say, for example, that the market, as it usually does in those between-swings times, fluctuates within a range of ten points; up to 130 and down to 120. It may look very weak at the bottom; or, on the way up, after a rise of eight or ten points, it may look as strong as anything. A man ought not to be led into trading by tokens. He should wait until the tape tells him that the time is ripe. As a matter of fact, millions upon millions of dollars have been lost by men who bought stocks because they looked cheap or sold them because they looked dear. The speculator is not an investor. His object is not to secure a steady return on his money at a good rate of interest, but to profit by either a rise or a fall in the price of whatever he may be speculating in. Therefore the thing to determine is the speculative line of least resistance at the moment of trading; and what he should wait for is the moment when that line defines itself, because that is his signal to get busy.

Reading the tape merely enables him to see that at 130 the selling had been stronger than the buying and a reaction in the price logically followed. Up to the point where the selling prevailed over the buying, superficial students of the tape may conclude that the price is not going to stop short of 150, and they buy. But after the reaction begins they hold on, or sell out at a small loss, or they go short and talk bearish. But at 120 there is stronger resistance to the decline. The buying prevails over the selling, there is a rally and the shorts cover. The public is so often whip-sawed that one marvels at their persistence in not learning their lesson.

Eventually something happens that increases the power of either the up-ward or the downward force and the point of greatest resistance moves up or down—that is, the buying at 130 will for the first time be stronger than the selling, or the selling at 120 be stronger than the buying. The price will break through the old barrier or movement-limit and go on. As a rule, there is always a crowd of traders who are short at 120 because it looked so weak, or long at 130 because it looked so strong, and, when the market goes against them they are forced, after a while, either to change their minds and turn or to close out. In either event they help to define even more clearly the price line of least resistance. Thus the intelligent trader who has pa-tiently waited to determine this line will enlist the aid of fundamental trade conditions and also of the force of the trading of that part of the community that happened to guess wrong and must now rectify mistakes. Such correc-tions tend to push prices along the line of least resistance.

And right here I will say that, though I do not give it as a mathematical certainty or as an axiom of speculation, my experience has been that acci-dents—that is, the unexpected or unforeseen—have always helped me in my market position whenever the latter has been based upon my determination of the line of least resistance. Do you remember that Union Pacific episode at Saratoga. . . ? Well, I was long because I found out that the line of least re-sistance was upward. I should have stayed long instead of letting my broker tell me that insiders were selling stocks. It didn't make any difference what was going on in the directors' minds. That was something I couldn't possi-bly know. But I could and did know that the tape said: "Going up!" And then came the unexpected raising of the dividend rate and the 30-point rise in the stock. At 164 prices looked mighty high, but as I told you before, stocks are never too high to buy or too low to sell. The price, per se, has nothing to do with establishing my line of least resistance.

You will find in actual practice that if you trade as I have indicated any important piece of news given out between the closing of one market and the opening of another is usually in harmony with the line of least resis-tance. The trend has been established before the news is published, and in bull markets bear items are ignored and bull news exaggerated, and vice versa. Before the war broke out the market was in very weak condition. There came the proclamation of Germany's submarine policy. I was short 150 thousand shares of stock, not because I knew the news was coming, but because I was going along the line of least resistance. What happened came out of a clear sky, as far as my play was concerned. Of course I took advan-tage of the situation and I covered my shorts that day.

It sounds very easy to say that all you have to do is to watch the tape, establish your resistance points and be ready to trade along the line of least resistance as soon as you have determined it. But in actual practice a man has to guard against many things, and most of all against himself—that is, against human nature. That is the reason why I say that the man who is right always has two forces working in his favor—basic conditions and the men who are wrong. In a bull market bear factors are ignored. That is human nature, and yet human beings profess astonishment at it. People will tell you that the wheat crop has gone to pot because there has been bad weather in one or two sections and some farmers have been ruined. When the entire crop is gathered and all the farmers in all the wheat-growing sections begin to take their wheat to the elevators the bulls are surprised at the smallness of the damage. They discover that they merely have helped the bears.

When a man makes his play in a commodity market he must not permit himself set opinions. He must have an open mind and flexibility. It is not wise to disregard the message of the tape, no matter what your opinion of crop conditions or of the probable demand may be. I recall how I missed a big play just by trying to anticipate the starting signal. I felt so sure of conditions that I thought it was not necessary to wait for the line of least resistance to define itself. I even thought I might help it arrive, because it looked as if it merely needed a little assistance.

I was very bullish on cotton. It was hanging around twelve cents, running up and down within a moderate range. It was in one of those in-between places and I could see it. I knew I really ought to wait. But I got to thinking that if I gave it a little push it would go beyond the upper resistance point.

I bought 50 thousand bales. Sure enough, it moved up. And sure enough, as soon as I stopped buying it stopped going up. Then it began to settle back to where it was when I began buying it. I got out and it stopped going down. I thought I was now much nearer the starting signal, and presently I thought I'd start it myself again. I did. The same thing happened. I bid it up, only to see it go down when I stopped. I did this four or five times until I finally quit in disgust. It cost me about $200 thousand. I was done with it. It wasn't very long after that when it began to go up and never stopped till it got to a price that would have meant a killing for me—if I hadn't been in such a great hurry to start.

This experience has been the experience of so many traders so many times that I can give this rule: In a narrow market, when prices are not getting anywhere to speak of but move within a narrow range, there is no sense in trying to anticipate what the next big movement is going to be—up or down. The thing to do is to watch the market, read the tape to determine the limits of the get-nowhere prices, and make up your mind that you will not take an interest until the price breaks through the limit in either direction. A speculator must concern himself with making money out of the market and not with insisting that the tape must agree with him. Never argue with it or ask it for reasons or explanations. Stock-market post-mortems don't pay dividends.

Not so long ago I was with a party of friends. They got to talking wheat. Some of them were bullish and others bearish. Finally they asked me what I thought. . . . "If you are sure you wish to make money in wheat just you watch it. Wait. The moment it crosses $1.20 buy it and you will get a nice quick play in it!". . .

As I told you, I had watched it a long time. For months it sold between $1.10 and $1.20, getting nowhere in particular. Well, sir, one day it closed at above $1.19. I got ready for it. Sure enough the next day it opened at $1.20, and I bought. It went to $1.21, to $1.22, to $1.23, to $1.25, and I went with it.

Now I couldn't have told you at the time just what was going on. I didn't get any explanations about its behavior during the course of the limited fluctuations. I couldn't tell whether the breaking through the limit would be up through $1.20 or down through $1.10, though I suspected it would be up because there was not enough wheat in the world for a big break in prices.

As a matter of fact, it seems Europe had been buying quietly and a lot of traders had gone short of it at around $1.19. Owing to the European purchases and other causes, a lot of wheat had been taken out of the market, so that finally the big movement got started. The price went beyond the $1.20 mark. That was all the point I had and it was all I needed. I knew that when it crossed $1.20 it would be because the upward movement at last had gathered force to push it over the limit and something had to happen. In other words, by crossing $1.20 the line of least resistance of wheat prices was established. It was a different story then. . . .

What I have told you gives you the essence of my trading system as based on studying the tape. I merely learn the way prices are most probably going to move. I check up my own trading by additional tests, to determine the psychological moment. I do that by watching the way the price acts after I begin.

It is surprising how many experienced traders there are who look incredulous when I tell them that when I buy stocks for a rise I like to pay top prices and when I sell I must sell low or not at all. It would not be so difficult to make money if a trader always stuck to his speculative guns— that is, waited for the line of least resistance to define itself and began buying only when the tape said up or selling only when it said down. He should accumulate his line on the way up. Let him buy one-fifth of his full line. If that does not show him a profit he must not increase his holdings because he has obviously begun wrong; he is wrong temporarily and there is no profit in being wrong at any time. The same tape that said UP did not necessarily lie merely because it is now saying NOT YET.

In cotton I was very successful in my trading for a long time. I had my theory about it and I absolutely lived up to it. Suppose I had decided that my line would be 40 to 50 thousand bales. Well, I would study the tape as I told you, watching for an opportunity either to buy or to sell. Suppose the line of least resistance indicated a bull movement. Well, I would buy 10 thousand bales. After I got through buying that, if the market went up 10 points over my initial purchase price, I would take on another 10 thousand bales. Same thing. Then, if I could get 20 points' profit, or one dollar a bale, I would buy 20 thousand more. That would give me my line—my basis for my trading. But if after buying the first 10 or 20 thousand bales, it showed me a loss, out I'd go. I was wrong. It might be I was only temporarily wrong. But as I have said before it doesn't pay to start wrong in anything.

What I accomplished by sticking to my system was that I always had a line of cotton in every real movement. In the course of accumulating my full line I might chip out 50 or 60 thousand dollars in these feeling-out plays of mine. This looks like a very expensive testing, but it wasn't. After the real movement started, how long would it take me to make up the 50 thousand dollars I had dropped in order to make sure that I began to load up at exactly the right time? No time at all! It always pays a man to be right at the right time.

As I think I also said before, this describes what I may call my system for placing my bets. It is simple arithmetic to prove that it is a wise thing to have the big bet down only when you win, and when you lose to lose only a small exploratory bet, as it were. If a man trades in the way I have described, he will always be in the profitable position of being able to cash in on the big bet. . . .

I sometimes think that speculation must be an unnatural sort of business, because I find that the average speculator has arrayed against him his own nature. The weaknesses that all men are prone to are fatal to success in speculation—usually those very weaknesses that make him likable to his fellows or that he himself particularly guards against in those other ventures of his where they are not nearly so dangerous as when he is trading in stocks or commodities.

The speculator's chief enemies are always boring from within. It is inseparable from human nature to hope and to fear. In speculation when the market goes against you you hope that every day will be the last day—and you lose more than you should had you not listened to hope—to the same ally that is so potent a success-bringer to empire builders and pioneers, big and little. And when the market goes your way you become fearful that the next day will take away your profit, and you get out—too soon. Fear keeps you from making as much money as you ought to. The successful trader has to fight these two deep-seated instincts. He has to reverse what you might call his natural impulses. Instead of hoping he must fear; instead of fearing he must hope. He must fear that his loss may develop into a much bigger loss, and hope that his profit may become a big profit. It is absolutely wrong to gamble in stocks the way the average man does.

I have been in the speculative game ever since I was 14. It is all I have ever done. I think I know what I am talking about. And the conclusion that I have reached after nearly 30 years of constant trading, both on a shoestring and with millions of dollars back of me, is this: A man may beat a stock or a group at a certain time, but no man living can beat the stock market! A man may make money out of individual deals in cotton or grain, but no man can beat the cotton market or the grain market. It's like the track. A man may beat a horse race, but he cannot beat horse racing.

If I knew how to make these statements stronger or more emphatic I certainly would. It does not make any difference what anybody says to the contrary. I know I am right in saying these are incontrovertible statements.

Jesse L. Livermore

DANA THOMAS

This vignette about the King of the Bears, Jesse Livermore, focuses on his early trading education and the development of his methods. Readers will quickly discover the genius of the man, and the combination of iron will, patience, and timing that characterized his operations.

Jesse L. Livermore began life humbly enough.

He was born on a farm in Shrewsbury, Massachusetts, and as soon as he got out of school, he obtained his first job marking the quotation prices for a display board in the Boston branch of the broker firm of Paine, Webber & Co. He was fast at figuring; he could add numbers, multiply and divide in his head without having to calculate on paper, and he would remember, down to the last fraction of a point, what such and such a stock had sold for in the previous trade. In watching the fluctuations of prices on the board day after day he came to develop a feel for price behavior. He became aware that the tape was a most powerful tool for analyzing the struggle taking place in the market. Instead of leaving the broker office when his work was done, he would stay for hours, jotting down the prices left standing on the board in a little memorandum book, studying the changes from the previous day's figures, searching for the repetitive patterns of market behavior.

Shortly after joining Paine, Webber, Livermore began frequenting bucket shops during his lunch hour to try his hand at the play. America in the 1890s teemed with shops that were ready to part the trader from his cash. They were to the stock market what the bookie today is to the racetrack. The trader did not buy and sell the actual stocks traded in the market but bet on the prices as they were reported on the quote board of the shop. The customer gave his money to a clerk and told him what he wished to trade in. He could bet either way, long or short. If he bet long and the market went up, he cashed in accordingly. If he bet on the short side and the stock tumbled, he made money that way. When the market turned against him, however, and the price went beyond the limit set by his margin, the deal was automatically concluded and the trader was cleaned out.

Livermore began playing the bucket shops and found that he had been born for the life. With a quick head for figures and an uncanny ability to anticipate price fluctuations, he presented an unusual threat to the shop owners—a customer who consistently won. This was unheard of and could not be tolerated, for the bucket shop owner was ordinarily as certain of coming out ahead in the long run as the croupier in a gambling casino. The very nature of the betting operation normally assured that he couldn't be beaten. And the shops practiced a variety of tricks to guarantee their edge.

It was standard practice for a shop to hold back from reporting sudden fast price moves on the Stock Exchange floor. If U.S. Steel, for instance, was selling at 90 and took a sudden climb to 100, the shop wouldn't announce this on the board immediately. It would let the stock advance only to 96 on a fake quotation, in the hope that some of the traders would be suckered into selling short, expecting the price to swing down again. After a few trades had been made at 96, the shop then would announce the rest of the run-up to 100, and the players who had gone short at 96 would be cleaned out.

But despite such sharp practices, Livermore continued to win. Gossip travels fast through the gamblers' grapevine, and in virtually no time most of the houses on the circuit were warned about him. Whenever Livermore walked in and plunked down his money, the clerks would stare at it as if they were hypnotized by the eyes of a snake. No one would lift a finger to take it. Livermore tried every dodge to force shops into letting him play. He took a fictitious name and traded in out-of-the-way houses. To allay suspicion he even tried losing deliberately on small stakes in the hope the house would let him get involved in big enough ones to make a killing. As more and more houses shut their doors, he had to travel further and further afield to get any action. But even under these handicaps, Livermore continued to win.

He had one consuming ambition—to accumulate enough money to enter the stock market as something more than a piker trader. And the day finally came when he was able to swing a big enough line for significant operations. He discovered that playing the stock market required a different strategy from playing the bucket shops. In the shops one bet on fluctuations of a few points, knowing exactly what price one was getting when one bought and when one sold. But the market was a different kettle of fish. The time that elapsed between the order a trader gave to buy or sell at the market and the actual price at the time of sale could vary sufficiently enough to wipe out his stake. Livermore found that while he was right more often than not in anticipating where a stock was heading, he was not making as much money as he should have because he was following the age-old psychology of the conventional trader—snatching at immediate gains instead of letting his profits ride. He took a 5-point profit only to see his stock continue up 15 or 20 points. He came to realize that the hardest thing for a trader was to put his anxieties on a leash. The market did not outwit the trader. He outwitted himself. The man who could sit still for as long as necessary for the market to confirm the accuracy of his judgment was a rare breed. The most important thing was to establish position, to keep one's eye on the long swing.

Livermore learned to play with nerves of steel. He had no predilections on moral grounds about going long or selling short. Frequently when he sold out a stock as a bull he simultaneously went short on it; for he reasoned that if it was poor judgment to continue to be long on a stock, it made equally good sense to turn bearish on it. He geared himself to make a profit coming or going.

Like other successful plungers, he seemed to be possessed of a mystical prescience. He had an instinct for foreseeing events in a way he could not explain rationally. Rumors spread among his friends that he acted on subconscious impulses. There were times when he just had to put away his golf clubs and rush to his broker's office to make a sudden short sale. There were occasions when he went fishing on which he put down his rod and hurried back to land and the local broker house to wire a buying order. His moods were unpredictable. At times he would move like lightning in his trading; on other occasions he would wait for months, doing nothing whatever, lying on the beach on the Riviera, 3,000 miles from Wall Street. And then, inexplicably, he would leap into action. Livermore himself disclaimed any extrasensory perception. And yet, some curious sixth sense divining the future led to one odd episode.

Early in 1906, Livermore took a vacation in Atlantic City. One morning he strolled along the boardwalk and sauntered into a brokerage office to see how the market was doing. It was climbing briskly. The Dow-Jones average was up several points. He looked casually over the quotation board until his eye lit on Union Pacific. The railroad stock was one of the market's star performers—deemed to be practically as invulnerable as the Rock of Gibraltar. The news about the road was overwhelmingly bullish. Livermore picked up a pad and wrote out a message for the office manager. It was an order to sell a thousand shares of Union Pacific short. The manager emitted a nervous little laugh as if to say, "That was a slip of the pen, wasn't it, Mr. Livermore? You meant *buy* a thousand shares." Livermore had no conscious reason for selling Union Pacific short. He had heard nothing about the road that everyone else didn't know. Its earnings' prospects were rosy. Freight and passenger revenues were on the rise. Its capital position was strong. And yet, deep within him, there was the feeling that all was not well.

He picked up a second order blank and wrote out orders to sell another two thousand shares short. He went out for a bite of lunch. When he had finished his coffee, he returned to the broker office and glanced at the quote board. The price of Union Pacific had climbed higher since his last sale. He was heavily short on a climbing market; yet he was strangely untroubled. The next day Union Pacific backed off a little. Livermore sold two thousand more shares short. That night he cut short his vacation and returned to New York to be closer to the action.

The following morning news came over the wires that stunned the nation. *San Francisco had been hit by an earthquake.* It was one of the greatest disasters in history. Whole city blocks had been leveled; hotels, office buildings and homes collapsed like splintered matchsticks. City Hall was demolished. The Grand Opera House and the entire financial district were reduced to ashes. Soldiers were rushed to the city with bayonets to hold in check the mobs. Livermore had acted on an uncanny premonition of disaster, for which there was no obvious ready explanation.

However, a curious thing happened. When the news reached New York, the stock market remained strong, yielding only a few points at first and then rebounding. The bulls who had been accumulating massive holdings for months weren't going to be dislodged easily. Although Union Pacific had miles of track in the disaster area and was bound to suffer, the stock refused to go down. Livermore was short almost a half million dollars, and his associates were gloomy over his prospects. A cataclysmic blow of nature had been unable to shake the Union Pacific stock. They urged Livermore to cover and take his losses before they grew heavier. But he held on. The hunch that had impelled him to sell in the first place continued to possess him.

And, sure enough, on the following day, as the details of the earthquake poured into New York and the full scope of the disaster became evident, the market began to slide. At first it was a measured, orderly retreat without any indication of panic. Then, twenty-four hours later, the break that Livermore had been waiting for developed. For several days now traders had been sifting the news from San Francisco to ferret out its implications. And at last they reacted; the market's critical threshold of resistance was penetrated and broken. At first, prices fell slowly; then they picked up momentum. Finally, the panic was on. Livermore doubled his ante; he unleashed wave after wave of selling and on the following day he covered, making a quarter of a million dollars on the play. He had held his fire until the last possible moment. He had learned through years of bitter experience a lesson that only the most successful speculators really take to heart. It is the most difficult thing in the world for one to keep himself on a leash, when he knows he is absolutely right in his judgment, waiting for the big swing. It is only on the big swing that the big money is made, but the market all too often takes an unconscionable time to behave as the astute speculator knows it eventually must. In the meantime, the trader has to sweat it out.

From then on Livermore's career as a short seller gained momentum. He became a master manipulator of the subterranean depths of fear, exploring the psychic caverns of suppressed anxieties with a touch approaching that of genius. He turned into an expert at sensing the nature and scope of mass hysteria, the threshold levels at which different men begin to panic. Everyone has some level beyond which he loses control of himself. And Livermore became adept at manipulating the conditions necessary to bring his bull opponents to this point. Wrestling with one's adversary was frequently a long, sustained cold war of nerves. Livermore developed an infinite patience for waiting out the enemy, an infinite cunning for accepting reverses and turning them into opportunities, and the courage to wait without moving a hair until the time was ripe for a decisive strike.

Utilizing these talents, Livermore was able to make a second killing within a year after the San Francisco earthquake. In 1907 he had studied economic conditions carefully and come to the conclusion that the money outlook was far more critical than most people realized. Money rates were rising ominously all over the world. Unemployment was growing in the United States. Livermore concluded that the nation was heading for a recession and that the stock market was bound to react accordingly.

He went heavily short. At first, as in the case of Union Pacific the previous year, the stocks he sold short stayed strong; and once again his associates were skeptical about his judgment. But Livermore was certain he was right. He felt that the longer the market hesitated about going down, the more drastic the final break would be. He sat through rally after rally without turning a hair. And he continued to put out heavier and heavier short lines. In the meantime, money got scarcer and call rates rose. The market broke, and the tumble accelerated as Livermore and other bears unleashed waves of selling.

Morgan sent word through his emissaries to Livermore and the other top bears warning them to let up or take the responsibility for consequences no one could foresee. Livermore listened and was convinced. He had already raked in over $1 million on paper. He was realistic enough to know that if the market became any weaker, he might be unable to turn these paper profits into cash. And if the Exchange were forced to close, this would freeze his assets.

So he agreed to let up on his pounding. Upon covering his lines, in one day alone—October 24, 1907—he took in over a quarter of a million dollars. And he never forgot—nor did Wall Street—that the market had been at his mercy and that of other big bears during its most critical hour. The bankers had been forced to come hat in hand to this onetime bucket shop trader because he had guessed right about the course of events against virtually the entire investment world.

Livermore emerged from the panic of 1907 a nationally known figure.

Joseph P. Kennedy

ROBERT CANTWELL and RICHARD J. WHALEN

Joseph P. Kennedy's skills and persistent striving enabled him to realize several ambitions: he established both a family fortune and a political dynasty. The first of these two pieces dates from 1937 and tells the Kennedy public story up to the time when his work for the New Deal was rewarded by appointment as U.S. Ambassador to the Court of St. James. The second is a brief snippet from a 1964 biography and reports on a revealing incident from young Joe Kennedy's Harvard years.

On the public career of Mr. Joseph Patrick Kennedy the curtain rose uncertainly at three o'clock on the afternoon of July 2, 1934, to the accompaniment of murmurs of discontent. . . . That day the ambiguous Mr. Kennedy, a highly successful Wall Street speculator, arrived to head a reform commission designed to curb Wall Street speculators like himself.

The off-stage muttering came from many sources. In the center of the stage with Joseph Kennedy (who had no idea of how big a show it was going to be) there was the keen, expressionless Mr. James Landis, one of the authors of the Securities Exchange Act and the man most frequently mentioned for the chairmanship. With him was the short, emotional Mr. Ferdinand Pecora, often mentioned for the same post, whose stock-market investigation had revealed, among other things, that Mr. Kennedy had made a killing in a large pool operation only a short time before. . . .

Excerpted from Robert Cantwell and Richard J. Whalen, *Fortune Magazine*, 1937, pp. 57–59, 138–44. Reprinted from *The Founding Father: The Story of Joseph P. Kennedy*. Regnery Publishing, Inc. Reprinted by permission of Time, Inc.

New Dealers scattered around Washington . . . looked on Kennedy's appointment as the final surrender of the New Deal to Wall Street's warmest embrace. These people knew that Mr. Kennedy had given $15,000 to the Democratic campaign fund, had lent $50,000 more, and they had heard that he had contributed another $100,000 indirectly. Almost to a man the New Dealers had tried to stop his appointment to the SEC, and there was a series of inspired, last minute, front page editorials, calling attention to Mr. Kennedy's record (which nobody had very straight). . . .

But if the heat, the protest, or the suspicions of his new colleagues fazed Joseph Kennedy at that first meeting, he did not show it. Pecora arrived a little late, frowning, and went into private conference with Landis, who was also looking glum. Mr. Kennedy waited with Commissioners Healy and Mathews. He had never met the commissioners until the day he became Chairman. He had never held a political job of any consequence. He was no reformer. Since the President had selected him for the Commission's five-year term, which was equivalent to presidential recommendation for the chairmanship, his election was reasonably certain; but Mr. Kennedy knew that a chairman without a majority was no chairman at all. Presently he limped four doors down the hall to join Pecora and Landis (he had fallen off a horse a few weeks before and broken his leg) and in about an hour they all emerged, smiling happily, to announce that Mr. Kennedy was Chairman, that Mr. Pecora would stay with the Commission, and that all was well. Joseph Kennedy had won over his first two critics. The next day he asked Landis, Cohen, and Corcoran to lunch. When they met in the inexpensive open-front Tally-Ho Tavern Coffee House, the ex-Wall Street speculator grinned as he shook hands with the authors of the bill designed to curb speculation, and asked them interestedly, "Why the hell do you fellows hate me?"

The curtain descended on the first act of Joseph Patrick Kennedy's public career some 15 months later when he resigned from the SEC. By that time it was generally considered the New Deal's most successful reform. Mr. Kennedy's opponents at the time it started—Landis, Pecora, Corcoran, Cohen, and the New Dealers by and large—had become his friends and partisans. . . .

When you think of Mr. Kennedy's career you think of a life that has been lived, not in terms of years, but of months, weeks, or even days. He was a bank examiner for 18 months and a bank president for three years. He was assistant general manager of Bethlehem Shipbuilding Corp.'s Fore River yards for 20 months, president of Film Booking Offices of America for two years and nine months, chairman of the board of Keith-Albee-Orpheum for five months, special adviser for First National Pictures for six weeks, reorganizer of Radio Corp. of America for two and a half months, a special adviser to Paramount Pictures for 74 days, and chairman of the Securities and Exchange Commission for the most consequential 431 days of his life.

You cannot discuss Joseph Patrick Kennedy's career with any fullness unless you discuss the stories that have always swirled around him. They are a part of his personality, like his pungent language or his habit of working in his shirt sleeves. Ten years ago, when he was in Hollywood producing about 50 movies a year, Hollywood considered him a Boston banker. . . . About the same time Wall Street identified Joseph Kennedy as a Hollywood producer. And Boston—where he had grown up and been in several kinds of business for 12 years—placed him as the son-in-law of one of her many ex-mayors. When he went into the SEC his New Deal colleagues, as has been indicated, eyed him suspiciously as a Wall Street speculator, and when he went back to Wall Street he was regarded just as doubtfully as an emissary of the New Deal. . . .

Mr. Kennedy was born on September 6, 1888, on Meridian Street in East Boston, and lived during his boyhood on Webster Street, near the terminus of the narrow gauge that ran down to Lynn, near the piers, in a little section of moderate dwellings set back from streets with seafaring names—Liverpool Street, Bremen Street, Hamburg, and Havre. His father had been a state representative at 28, a state senator at 32, and went from politics into neighborhood banking, into a coal company, the wholesale liquor business, partnership in two East Boston saloons, eventually to become Boston's election commissioner and fire commissioner. He was a familiar figure in that strange, provincial, pre-war Boston political and financial world—the city of Brandeis and Charles Mellen, and of the great New Haven scandal, in the period when it was possible to be a national figure in Boston and yet remain unknown to the rest of the country. . . .

One of the main tendencies in Boston finance from 1910 to 1914 was the consolidation of small trust companies about the size of Columbia Trust. At the end of 1913 Columbia Trust was at the point of being taken over by the First Ward National. The Kennedys had a sentimental as well as financial interest in the bank, and by combining the assets of relatives, drawing on uncles for help, Joe got together $45,000 to buy stock in Columbia Trust, collected proxies around East Boston to keep control of it there, and was elected President by the Board of Directors. So he became a bank president at 25, widely publicized as the youngest in the country, just about the time Boston finance froze up tight and the Exchange closed for six months, at the outbreak of the war.

Joe had borrowed heavily to buy Columbia's stock, and his family had borrowed heavily to help him. He borrowed another $2,000 when he married Miss Rose Fitzgerald in October 1914, and made his down payment on a $6,500 house in Brookline. His bride had graduated from the Sacred Heart Convent in Boston, taken a postgraduate course at Aix-la-Chapelle, where she was a piano gold medalist. . . .

Joe's debts were crowding him hard and the Kennedy family grew rapidly—the first son was born in 1915, the second in 1917, followed by five girls and another son by 1928 and a youngest son in 1932—so that by the time Joe Junior was 10 there were seven children in the household. But before that time Joe had left Columbia Trust to become assistant general manager of Bethlehem's Fore River yards during the war, served on the Board of Trustees of the Massachusetts Electric Co., learned market operations in the investment banking house of Hayden, Stone after the war, and acquired an aptitude as a market operator that made him his fortune during the bull market.

He met Galen Stone in trying to persuade Stone (who was chairman of the board of Atlantic, Gulf & West Indies) to have his ships built by Bethlehem; he studied Stone's habits, took a seat next to him on the train, and while he could not interest Stone in ordering ships, he interested Stone in himself. As a result he was hired to head the stock department of Hayden, Stone's Boston office. About that same time something happened that steered Boston capital, especially small capital, toward the movies. In 1919 the president of a small trust company much like Kennedy's Columbia Trust backed a suburban retail merchant in producing a movie. It was *The Miracle Man*, and it grossed $3,000,000 on an investment of $120,000. In those days before Hollywood's unquestioned dominance, movies were still being produced on shoestrings in 13 U.S. cities, in enterprises that were more nearly akin to wildcat oil drilling than to modern large-scale production. The backer of *The Miracle Man* put his winnings into an effort to repeat, and when his company went under it was offered to Kennedy. He turned it down, but with a group of young Bostonians bought control of a chain of 31 small movie theatres scattered over New England and took a brief flier into production himself. But he was still dealing in thousands of dollars, and it was not until 1924 that he began to deal in millions. . . .

The first of [two features starring Gloria Swanson] was the ill-fated *Queen Kelly*, directed by Von Stroheim and never released. Kennedy had approved the script, and was in Palm Beach on vacation when Gloria Swanson called to tell him that difficulties had developed about the end of the picture. He had some $750,000 invested in it by that time, and it was still far from concluded. Kennedy hurried to Hollywood. There he saw unreeling a picture that he had not visualized from the script, opening with a scene of a priest administering the last sacrament to the madam of a bawdy-house, and including a vividly presented scene of the seduction of a convent girl. He thought of that appearing under "Joseph P. Kennedy Presents." Although he was no moralist, and although he recognized that Von Stroheim had done a beautiful job, it was too much for him. He spent another $100,000 trying to salvage it, asking Goldwyn and Irving Thalberg for advice, and hired Edmund Goulding on their recommendation. Still *Queen Kelly* would not end, and after he had sunk some $950,000 in it, he shelved it. He had wanted to get out of production. But rather than quit on a failure he made one more feature, *The Trespasser*, in which Gloria Swanson starred in Edmund Goulding's script. By the time it began breaking records at its opening, he was well enough satisfied to get out.

Kennedy moved so fast that opinions still differ as to whether he left a string of reorganized companies or a heap of wreckage behind him. When he left the movies after that drive he had a fortune of about $5,000,000 and was 32 pounds underweight. Losing 32 pounds still left him with 168. But for Kennedy, who works with whole-souled concentration at some periods, and relaxes as completely at others, and whose exercises are always strenuous, it was alarming. He went to the hospital. When he emerged the depression was at that point where no fortune promised security and where others besides Joseph Kennedy were wondering if a house in Palm Beach (which he had) was a refuge or a target. And relaxing at his Palm Beach house, or at his house in Bronxville, or at Cape Cod (where he stretched out in the sun on the porch while his personal stock ticker chattered out its bad news inside), he began belatedly to clarify his social views. He has expressed them tentatively in his campaign volume, *I'm for Roosevelt*, which contains, among other things, an observation that at the low point of the depression his friends were murmuring that if they were sure they could keep half of what they had, they would be content. That was his feeling: he had made his money to provide security for his children, and it was plain that there could be no security for them while the social system itself was in danger. By such steps Mr. Kennedy reasoned from the particular to the general. He could not disagree with the social objectives of many of the New Deal reforms, and if he criticized the way the laws were drafted, as he did, or the way they were administered, as he did also, he could criticize more effectively if he had the authority that came with work accomplished. So he was conditioned, in 1934, to go to Washington when the chairmanship of the SEC was offered him.

But in the realm of practical politics his progress was not so plain. When he traveled with the Roosevelt campaign train in 1932 he was rumored to be slated for Secretary of the Treasury; newspaper reports discussed his millions, and there were stories that he had won Hearst's support for Roosevelt. Moving so rapidly through so many fields, with friends and contacts in each, had left him in a position that was as influential as it was obscure: he was in circles as far apart as the movies in their pre-Legion-of-Decency days and the Catholic church; and as a devout Catholic, a friend of Cardinal Pacelli and of Father Coughlin, he occupied a special position among the early supporters of Roosevelt. To Louis McHenry Howe, as to the New Dealers in the SEC later on, Joseph Kennedy was a political and financial enigma, and no political appointments followed his work in the 1932 campaign. In the summer of 1933 he was again on Wall Street, active in a pool in the stock of Libbey-Owens-Ford Glass Co.—an episode that was to form the substance of the liberal criticism against him when he went into the SEC the next year. He had met Raymond Moley during the campaign, and in the period that Landis and Pecora were being discussed for chairmanship of the SEC, Moley was urging Kennedy's candidacy at the White House. . . .

When Mr. Kennedy went into the SEC he had a very clear idea of when his own work would be finished. It would be when the capital market was restored. Other parts of the job—perfecting the internal organization of some 700 people, reassuring small investors by cleaning up the worst abuses, revising the complicated registration forms—were big tasks, but underlying them was the tremendous one of restoring the capital market. Unlike many of his New Deal colleagues, Kennedy did not regard the market as a mere barometer reflecting the condition of the country's business. He considered it the generator, which meant that he looked upon the issuing of new securities as the surest index of prosperity. And the thin trickle of new financing had almost entirely dried up. During the 17 months before March 1935, new issues, secured bonds and debentures, amounted to only $89,000,000. In January, for instance, there were no new issues of any consequence, and in February the total was only $1,875,000. The New Dealers had a name for this condition. They called it a strike of capital. Kennedy himself referred to it more tactfully as lack of confidence. The theory of the New Dealers was that the log jam in the capital market was artificial; as they saw it the big Wall Street underwriting houses were holding back because they believed that in so doing they would force the SEC to liberalize its restrictions.

So again Kennedy was playing a waiting game against a number of opponents—but this one ended sensationally. In February 1935, Swift & Co. opened negotiations with the SEC for listing a $43,000,000 bond issue. But the novelty of that issue lay in the fact that it was sold directly to the public by the firm of Salomon Bros. & Hutzler (afterward, it was said, boycotted into abandoning the practice), which handled the issue for a fraction of a point instead of the two or three point spread usually received by the bankers. According to Mr. Kennedy's New Deal audience, which by this time was watching him with enthusiasm tinged with awe, the Swift & Co. issue was not only new financing. It was a threat to the established spread. Whatever the reason, the log jam in the capital market broke immediately. In March new issues of secured bonds amounted to $97,000,000, or more than the total of secured bonds and debentures for the previous 17 months. In April the total was $82,000,000; in May it was $110,000,000; in June it was $151,000,000. By July the trickle of new financing had become a flood, and the total was $401,000,000; in August it was $193,000,000; in September, the month Mr. Kennedy resigned, it was $235,000,000; and by the end of the year it had added up to a grand total of $1,868,000,000. Mr. Kennedy had intended to resign in March, when the flood began. But as he was on his way to the White House with his resignation in his pocket, on March 27 (the day the Swift issue was released), he read the headlines announcing the Supreme Court decision on the NRA, and went back to work for another six months.

• • •

The gentleman from the *Boston Evening Transcript*, aware that he was covering an event of utmost importance to Proper Bostonians [the 1911 Harvard-Yale baseball game] . . . hurriedly scribbled the pregame story for page one of that afternoon's edition. The grandstand was filled well before two o'clock, and a large overflow crowd stood behind ropes in the outfield. The reporter estimated the attendance at 15 thousand persons. Also worthy of prominence in his story was the starting pitcher for Harvard: Captain Charles B. (Chick) McLaughlin, playing the last game of his brilliant career. . . . As McLaughlin warmed up, few spectators noticed the rangy, red-haired player who took a seat near the end of the Harvard bench. But his unexpected appearance in uniform drew curious stares from the players. He had failed to make the team that spring, had not appeared at other games, and, so far as anyone knew, wasn't a member of the squad. Yet there he sat. . . .

This minor mystery was forgotten as the game began. . . . The ninth inning opened with Harvard leading, 4–1. After retiring the first two Yale batters, McLaughlin turned to the umpire and asked for time. To the surprise of his teammates, he called the redhead from the bench and waved him to first base. The next Yale batter hit a grounder to the infield and was retired at first. As the Harvard team came off the field, McLaughlin, who had assured the last-minute first baseman of his coveted *H*, asked him for the game-winning ball. The substitute shook his head.

"I made the putout, didn't I?"

With that, Joe Kennedy stuck the ball in his pocket and walked away. . . .

About a year after the puzzling incident, a teammate asked McLaughlin why he had treated his sworn enemy so generously. Shamefacedly, McLaughlin said perhaps he had done the wrong thing. A few days before the game, he said, some friends of Joe's father had come to see him. They knew he intended to apply for a license to operate a movie theater when he was graduated from Harvard that June. If McLaughlin wanted the license, they clearly implied, he had better see that young Kennedy won his letter.

Said the former Harvard player to whom McLaughlin related the story: "Joe was the kind of guy who, if he wanted something bad enough, would get it, and he didn't much care how he got it. He'd run right over anybody."

William O. Douglas

MAX LERNER

William O. Douglas distinguished himself as the third chairman of the Securities and Exchange Commission—and went on to long and fruitful service on the U.S. Supreme Court.

Like any body of men that makes prowess and luck its *summum bonum*, Wall Street personalizes the forces with which it has to deal. Since 1934, when the SEC was created to watch over men who manipulate other people's money, its chairmanship has, for the Street at least, ranked in interest beyond most Cabinet portfolios. The first chairman, Joe Kennedy, was definitely "one of ours"—a boy from the Wall Street slums who had somehow grown up in the financial Dead End without succumbing to its gangsterism, but who was nevertheless known and trusted by the big shots on the Street. His successor, Jim Landis, being a Harvard law professor, a former Frankfurter disciple, a drafter of the Securities Act, and seemingly a brash young man, aroused Wall Street fears at first, but soon managed to allay them. Now comes, as the new chairman, William O. Douglas. And Wall Street wants to know, in his own words, "what kind of a bird" he is.

Apparently the Street has some basis for its jitters about Douglas. His record thus far is that of the most uncompromising member who ever sat on the commission, and despite Joe Kennedy's belief in him and support of him, Wall Street fought his selection as chairman with every means it knew how to employ. Now, nervous over the stock-market slump, aware that the first two chairmanships of the SEC were merely preparatory and that this one is likely to be crucial, it wants to know how "safe" its new mentor is.

Whatever he is, whether radical or conservative, Bill Douglas is the West Coast brand. At 39 he has not lost the look of the Western college boy, lanky, sandy-haired, earnest, able, who has come East and made good. The first impression he makes is bucolic—a big fellow, very blond, with light eyebrows and childlike blue eyes—a slow-moving fellow, low-voiced and deliberate in speech—a simple sort of fellow, with slouching ways and carelessly chosen clothes. As you get to know him, however, you discard any notions you may have had of his being either bucolic or simple. He has one of the sharpest and deftest minds in Washington, a capacity for

Excerpted from Max Lerner on William O. Douglas, *The Nation*, October 23, 1977, pp. 429–31. Reprinted by permission from *The Nation* magazine. © The Nation Company, L.P.

handling people and a calculated skill in winning them over or shocking them, as occasion may require, a sense of strategy, and an air of quiet authority. You begin to see him tentatively as a man of immense native ability, who has fitted the standards of an American university training and the skills acquired in the world of law and finance into the ideals of the western lower-middle class.

Douglas's boyhood was nomadic in the best frontier tradition. His father, who was a home missionary, moved from one western small town to another. After the father's death, the family finally settled in 1903, when the boy was five, at Yakima, Washington. Yakima was a small town, with the narrow conservatism only a small town can show. . . .

High school was for Douglas an intellectual awakening, chiefly because of good teachers. They made dents in the armor of his conventionality. . . . At Whitman College, in Walla Walla, young Douglas majored in economics, but the principal impressions made on him came slantwise from unlikely sources—from an English professor who, apart from his subjects, was a great stirrer-up of young men, and from a professor of geology and physics whom Douglas considers the greatest teacher he has ever met and of whom he still speaks with fervor. As for books, Douglas was too busy working outside class hours to read any. One still gets from him the feeling of a man who has never had leisure and wouldn't know what to do with it. During the harvest season he went into the wheat fields with the casual laborers, mostly IWWs, and after work he sat around with the "wobblies" on sacks of wheat, while they talked of their experiences and their prowess and the dream of revolution. Curiously, Douglas seems completely untouched by their social doctrine. I have rarely seen a man regarded as a radical, even a western radical, who had less interest in labor or revolutionary doctrine.

How Douglas made the transition from all this to his present place has become by now a set of minor myths. He wanted to study law in the East, but he had no money. He taught Latin and English for a few years at the Yakima high school and coached the debating team, but most of what he saved he lost through an unlucky insurance venture. Finally in 1922 he set off desperately for New York. How he took charge of a herd of sheep as far as Montana, rode the rods the rest of the way into Chicago, and then spent his last dollar on railway fare to New York has been told several times. What has not been told is how miserable this western boy felt when he first encountered New York. He found none of the warmth of the West; he found only cold, reserved men, intent on success. He could get no work, failed to pay either his room rent or his tuition, and was put out of his dormitory room. He soon managed, however, to pick up about $600 by taking a correspondence-school textbook on commercial law and fitting each lesson out with an armory of actual cases, and it tided him over his difficulties. But the study of law still seemed to him heavy, dogmatic, and stultifying. He felt he had made a mistake to come East at all, but he stuck the year out. The last two years of law school were, however, transformed for him by the work on the relation between law and business that he did with Underhill Moore, whom he regards as the best teacher in the entire field of law.

For two years after graduating from law school, Douglas went out, like an anthropologist, into Wall Street to study the facts of law and life among the natives. He interviewed the high-powered lawyers in the financial district, right down the line. It was hard not to succumb to the magic of the power that surrounded them, and for a moment at least—so Douglas confesses now—he had a vision of becoming one of them. The firm he entered was Cravath, De Gersdorff, Swaine, and Wood, and what he found in his new work was something he had been entirely unprepared for. It was not so much law as corporation finance, intricate, subtle, compelling. He threw himself into its mysteries and how well he mastered them many a lawyer and broker has since ruefully acknowledged. . . .

A bright future beckoned Douglas if he stayed with the firm. The boom market of the twenties was in full swing, his contacts with the Exchange were numerous and intimate, his friends were all playing the market. But a single plunge, although it netted him a profit, proved enough for him. He never went in again; it was too much like rolling dice. Despite the temptations to stay in Wall Street, Douglas managed to build up a curious detachment about the whole business. Moore, who was a Veblen enthusiast, had introduced him to "Absentee Ownership," which made a deep impression on him, and evoked that mood of pitiless aloofness that gave Veblen's thought about business its strength and its stringency. He was even more impressed by Brandeis's "Other People's Money," phrases from which still keep cropping up in his speeches. So, in 1927, he left New York and went back to Yakima to hang out his shingle. He had a strong feeling for the western country and was sure his roots were there. But arriving at Yakima, he found he was one of 65 lawyers in a town of 20,000. After 10 days he came back to Columbia to teach and he has been teaching law ever since. Even now, as chairman of the SEC, he is on leave of absence from the Yale Law School.

Douglas came to the SEC in October 1934, as head of its investigation of protective committees, held hearings for 15 months, established a reputation as an unyielding and infrangible inquisitor, and was on the point of writing his report in January 1936, when Joe Kennedy resigned from the commission and Douglas was appointed to succeed him. . . .

Douglas has worked out a formula about the history of the commission which is tactful yet fairly true. Kennedy's chairmanship he sees as the period of consolidating the legislative victory of the Securities Act, when everything depended on good relations with Wall Street; Landis's chairmanship he sees as the period when the tools were sharpened with which the commission would have to work; but both periods took too long, he adds, and it is high time now that the commission got things done.

Whether he will be able to get anything done depends on a good many factors. He has to reckon with the fiercest potential opposition from the financial community that any government agency in Washington has encountered. He has, secondly, to do his work in the framework of Washington politics, both sacred and profane; that is, he has to deal with Morgenthau of the Treasury and Eccles of the Federal Reserve Board, as well as with Farley and Congress. Finally, he has in his own commission a still unknown quantity. . . .

Douglas believes that, given the passage of the three bills now before Congress, the commission would have ample legal power to achieve its purposes. As for the purposes themselves, he sees them as a pretty complete reconditioning of the financial structure of the country.

That will sound to most Wall Street men, and even to most liberals, sweepingly radical. But when stress is laid upon the word "reconditioning," it becomes clear that if his plans are radical, it is only in an ethical sense. Douglas is both ironically and genuinely honest when he calls himself "a conservative of the old school." What he is driving at is that, given a capitalist structure, there is nothing wrong with the conservative theory of finance. What is wrong is the wild and unscrupulous departure from that theory in actual practice. And he knows as well as anyone in the country what excesses that practice has involved. For years he conducted a bankruptcy clinic at Yale Law School. During his three years with the commission he has spent most of his time studying reorganizations. He has become a specialist in ruins, and as a result there has crept into his thinking the macabre moral note that you will find in most undertaking establishments. In fact, the reason his speeches have been so frightening to those high financiers who live by respectable crookedness is that he takes their professions at face value and demands that they be translated into action. And that involves, of course, not a new framework of ideals but a change in behavior.

The infuriating thing from Wall Street's standpoint is that Douglas has taken an impregnable position.

GREAT PLAYERS IN AMERICAN FINANCE

Robert Morris

ARMINE NIXON HART

Robert Morris, who came to America from England at the age of six, was a wealthy Philadelphia merchant when Congress made him Superintendent of Finance during the American Revolution. In this post he borrowed, primarily from France through the influence of Ambassador Benjamin Franklin, the money needed to finance Washington's army. He lost his fortune in land speculations after the war although his holdings once included, through syndicates, most of New York State.

In presenting a brief memoir of the life of Robert Morris, it is impossible to forget the biting sarcasm and sharp wit of Rufus Choate's memorable toast: "Pennsylvania's two most distinguished citizens, Robert Morris, a native of Great Britain, and Benjamin Franklin, a native of Massachusetts." It is to portray the life of one of these *"citizens"* that I have been invited here today.

Robert Morris, the financier of the American Revolution, was born in Liverpool, Kingdom of Great Britain, on the 20th of January, 1733–34, old style, or what would be, according to the modern method of computation, January 31, 1734. His father, also Robert Morris, came to this country and settled at Oxford on the eastern shore of Maryland prior to the year 1740. He was there engaged in the tobacco trade as the factor of Foster Cunliffe, Esq., of England. His tombstone in Whitemarsh burial ground, Talbot County, Maryland, records, that "A salute from the cannon of a ship, the wad fracturing his arm, was the signal by which he departed, greatly lamented, as he was esteemed, in the fortieth year of his age, on the 12th day of July, MDCCL."

Robert, the son, at an early age came to Philadelphia, and entered the counting-house of Mr. Charles Willing, one of the first merchants of his day, and subsequently in 1754, at the age of 20, formed a copartnership with his son Thomas Willing, which lasted until 1793, a period of thirty-nine years, and the firm of Willing & Morris became the best known and largest importing house in the colonies. In October 1765, upon the arrival of the *Royal Charlotte*, carrying the obnoxious stamped paper for the colonies, a town meeting was held at the State House, to prevent the landing of the stamps, and a committee was appointed to wait upon John Hughes,

Excerpted from Armine Nixon Hart, "Robert Morris," *The Pennsylvania Magazine of History and Biography 1*, (1877), pp. 333–341. Reprinted by permission of The Historical Society of Pennsylvania.

the stamp distributor, and demand his resignation of the office. On this committee Mr. Morris was appointed, and from Hughes' letters . . . it would appear that he and James Tilghman were the spokesmen on the occasion. Later in the same year Mr. Morris signed the Non-Importation Resolutions and Agreement of the Merchants of Philadelphia, and in January 1766, was appointed one of the first wardens of the port of Philadelphia, by the Assembly of Pennsylvania. Upon the formation of a Committee of Safety for the Province, in June 1775, Mr. Morris was made vice-president, Franklin being the head, and continued in the office until the dissolution of the committee, in July 1776.

The appointment of Mr. Morris, by the Assembly of Pennsylvania on the 3d of November 1775, as one of the delegates to the second congress, then in session at Philadelphia since May 10th, was his first entrance into important public life. Soon after he had taken his seat he was added to and made chairman of the Secret Committee, which had been selected in September, to contract for the importation of arms and ammunition. On the 11th of December, he was designated as one of the committee to devise ways and means for furnishing the colonies with a naval armament, and subsequently, on the formation of a naval committee, he was made a member. In April 1776, Mr. Morris was specially commissioned to negotiate bills of exchange, and to take other measures to procure money for the Congress. When Richard Henry Lee's resolution of June 7th came up for final action on July 2d, the day we celebrate, he, with John Dickinson, Thomas Willing, and Charles Humphreys, voted against independence; and afterwards, on the FOURTH, when the Declaration was submitted for approval, he and Dickinson absented themselves from their seats in Congress. His action was of course much commented upon, and John Adams, the most ardent and at the same time the most severe and censorious of his contemporaries, wrote to General Gates: "You ask me what you are to think of Robert Morris? I will tell you what I think of him. I think he has a masterly understanding, an open temper, and an honest heart; and if he does not always vote for what you and I think proper, it is because he thinks that a large body of people remains who are not yet of his mind." This query was doubtless occasioned by the apparent inconsistency of Mr. Morris's action with his views. . . .

Mr. Morris' reason for this course was that he considered the act premature and unnecessary, that the colonies were not yet ready for independence; and that his motives were respected and sanctioned by his constituents, and his patriotism never questioned, are shown by the fact that on the 20th of the same month, he, alone of the members who had voted with him, was re-elected a delegate. On this same day he wrote. . . . "Whilst I think this a duty, I must submit, although the councils of America have taken a different course from my judgment and wishes, I think that the individual who declines the service of his country because its councils are not conformable to his ideas, makes but a bad subject; a good one will follow if he cannot lead." Subsequently, on the 2d of August, when the engrossed Declaration was laid on the table to be signed, he subscribed, with firm hand and unfaltering heart, his signature to our Magna Carta. . . .

In December 1776, when Congress retired to Baltimore on the approach of Cornwallis, a committee, consisting of Mr. Morris, George Clymer, and George Walton, was appointed to remain in Philadelphia, with extensive power to execute all necessary public business. It was just at this period that Washington wrote to Morris, from above Trenton, that unless he had a certain amount of specie at once, he would be unable to keep the army together, and could not foretell the result. Morris on his personal credit borrowed a sufficient sum, forwarded it to Washington, and enabled him to finish the victory over the Hessians at Trenton, by his success at Princeton. . . .

In August, he was appointed a member of the Committee of Finance, and in the spring of 1780, organized the Bank of Pennsylvania, "to supply the army with provisions for two months," and to it subscribed £10,000. Early in the year 1781, Congress found it necessary to organize the Executive departments of the government, and, "whatever may have been thought, in regard to the candidates suitable for the other departments, there was but one opinion in Congress and in the nation as the proper person for taking charge of the finances, then in a dilapidated and most deplorable condition. The public sentiment everywhere pointed to Robert Morris, whose great experience and success as a merchant, his ardor in the cause of American liberty, his firmness of character, fertility of mental resources, and profound knowledge of pecuniary operations qualified him in a degree far beyond any other person for this arduous and responsible station.". . . Accordingly, on the 20th of February, at a time when Mr. Morris was a member of the Assembly of Pennsylvania, he was unanimously chosen to the office of Superintendent of Finance. . . .

In his letter of acceptance, which is a noble eulogium upon the man who wrote it, he says: "In accepting the office bestowed on me, I sacrifice much of my interest, my case, my domestic enjoyments, and internal tranquillity. If I know my own heart, I make these sacrifices with a disinterested view to the service of my country. I am ready to go further; and THE UNITED STATES MAY COMMAND EVERYTHING I HAVE EXCEPT MY INTEGRITY, AND THE LOSS OF THAT WOULD EFFECTUALLY DISABLE ME FROM SERVING THEM MORE." From this period until November 1st, 1784, when he resigned, he continued to fill this arduous and responsible post.

In so brief a notice it is impossible to recount the duties which this appointment imposed; but it was a herculean task, which he managed so as to bring order out of chaos and success out of doubt. When the exhausted credit of the government threatened the most alarming consequences; when the army was utterly destitute of the necessary supplies of food, clothing, arms, and ammunition; when Washington almost began to fear for the result, Robert Morris, upon his own credit and from his private resources, furnished those pecuniary means without which all the physical force of the country would have been in vain; without Robert Morris the sword of Washington would have rusted in its sheath. . . .

One of the earliest official acts of Mr. Morris was to submit to Congress, in the same month as he accepted his appointment, "A Plan for Establishing a National Bank for the United States," and, on the 31st of the following December, "The President, Directors, and Corporation of the Bank of North America" were incorporated. This was the first incorporated bank in the United States. . . .

When peace had once again fallen upon the land of his adoption, and a fundamental law was necessary to be formed for its governance, Mr. Morris was chosen a delegate to the memorable convention which met in Philadelphia, May 25, 1787, and framed the Constitution of the United States. It was he who proposed Washington for president of that convention, and during its entire session Washington was his guest. . . . In October, 1788, he received a renewed mark of the high confidence his fellow-citizens entertained for him, by being chosen the first Senator from Pennsylvania, to the first Congress of the United States under the Constitution, and which assembled in New York on the 4th of March, 1789. It was mainly through his instrumentality that the seat of government was removed, the next year, to Philadelphia, where it remained, *temporarily*, for 10 years, until the buildings were completed in the District of Columbia. He served a full term in the Senate, retiring in 1795. Washington desired Mr. Morris to become his Secretary of the Treasury, and upon his declining requested him to name the person most competent, in his opinion, to fill the office, which he did by naming Alexander Hamilton.

On Mr. Morris' retirement from public life, he began to speculate largely in unimproved lands in all sections of the country, and in February 1795, organized, with John Nicholson and James Greenleaf, the North American Land Company, which, through the dishonesty and rascality of Greenleaf, finally caused his ruin, and burdened the closing years of his life with utter poverty. The government, that he had carried on his own shoulders through adversity to prosperity, allowed him to remain from the 16th of February, 1798, until the 26th of August, 1801, a period of *three years, six months, and ten days*, an inmate of a debtor's prison, without raising a hand to help him, thus adding another link to the chain which proves that "Republics are ungrateful."

Mr. Morris survived his imprisonment not quite five years, dying on the 7th of May, 1806, in his seventy-third year, and his remains repose in the family vault, Christ Church, Second Street above Market Street, Philadelphia.

George Peabody

KATHLEEN BURK

George Peabody developed—from nothing—the leading firm of its kind
in London. By taking Junius Morgan (J. Pierpont's father) into partnership, he put in place the foundation for what became in three generations one of the Western world's great financial houses. So well regarded
was he in the City that his statue sits before the Royal Exchange.

George Peabody was born in 1795 in [a] . . . Massachusetts [town] which
was subsequently renamed Peabody in his honour. . . . George came from
one of the poorer branches of the Peabody family, whose common ancestor
had emigrated from Hertfordshire, England, in 1635. . . . At the age of
eleven, George started work in a country general store, and it was from the
owner of this store that he learned to keep accounts in a clear handwriting
and to organize and discipline his daily activities. . . .

During the War of 1812 with Great Britain, Peabody met the merchant
Elisha Riggs, who traded in a number of commodities, including wheat,
whiskey, and hams. . . . In 1814 the two . . . went into partnership . . . trading as Riggs, Peabody and Company, and specializing in dry goods imported from Britain. This was the turning-point in Peabody's business
career: his face was now turned towards Britain, and in 1827 he made his
first business trip there. In 1829 Elisha Riggs retired, and the firm was re-
constructed as Peabody, Riggs & Co., with Elisha Rigg's nephew Samuel
becoming the junior partner. Each partner contributed $25,000 in capital:
Peabody as the senior was to undertake the purchasing in Europe and
Riggs as the junior was to concentrate on selling the goods in the
United States. . . .

In the years 1829–37, Peabody made four further trips to Britain.
Clearly he found the experiences more than pleasant, for in 1838 he was to
take up residence there. These were prosperous years for both Peabody
and the firm: in 1815 Peabody had had very little capital, while by 1837 he
had over $300,000, or £65,000. . . . The basic strength of Peabody, Riggs &
Co. and of Peabody himself meant that both were to come through the
panic of 1837 with enhanced reputations. . . .

Early in 1836, in response to the warning signs he could see for himself as well as the warnings of friends, Peabody had returned to the

Excerpted by Kathleen Burk, *Morgan Grenfell: 1838–1988* (1990), Chapter 1, pp. 1–7,
10–27. Reprinted by permission of Oxford University Press.

United States and begun curtailing operations. He concentrated on collecting debts owed to the firm and in remitting the funds to England: both of these operations would soon become difficult for other firms, as their customers became unable to pay their bills and as the US exchange rate weakened. At the same time, Peabody ceased operations on his own account and reserved all of his private means and credit for the use of the firm. By the spring of 1837 Peabody was instructing his partner Riggs to realize their assets even if little profit was forthcoming, and Peabody himself made sales at a loss in order to get rid of stock and to get cash. As far as he was concerned, the priority was the state of their credit and reputation. . . . By September 1837, Peabody could write to Riggs that 'With respect to the standing of our house. . . I believe we are almost the *only* American importers of European goods that have met every engagement on both sides of the Atlantic with punctuality.' . . .

• • •

It should not be thought, however, that Peabody travelled a singular path as, over the years, he gradually changed from being primarily a merchant to acting primarily as a merchant banker: in fact, most of the leading merchant banks grew up in precisely the same manner. That is, they moved from merchanting to banking when they had built up a sufficient reputation for soundness and reliability—and wealth—which warranted their colleagues' trust. They gradually concentrated on banking because the profits were higher and the risks were lower. . . .

During the period 1837–39, renewed confidence in American bills—as long as they were not cotton acceptances—meant that British lending to Americans had continued. . . . By 1839, however, incredulity began to set in, and with Belgian and French banking collapses in 1838, the European liquidations were added to the American difficulties to ensure that the ensuing panic was international in scope. Work stopped on railways and canals, people were thrown out of work, banks closed their doors, and depression settled over the western part of the United States. In 1839, $200 million of American securities were owned in England, and by 1841, when the Bank of the United States failed, $120 million of these were in danger of suspension. Banks south of New York suspended payments for the third time since 1837, and the next year Illinois, Indiana, Louisiana, Michigan, Alabama, Maryland, Mississippi, Florida, and Pennsylvania either defaulted on the interest due on their state bonds or repudiated them altogether. This, of course, made the sale of American securities in Britain almost impossible. The British lobbied to have the Federal government assume the obligations of the defaulting states, and when this proved impossible the reaction was ferocious. . . . Even the Federal government, when attempting to issue a loan in Europe in 1842, was essentially thrown out of bankers' offices:

"You may tell your government," said the Paris Rothschild to Duff Green, the American agent, "that you have seen the man who is at the head of the finances of Europe, and that he has told you that they cannot borrow a dollar, not a dollar.". . .

George Peabody suffered personally from this reaction. In spite of his high standing—he was referred to by the London *Times* as "an American gentleman of the most unblemished character"—he was refused admission to the Reform Club because he was a citizen of a nation that did not pay its debts. . . .

Peabody, Riggs and Co. suffered from both the trading slump and the slump in American securities. . . . The firm, however, pulled through, and by late 1842 or 1843 was reasonably secure again. . . .

In 1843, when the upturn came, Peabody withdrew. . . his capital from Peabody, Riggs & Co. Nevertheless, the firm continued to use his name: he received an annual fee of $3,000 for executing the firm's financial business, and the firm itself was helped by the Peabody name. By 1845, however, he decided to sever himself completely from the dry goods business, and the firm was closed. . . .

During the period 1837–45 . . . Peabody had been gradually turning himself more and more into what would later be termed a merchant banker.

• • •

Although he continued to engage in banking business, the bulk of his time for the remainder of the 1840s was spent on transactions in American stocks, for which he seems to have been the major London specialist dealer. . . . He bought and sold securities in the London market, and when prices were higher in the United States he shipped them across the Atlantic and sold them there. He took parts of new issues in the United States and sold them in Europe, usually on joint account with firms such as Baring Brothers, then the most important English house in American finance.

It was some time before he ventured to lead in issuing American securities in Britain. After the repudiations by the states, American securities were seen as risky, and Peabody spent no little energy in trying to restore confidence in them. He had, in fact, great faith in their ultimate value, so he was prepared to buy at low prices with the confidence that he would eventually reap a profit. . . . He made his office a centre of transactions, and he developed the reputation of being willing to buy or sell any American securities. . . . In short, Peabody was, in modern parlance, a "market maker". . . . One result of market making, of course, was and is that investors will show the man in that position the business first, because they know he will always make a price, which has a clear business advantage. . . . Brokers also came to Peabody because he was willing to pay the full brokerage commission, unlike others who tried to save on their commissions. . . .

Even when American securities were not very popular, Peabody made a good business. . . . The possibilities after 1848, then, when the whole market for American securities had altered, were exploited to the full. . . .

But Peabody did not restrict his activities to Britain itself, and he worked to build up a market on the Continent, in particular in Germany. Not only did money frightened by revolution flow into American bonds, but they were bought especially by German emigrants to the United States: bearer bonds were easily transferable and preferable to carrying cash on the long voyage. His main trading, then, was in American state and railroad securities, which he sold in Britain and on the Continent, although he also traded in Mexican and Peruvian bonds. . . . by the late 1840s he had become a wealthy man. Beyond that, he had prestige and useful business connections, both in the United States and in Britain, for example with Barings. It was time, as his friends repeatedly told him, to turn his attention to building up an outstanding American house in London. . . .

There was in the late 1840s no important American-run house in London, and had been none since the collapse of the three American trading houses in the panic of 1837. Peabody had the capital and connections, and he also had the ambition to build a house which would be the centre, not only of the American trade, but for Americans in that trade. . . .

Because of his growing success, Peabody had for some time felt the need to take a partner. He had, it is true, declared in 1849 that he would never have a partner again, but by 1851 he was working ten hours a day and had not been absent from the office on two consecutive business days for twelve years. He was nearly fifty-seven, and his correspondents in the United States were somewhat alarmed at the fact that it was essentially a one-man business: if anything happened to Peabody there would be no continuity. Finding a partner, however, was no easy task: his was an American house and he wanted it to continue to be so in all ways, and therefore he required an American of standing and business talent. . . . He had not found one by 1849. . . .

In 1851, however, Peabody took a further step in regularizing matters: on 22 December a circular announced the formation of George Peabody & Co. The interests of the firm were to include "American and other Stocks, Foreign Exchange, Banking and Credits, the execution of Railroad Orders, purchase and sale of Produce and general Mercantile Transactions". . . . It is this organization which can be said to constitute the institutional beginning of Morgan Grenfell; it was not, however, until 1854 that a Morgan became part of the firm.

• • •

Upon the death of his father in 1847, Junius Morgan, at the age of thirty-four, came into a sizeable fortune. His own record as an established merchant joined with his inherited estate to make him a member of New England's commercial élite. . . . His connections, his proven abilities, and his increased capital opened up greater opportunities: in February 1850 he became a senior partner in the firm, now called Mather Morgan & Company, and in May 1850 he left on his first business trip to Europe. His intention was to meet some of London's leading merchant bankers and transatlantic traders and to learn what opportunities there were for his own firm to move into that business. . . . He was clearly looking for larger opportunities than were available in Hartford. . . .

One of the people Morgan called on in London was Peabody. . . now fifty-eight. . . .

Peabody invited Morgan and his wife to attend a large dinner, for 150 English and American guests, which he was giving on 18 May at the Star and Garter Hotel in Richmond in honour of Joseph Reed Ingersoll, the new American Minister in London. Peabody was particularly pleased by Morgan's ability to mix well with many kinds of people, an attribute on which he placed very high value. Shortly thereafter, Peabody had a long talk with Morgan and discussed with him a possible partnership. Morgan was interested and promised to think seriously about the proposal, and after his return to the United States the two exchanged letters regularly. . . . In November 1853, Peabody initiated serious negotiations, and early in February 1854 Morgan returned to London; he examined the firm's accounts and satisfied himself with the way Peabody and the firm conducted business, and after further discussions the two agreed that he should become a partner. . . .

Morgan was joining the premier American house in London, although it was not yet the premier house in the American trade: this was a position more likely to be contested between Baring Brothers & Co. and Brown, Shipley & Co., the English branch of Alexander Brown & Sons. . . .

Between 1 August 1848 and 30 September 1854 Peabody, and George Peabody & Co., had made £311,546, and by December 1851 Peabody himself was worth £1.2 million. . . .

Meanwhile, apparently at the suggestion of Morgan, Peabody Co. began to engage in a very un-English activity: they began soliciting accounts through agents in American and continental ports at ½% commission, which was lower than that normally charged. Barings, whose business was affected, felt that this was very wrong for two reasons: "it was dishonourable to apply to the correspondent" of a competitor for his business and "doubly wrong" to offer to work at a reduced commission. Further, Peabody agents emphasized that the two leading partners were American citizens and that arrangements could be made which would eliminate the need for the customer to buy bills for remittance to London. Barings, although the firm most hit by this procedure, merely shared a belief common in the City that this approach was not what was expected of the highest firms. . . . But what

Peabody & Co. were doing was quite acceptable in the United States: this was not to be the last time that the difference in American and British business practices would be noticeable, and City reaction to American Morgan practices would in the future—and particularly at the turn of the century—rebound to the harm of the firm. The outcome of this push for business would in fact nearly be disastrous. . . .

On 17 November 1857, George Peabody & Co. was forced to ask the Bank of England for help. . . .

There is no evidence that Peabody and Morgan were particularly apprehensive as to whether the Bank would lend . . . after all, they were a large, well-managed firm whose difficulties were not obviously of their own making; furthermore, . . . Peabody had in the previous panic in 1837 assisted the Bank in its attempts to aid the Liverpool firm of W. & J. Brown & Co. . . .

It is notable that during the week when negotiations between Peabody & Co. and the Bank were taking place, commercial rivals tried to take advantage of the firm's weakness to force them out of business. The story goes that a confidential proposal was relayed to Junius Morgan that "certain individuals" would guarantee a loan to Peabody on the condition that the firm would cease business by the end of 1858. . . .

Far from crashing during the panic, Peabody & Co. appear to have survived with their credit intact. Indeed, the fact that the Bank of England had felt it necessary to come to the firm's aid was taken in the United States as evidence of the firm's strength and importance; the *New York Herald* wrote on 3 December 1857 that the loan "speaks volumes for the character of the house". . . .

The favourable outcome of the crisis was . . . the signal for a change in the leadership of the firm. George Peabody was now sixty-three, tired, and ill. He had many things he wanted to accomplish before he died, and he seems to have felt that time was beginning to run out. He was to remain as the firm's senior partner, but from the spring of 1858 Junius Morgan was the effective head. Peabody returned to the firm for some months in the autumn and winter, but this was his last extended period in the offices, and in February 1859 he gave Morgan full control of the business. . . .

Peabody was a bachelor, with no direct heirs, and he was preoccupied with the dispersal of his fortune; the main reason he wished to retire from active business was to devote his time to philanthropy. . . .

He wanted to leave London some token of his affection for the city. He thought first of an elaborate system of drinking fountains; then he considered helping Lord Shaftesbury's Ragged Schools for the children of the very poor. In the end, Shaftesbury convinced Peabody that it was more important to provide better housing conditions for the working classes: in March 1859 Peabody decided that his gift to London would be a number of model dwellings. The American Civil War began before the gift could be organized, and it was not until 26 March 1862 that the Peabody Donation Fund was announced. His donation was to be £150,000 (later increased to £500,000), which was to be used to build houses to be inhabited by poor Londoners who had good moral characters and who were good members of society. (By 1882 the Fund owned 3,500 dwellings and housed more than 14,600 people). . . . As a result of this gift, Peabody in July 1862 was made a Freeman of the City of London, the first American to receive the honour. A more enduring monument is the statue of Peabody on Threadneedle Street near the Royal Exchange: the funds were raised by popular subscription, and it was unveiled on 23 July 1869. . . .

In October 1864 the ten-year partnership agreement was due to expire: what was to happen to the firm? J. S. Morgan certainly wanted things to go on as they were: after all, the firm had Peabody's name, a well-known and respected one, and Peabody capital, but he had untrammelled control. The partnership had been a profitable one for all concerned: after setting aside about £241,000 in the firm's "suspense" account, to cover bad and doubtful debts, the partners had, over the ten-year period, divided a total of £444,468 amongst the three of them. . . . Accordingly, in August 1864 Morgan wrote to Peabody, then staying in the Scottish Highlands, urging him to continue the partnership for some months beyond October: his concern was that many securities held by the firm would have to be sold when the partnership came to an end, and their precipitate sale would result in losses. But Peabody refused: he was nearly seventy, and with the uncertainty of life, a month for Morgan would appear as a year for him; and before he died he wished to arrange his "wordly [sic] affairs" and devote himself to his philanthropies, of which the Peabody Donation Fund was merely a part (Peabody's fortune amounted to something over $10 million). . . . Morgan of course had to accept this. He also had to accept the fact that Peabody refused to allow the firm to remain George Peabody & Co.: he did not wish to have his name used in business affairs over which he had no control. Therefore, on 30 September 1864 George Peabody & Co. ceased to exist, and on 1 October J.S. Morgan & Co. was born. . . .

The career of George Peabody is an exemplification of much which the nineteenth century found admirable. . . . His personal traits encouraged trust: he was personally austere while publicly generous. He ended his life wealthy and respected.

He died on 4 November 1869, and both his native and his adopted countries paid him public honour. His funeral was held in Westminster Abbey, after which his body was carried by special train to Portsmouth. Queen Victoria and W. E. Gladstone, the Prime Minister, had jointly requested the Royal Navy to provide HMS *Monarch*, the Navy's newest ironclad, to take Peabody's body back home, and the *Monarch*, on the orders of President Grant, was escorted by the USS *Plymouth*. The American authorities received the body at Portland, Maine, and there were elaborate services both there and in Peabody (his old hometown of South Danvers, renamed in 1868), before he was finally laid to rest near Salem, Massachusetts. . . .

He left behind him in London a firm which he had built from nothing to become the major American house in London. He also left behind him a partner who intended to make the firm more than that: Morgan was determined that J.S. Morgan & Co. would become a major international house.

Andrew Carnegie

ANDREW CARNEGIE

Andrew Carnegie exchanged his personal interests in the industry he dominated for $225,639,000 in bonds of the new enterprise, giving J. Pierpont Morgan his great triumph in organizing the giant U.S. Steel Corporation. Later, in a chance meeting on a ship, Carnegie said to Morgan, "I made one mistake, Pierpont, when I sold out to you . . . I should have asked for $100,000,000 more than I did." "Well," said Morgan, "you would have got it if you had." Carnegie's business philosophy is revealed in the final pages of this sketch.

Complete success attended a negotiation which I conducted about this time for Colonel William Phillips, president of the Allegheny Valley Railway at Pittsburgh. One day the Colonel entered my New York office and told me that he needed money badly, but that he could get no house in America to entertain the idea of purchasing five millions of bonds of his company although they were to be guaranteed by the Pennsylvania Railroad Company. The old gentleman felt sure that he was being driven from pillar to post by the bankers because they had agreed among themselves to purchase the bonds only upon their own terms. He asked ninety cents on the dollar for them, but this the bankers considered preposterously high. Those were the days when Western railway bonds were often sold to the bankers at eighty cents on the dollar.

Colonel Phillips said he had come to see whether I could not suggest some way out of his difficulty. He had pressing need for $250 thousand, and this Mr. Thomson, of the Pennsylvania Railroad, could not give him. The Allegheny bonds were 7 percents, but they were payable, not in gold, but in currency, in America. They were therefore wholly unsuited for the

From Andrew Carnegie, *The Autobiography of Andrew Carnegie*, Riverdale Press, Cambridge, Chapter 12, pp. 161–166 & 170–171.

foreign market. But I knew that the Pennsylvania Railroad Company had a large amount of Philadelphia and Erie Railroad 6 percent gold bonds in its treasury. It would be a most desirable exchange on its part, I thought, to give these bonds for the 7 percent Allegheny bonds which bore its guarantee.

I telegraphed Mr. Thomson, asking if the Pennsylvania Railroad Company would take $250 thousand at interest and lend it to the Allegheny Railway Company. Mr. Thomson replied, "Certainly." Colonel Phillips was happy. He agreed, in consideration of my services, to give me a 60-days option to take his five millions of bonds at the desired ninety cents on the dollar. I laid the matter before Mr. Thomson and suggested an exchange, which that company was only too glad to make, as it saved one percent interest on the bonds. I sailed at once for London with the control of five millions of first mortgage Philadelphia and Erie Bonds, guaranteed by the Pennsylvania Railroad Company—a magnificent security for which I wanted a high price. And here comes in one of the greatest of the hits and misses of my financial life.

I wrote the Barings from Queenstown that I had for sale a security which even their house might unhesitatingly consider. On my arrival in London I found at the hotel a note from them requesting me to call. I did so the next morning, and before I had left their banking house I had closed an agreement by which they were to bring out this loan, and that until they sold the bonds at par, less their 2½ percent commission, they would advance the Pennsylvania Railroad Company four million dollars at 5 percent interest. The sale left me a clear profit of more than a half million dollars.

The papers were ordered to be drawn up, but as I was leaving Mr. Russell Sturgis said they had just heard that Mr. Baring himself was coming up to town in the morning. They had arranged to hold a "court," and as it would be fitting to lay the transaction before him as a matter of courtesy they would postpone the signing of the papers until the morrow. If I would call at two o'clock the transaction would be closed.

Never shall I forget the oppressed feeling which overcame me as I stepped out and proceeded to the telegraph office to wire President Thomson. Something told me that I ought not to do so. I would wait till tomorrow when I had the contract in my pocket. I walked from the banking house to the Langham Hotel—four long miles. When I reached there I found a messenger waiting breathless to hand me a sealed note from the Barings. Bismarck had locked up a hundred millions in Magdeburg. The financial world was panic-stricken, and the Barings begged to say that under the circumstances they could not propose to Mr. Baring to go on with the matter. There was much chance that I should be struck by lightning on my way home as that an arrangement agreed to by the Barings should be broken. And yet it was. It was too great a blow to produce anything like irritation or indignation. I was meek enough to be quite resigned, and merely congratulated myself that I had not telegraphed Mr. Thomson.

I decided not to return to the Barings, and although J. S. Morgan & Co. had been bringing out a great many American securities I subsequently sold the bonds to them at a reduced price as compared with that agreed to by the Barings. I thought it best not to go to Morgan & Co. at first, because I had understood from Colonel Phillips that the bonds had been unsuccessfully offered by him to their house in America and I supposed that the Morgans in London might consider themselves connected with the negotiations through their house in New York. But in all subsequent negotiations I made it a rule to give the first offer to Junius S. Morgan, who seldom permitted me to leave his banking house without taking what I had to offer. If he could not buy for his own house, he placed me in communication with a friendly house that did, he taking an interest in the issue. It is a great satisfaction to reflect that I never negotiated a security which did not to the end command a premium. Of course in this case I made a mistake in not returning to the Barings, giving them time and letting the panic subside, which it soon did. When one party to a bargain becomes excited, the other should keep cool and patient.

As an incident of my financial operations I remember saying to Mr. Morgan one day:

"Mr. Morgan, I will give you an idea and help you to carry it forward if you will give me one quarter of all the money you make by acting upon it."

He laughingly said: "That seems fair, and as I have the option to act upon it, or not, certainly we ought to be willing to pay you a quarter of the profit."

I called attention to the fact that the Allegheny Valley Railroad bonds which I had exchanged for the Philadelphia and Erie bonds bore the guarantee of the Pennsylvania Railroad Company, and that that great company was always in need of money for essential extensions. A price might be offered for these bonds which might tempt the company to sell them, and that at the moment there appeared to be such a demand for American securities that no doubt they could be floated. I would write a prospectus which I thought would float the bonds. After examining the matter with his usual care he decided that he would act upon my suggestion.

Mr. Thomson was then in Paris and I ran over there to see him. Knowing that the Pennsylvania Railroad had need for money I told him that I had recommended these securities to Mr. Morgan and if he would give me a price for them I would see if I could not sell them. He named a price which was then very high, but less than the price which these bonds have since reached. Mr. Morgan purchased part of them with the right to buy others, and in this way the whole nine or ten millions of Allegheny bonds were marketed and the Pennsylvania Railroad Company placed in funds.

The sale of the bonds had not gone very far when the panic of 1873 was upon us. One of the sources of revenue which I then had was Mr. Pierpont Morgan. He said to me one day:

"My father [Junius S. Morgan in London] has cabled to ask whether you wish to sell out your interest in that idea you gave him."

I said, "Yes, I do. In these days I will sell anything for money."

"Well," he said, "what would you take?"

I said I believed that a statement recently rendered to me showed that there were already $50 thousand to my credit, and I would take $60 thousand. Next morning when I called Mr. Morgan handed me checks for $70 thousand.

"Mr. Carnegie," he said, "you were mistaken. You sold out for $10 thousand less than the statement showed to your credit, and the additional 10 makes 70."

The payments were in two checks, one for $60 thousand and the other for the additional 10 thousand. I handed him back the $10-thousand check, saying:

"Well, that is something worthy of you. Will you please accept these 10 thousand with my best wishes?"

"No, thank you," he said, "I cannot do that."

Such acts, showing a nice sense of honorable understanding as against mere legal rights, are not so uncommon in business as the uninitiated might believe. And, after that, it is not to be wondered at if I determined that so far as lay in my power neither Morgan, father or son, nor their house, should suffer through me. They had in me henceforth a firm friend.

A great business is seldom if ever built up, except on lines of the strictest integrity. A reputation for "cuteness" and sharp dealing is fatal in great affairs. Not the letter of the law, but the spirit, must be the rule. The standard of commercial morality is not very high. A mistake made by any one in favor of the firm is corrected as promptly as if the error were in favor of the other party. It is essential to permanent success that a house should obtain a reputation for being governed by what is fair rather than what is merely legal. A rule which we adopted and adhered to has given greater returns than one would believe possible, namely: always give the other party the benefit of the doubt. This, of course, does not apply to the speculative class. An entirely different atmosphere pervades that world. Men are only gamblers there. Stock gambling and honorable business are incompatible. In recent years it must be admitted that the old-fashioned "banker," like Junius S. Morgan of London, has become rare. . . .

I had become interested, with my friends of the Pennsylvania Railroad Company, in building some railways in the Western states, but gradually withdrew from all such enterprises and made up my mind to go entirely contrary to the adage not to put all one's eggs in one basket. I determined that the proper policy was "to put all good eggs in one basket and then watch that basket."

I believe the true road to preeminent success in any line is to make yourself master in that line. I have no faith in the policy of scattering one's resources, and in my experience I have rarely if ever met a man who achieved preeminence in money-making—certainly never one in manufacturing—who was interested in many concerns. The men who have succeeded are men who have chosen one line and stuck to it. It is surprising how few men appreciate the enormous dividends derivable from investment in their own business. There is scarcely a manufacturer in the world who has not in his works some machinery that should be thrown out and replaced by improved appliances; or who does not for the want of additional machinery or new methods lose more than sufficient to pay the largest dividend obtainable by investment beyond his own domain. And yet most business men whom I have known invest in bank shares and in faraway enterprises, while the true gold mine lies right in their own factories.

I have tried always to hold fast to this important fact. It has been with me a cardinal doctrine that I could manage my own capital better than any other person, much better than any board of directors. The losses men encounter during a business life which seriously embarrass them are rarely in their own business, but in enterprises of which the investor is not master. My advice to young men would be not only to concentrate their whole time and attention on the one business in life in which they engage, but to put every dollar of their capital into it. If there be any business that will not bear extension, the true policy is to invest the surplus in first-class securities which will yield a moderate but certain revenue if some other growing business cannot be found. As for myself my decision was taken early. I would concentrate upon the manufacture of iron and steel and be master in that.

John D. Rockefeller

PETER COLLIER and DAVID HOROWITZ

John D. Rockefeller rationalized the U.S. petroleum industry, built
Standard Oil into one of the world's great business organizations, and
created an enormous fortune. On a number of occasions, however, he
was to see his name publicly identified with the worst examples of conspiratorial corporate excess.

The training and discipline to which Rockefeller had subjected his life
soon began paying business dividends. A reputation as one of the
shrewdest dealers in a town filled with sharp operators took hold. His very
narrowness was an invaluable asset in driving the hardest bargain possible:
he had made himself into a perfect instrument for the conduct of business,
and the only pleasure he allowed himself came from success in his transactions. When she was compiling her history of Standard Oil, Ida Tarbell
was told by an acquaintance of Rockefeller: "The only time I saw John
Rockefeller enthusiastic was when a report came in from the Creek that
his buyer had secured a cargo of oil at a figure much below the market
price. He bounded from his chair with a shout of joy, danced up and down,
hugged me, threw up his hat, acted so like a madman that I have never forgotten it."

Early in 1865 the thriving firm of Andrews, Clark and Company was
split by dissension. Rockefeller, the formerly silent but now most enthusiastic partner, had become increasingly annoyed with Clark's timid attitude toward expansion. The firm was $100,000 in debt, but Rockefeller
wanted to extend the operation further and take advantage of the booming
market. An impasse resulted, and it was mutually agreed to sell the business to the highest bidder.

The auction was held on February 2, 1865, with Rockefeller represent-
ing Andrews and himself against Clark. Clark began the bidding at $500,
which Rockefeller raised to $1,000. The price went up and up, to $40,000,
to $50,000, and then to $60,000. Gradually, with both sides unyielding, it
crept up to $70,000. There was a long silence.

"Seventy-two thousand," said Maurice Clark in desperation.

"Seventy-two thousand five hundred," Rockefeller replied without
hesitation.

Excerpted from Peter Collier and David Horowitz, *The Rockefellers: An American Dynasty*,
Holt, Rinehart & Winston, 1976, pp. 18–19 and 22–24.

Clark threw up his hands: "The business is yours."

Looking back in a later reminiscence with a friend, Rockefeller said that this day was "one of the most important in my life. It was the day that determined my career. I felt the bigness of it, but I was as calm as I am talking to you now." It was the calm of absolute confidence, of one who had methodically taken the measure of the field and the opponent, and knew what the outcome would be.

Although only twenty-six years old, he already had good enough standing in Cleveland's financial community to be able to borrow the purchase price. He took control of the business—rechristened Rockefeller and Andrews—on the crest of an oil boom that was making Cleveland rich, and at the apex of the great Civil War business bonanza that would introduce the word "millionaire" into the vocabulary of Americans. Rockefeller and Andrews was already the largest refinery in Cleveland, with a capacity of 500 barrels a day, or twice that of its nearest competitor, and annual revenues of $1 million, which grew to $2 million the following year. Rockefeller had been right. For the moment, expansion, not restraint, was the rule of success. A tremendous confidence in the future of the industry and in his own future possessed him. He convinced his brother William to come into the business and sent him to New York to handle the export trade, which accounted for two-thirds of the sales of Cleveland oil. It was about this time that a startled bystander watched one day as Rockefeller, thinking himself alone in his office, jumped up in the air, clicked his heels together, and repeated to himself, "I'm bound to be rich! Bound to be rich! *Bound to be rich!*"

If the other robber barons, with their mistresses, excesses of body and spirit, and artistic booty imported from the Old World, made Rockefeller seem a dull and predictable man, it was simply that he poured his passion and genius into this work, into the creation of Standard Oil, instead of his life. . . .

Eighteen seventy was a depression year. Total freight-car loadings were falling, and the heads of the mighty but hard-pressed railroads began to seek better solutions to their problems than the free market afforded. Why suffer the ravages of a competitive situation that was costing them money, they asked, when they could pool their resources with the largest refiners and plot out their own prosperity? They conceived a plan. It bore the innocuous name of the South Improvement Company. . . .

The railroads would combine with the largest refiners in each major refining center to plan the flow of oil for their mutual benefit. Freight rates would rise, but the rebate to members of the scheme would more than compensate them. Those who refused to join the cartel would be driven to the wall. Participating refiners would not only receive rebates on their own shipments, but "drawbacks" on the shipments of nonmembers as well.

Throughout the winter of 1871, the scheme went forward in absolute secrecy, with Rockefeller and other large refiners frequently journeying to New York to hold clandestine summit meetings with . . . the . . . railroad bosses. The promoters in each area decided which refineries they wanted in on the scheme and circulated an oath that prospective participants were forced to sign before learning the particulars of the plan. . . . Among those holding the original 2,000 shares of South Improvement Company stock, Rockefeller, his brother William, and Flagler each had 180 shares, which gave the Standard more than any other single interest.

Rockefeller saw the plan as a way of eliminating the Standard's annoying competitors in Cleveland. They had two alternatives—collapse their businesses into his in return for stock, or go it alone and be bankrupted by the rebate system. Starting with his largest competitors and working downward, he would make an appointment to see a rival and then with his usual civility explain how the plan would work to the benefit of all. The offer could be refused only by those who valued principles more than economic survival. To add leverage to the already crushing advantage of the secret rebates and "drawbacks," Rockefeller had offered the executives of Cleveland's leading banks stock in the Standard; thus independent refiners who held out would have a hard time financing their lonely uphill battles.

Isaac Hewitt, Rockefeller's former employer, who had since become a partner in the large refinery of Alexander, Scofield and Company, was urged to commit himself to the scheme and to take stock in the Standard. When he questioned the plan, Rockefeller shrugged him off cryptically: "I have ways of making money that you know nothing of." Others who were reluctant to join because they were already doing a good business were shown a hint of the iron fist underneath the velvet glove Rockefeller habitually wore. Frank Rockefeller, by then a partner in a firm competing against the Standard, was told by his older brother: "We have a combination of the railroads. We are going to buy out all the refiners in Cleveland. We will give everyone a chance to come in. . . . Those who refuse will be crushed. If you don't sell your property to us, it will be valueless." Frank did not sell and, when his brother's prophecy came true, remained bitter for the rest of his life, testifying publicly against him on several occasions and eventually moving his two children's bodies from the family burial plot in Cleveland lest they be forced to spend their eternity with John D.

The cabal went along smoothly for almost two months. When word accidentally leaked out revealing the nature of the South Improvement Company, there was immediate panic in the Oil Regions: all-night meetings, torchlight parades, angry petitions (one of them ninety-three feet long) carried to legislators, and threatening telegrams to railroad presidents. It was not only the creation of a combination that outraged the producers; they too had tried to form associations in order to keep prices of crude high. It was rather the cold and calculating nature of the plot, the combination of the strong against the weak, and most of all the use of the loathsome "drawback" that aroused them. As Ida Tarbell later wrote: "The rebate system was considered illegal and unjust, but men were more or less accustomed to it. The drawback on other people's shipments was a new device, and it threw the Oil Regions into a frenzy of rage."

Until this time, the name of Rockefeller had been unknown outside a small circle in Cleveland. Almost overnight, it became identified with infamy. For the duration of the conflict, the *Oil City Derrick* printed the names of the conspirators in a black-bordered box on the front page of each edition; notable among them was John D. Rockefeller. It was the first of many public battles Rockefeller would fight, the first time that words like "octopus" and "anaconda" would be used to describe the organization built by his methodical talent.

Yet, at the height of the South Improvement furor, Rockefeller displayed that characteristic inner discipline and iron self-confidence, the unflagging belief in his own rectitude, which he would always possess under fire. As he said later: "It was right. I knew it as a matter of conscience. It was right between me and my God.". . . "We will do right and not be nervous or troubled by what the papers say."

George F. Baker

George F. Baker was one of America's truly great financiers. The dean of American banking, he was also the founding benefactor of Harvard's Business School. Believing silence to be a key factor in business success, he did not speak in public until, at age 84, he addressed a group of 1,000 corporate leaders, saying exactly six words: "Thank you and God bless you." News of his death at age 91 was the lead story on the front page of the *New York Times* of May 3, 1931, in which this obituary appeared.

George Fisher Baker, the last of the "Old Guard" in the world of American finance, whom the late Judge Elbert H. Gary hailed as "the first citizen of New York," was Wall Street's inscrutable sphinx. An outstanding figure in the financial, industrial and railroad world and at one time a director, if not the directing genius, of scores of corporations, the vicissitudes of Mr. Baker's career extended from the critical days of Civil War financing through the phenomenal development of the post World War period.

Excerpted from the *New York Times*, May 3, 1931.

The power that he wielded, or was assumed by the financial world to hold, was graphically shown on November 9, 1927, when a report that Mr. Baker was critically ill caused a wave of selling that depressed by several points many of the soundest stocks on the Exchange.

It took a Congressional investigation, the Pujo money trust inquiry in 1913, to make known Mr. Baker's important position in Wall Street. Not until then was there revealed to the world the vast network of financial interests of the man who, together with the late J. Pierpont Morgan and James A. Stillman, "the big three," breathed the breath of life into many corporations.

* * *

George F. Baker was born in Troy on March 27, 1840. When he was eight years old his family moved to Brooklyn. His father cared little for business and worked under Horace Greeley on the *New York Tribune*. Young Baker was sent to live with his grandparents at Dedham, Massachusetts. It was there he observed his uncle John sitting on a porch while others were at work. On inquiry he was told his uncle did not have to work but lived on interest money. The lad, too, determined to live on interest money. His first start was said to have been from the sale of a load of cranberries for $7.

From Williamsburg School the boy went to Seward University, a boarding school at Florida, New York, founded by William Seward. He completed his schooling at 16 and returned to Albany. Little is known of his life for the next four years. One story, probably apocryphal, is that he went to work in a grocery store as a clerk for $2 a week and later added to his income by taking on the duties of night watchman at $5 a week.

Soon after the outbreak of the Civil War, young Baker, a clerk in the State Banking Department, was named assistant military secretary to Governor Edwin D. Morgan of New York. He remained in that post for about six months and then returned to the banking department, and by 1863 he was looked upon as the most able clerk in the department, a reputation that brought him the best salary.

His first real opportunity to advance in the world of finance came through his association with John Thompson, New York City banker, for whom he had transacted business in the State capital. Mr. Thompson had established his two sons, Samuel and Frederick, in business as brokers at 2 Wall Street. Said Mr. Thompson of the young Baker of that time:

"I often had business at the banking department and I soon learned that I could get more information and intelligent aid there from George Baker than from any one else, so I carefully kept my eye on him for years, feeling that he was destined to a high place in finance."

In the course of their friendship the young clerk had suggested to Mr. Thompson that he found a bank, and when the Civil War arrived, with a consequent overwhelming need for national government funds, the suggestion was acted upon.

In 1863 Salmon P. Chase, Secretary of the Treasury in Lincoln's Cabinet, advanced the proposal that the banks should become the only important agents for sale of government bonds and should be allowed to pledge them as a basis for their circulation up to 90 percent of their value.

The youthful clerk was struck particularly with this latter provision and Mr. Thompson also saw the possibilities for starting a national bank. Mr. Thompson advised his two sons in the brokerage business to take advantage of the situation and branch out into banking.

Mr. Thompson, according to the stories told, suggested to Mr. Baker that he take as much stock in the new institution as he wanted. Mr. Thompson said he would underwrite the subscription. The young clerk, unwilling to go into debt, insisted on paying for his own stock. He had saved some $3,000 and with this he purchased 30 shares.

It was on July 25, 1863, that the First National Bank opened its doors at 2½ Wall Street. Mr. Thompson was president, James Curphey was cashier and Mr. Baker was teller and a director. The capital of the institution was $200,000 when the bank opened for business, but within five months it rose to $300,000 and in April of the next year it went up to $500,000, as the institution did a thriving business in sale of government bonds.

The new bank won its place only after a hard fight. Some of the older banks were opposed to [a] national banking system and the rivals attempted to head off the new institution. The privilege of the Clearing House was denied for some time and considerable inconvenience was caused by this. Eventually the First National won recognition by the Clearing House, although it was not until many years later that Mr. Baker was named president of the Clearing House.

The First National began to prosper rapidly and in 1865 Mr. Baker became cashier and began to assume the place of active head of the bank. His own stock holdings increased. Although he was still under 25, he had achieved a position of respect in the financial world and his judgment was sought by far older men. Due to his growing importance he often was called to Washington for conferences with Secretary Chase and during these meetings he several times encountered President Lincoln, Secretary of State Seward and others in the Civil War Cabinet.

• • •

In 1877 Mr. Baker became president of the First National. Five years later, he began his railroad career by buying the Richmond & Danville Railroad, which later became the basis of the Southern Railway. Later he made connections with the Jersey Central, the Delaware, Lackawanna & Western, the New York Central and other roads. His hobby was buying roads when they were down at the heel and building them up until their securities were of great value.

In entering the railroad field, Mr. Baker acquired a close knowledge of construction and operations and was fully acquainted with the many intricate phases of the industry besides its financing. When his group took over the Richmond & Danville system the stock had a market value of $51 a share. Under the new management trackage and equipment were replaced, payment of dividends to shareholders rose and the stock after seven years sold at $240 a share. . . .

Mr. Baker's sphere of influence extended to the Guaranty Trust Company, the Mutual Life Insurance Company and a long string of railroads. He was made a member of the finance committee of the United States Steel Corporation when Mr. Morgan organized it.

• • •

At the height of his career he held directorates in 43 banks and corporations, including the American Telephone and Telegraph Company, of which he was said to be the largest individual stockholder, the Pullman Company, the Consolidated Gas Company, First Security Company, Lehigh & Wilkes-Barre Coal Company, Metropolitan Opera and Real Estate Company, New York Edison Company and the United Electric Light and Power Company.

The panic of 1893 found Mr. Baker again a "rock" in the swirling tides of financial frenzy. In June, 25 national banks suspended. The next month 78 were suspended and 38 more halted activities in August. By the end of that month 415 private and State banks had failed with liabilities of nearly $100,000,000.

It was a time of real financial stress. Numerous banks stopped cashing checks and currency went to a premium of 5 percent or more. Lack of ready money compelled some businesses to halt because funds were not available to pay the employees' wages.

The First National held firm. Confronted with a heavy run, it paid off every depositor that sought payment and no regular patron was refused. Mr. Baker stood by his guns and insisted that the condition was temporary.

James J. Hill, railroad builder and a close associate, paid this tribute to Mr. Baker's work in the 1893 panic in a speech in Seattle later:

"When the panic of 1893 came along and currency was almost impossible to get, or credit either, for that matter, I asked the First National for some assistance, and George Baker sent me this answer:

"'I send you by express tonight what you asked for. If you actually need more I will take off my coat and go to work.'

"It was $300,000, but at [a] time like that it seemed almost as big as a million in flush times. That transaction and that reply won me to George Baker for life. I would rather have his friendship and I would rather have his judgment in time of panic than that of all the other men between Trinity Church and the East River."

Interest was focused on Mr. Baker's bank one day in 1901 when [an] announcement was made that the institution was preparing to double its capital and declare a dividend equal to $10,000,000. After that the elder Mr. Morgan sought Mr. Baker's counsel, and he was asked for aid by James J. Hill in the expansion of the Great Northern and the Northern Pacific Railroads. He fought beside Morgan and Hill against E. H. Harriman in 1901 for control of the Northern Pacific.

"The profits of Mr. Baker's bank make the rest of us look like novices at the banking game," a prominent banker once said.

Writing in *Leslie's* of February 15, 1917, B. C. Forbes said that Mr. Baker was the first New York banker "to conceive the idea of doing things forbidden by the national bank act by means of a separate enterprise, but whose ownership in reality was and is identical with that of the bank itself, each share of the bank simply carrying with it a share in the 'other' enterprise."

"One could not be sold without the other," said Mr. Forbes. "The invention has proved highly profitable."

• • •

Until the Pujo investigation of the "money trust" in 1913, the name of George F. Baker meant little to the mass of the people despite the vast power the silent man wielded in "the Street." One of the financier's friends remarked after the inquiry had put him forward as a dominating force in American economic life:

"It required an investigation committee to get before the public the importance of George Baker's activities in the nation's financial affairs."

Mr. Baker's appearance on the witness stand before the Pujo committee on January 9 and 10, 1913, made financial history. The financier spoke frankly, revealing his strength under the questioning of Samuel Untermyer. . . .

When the committee was through with the head of the First National he had been definitely placed in the first rank of leaders in the American financial world along with the elder J. P. Morgan and the elder James A. Stillman.

The part played by Mr. Baker in the panic of 1907 was brought out by Mr. Untermyer. It was then he admitted that he and Mr. Stillman were the "lieutenants" and Mr. Morgan was the "general" in the world of finance who "had no superior."

• • •

Just before the elder Morgan sailed for Europe, where he died, he placed his hands on Mr. Baker's shoulders and said:

"If anything happens to me, I want you to know that my association with you has been one of the most satisfactory parts of my life."

Mr. Morgan left word with his associates that when they were puzzled and did not know which course to follow to go to Mr. Baker for advice. Mr. Morgan's son, present head of the firm, continued his friendship with Mr. Baker, and in one of his rare public utterances held up Mr. Baker as the embodiment of banking ethics.

George W. Perkins

This multitalented man made three successful careers: in life insurance, in investment banking, and in politics (as Chairman of the National Executive Committee of Theodore Roosevelt's Progressive Party). When Perkins told J. P. Morgan that he wouldn't accept an offered Morgan partnership because of his allegiance to the New York Life Insurance Company, Morgan so wanted him in the firm that he allowed Perkins to keep the insurance affiliation and become a partner. He left business life in 1910 to pursue social goals revolving around the working man and died in 1920 before he was 60. This portrait is from his obituary.

The versatility of George W. Perkins enabled him to rise to a commanding position first in the field of insurance, then in banking, and finally in the politics of the nation. The second phase of his career, embracing the 10-year period when he was a power in Wall Street, was devoted for the most part to industrial organization. When he became active in politics he made effective use of his business experience, and his interest in business and politics gave birth to still another development of his work, which in his last years was concerned principally with corporate reforms which he advocated and progressive plans he suggested for the benefit of the American people.

The place of Mr. Perkins in the financial world was assured when the late J. P. Morgan invited him to become a member of the firm of J.P. Morgan & Co., only to have the invitation declined, probably to the great surprise of Mr. Morgan, who knew that such an opportunity would have been jumped at by most young men in the same circumstances as George W. Perkins. An

Excerpted from the *New York Times*, June 19, 1920. ©1920 by New York Times, all rights reserved. Reprinted by permission.

interesting story has been preserved of the way in which Mr. Perkins became Mr. Morgan's partner.

Theodore Roosevelt, then Governor of New York, called Mr. Perkins on the telephone to inform him that he had appointed Mr. Perkins president of the Palisades Interstate Park Commission. . . . Mr. Perkins intervened with an excuse that he was too busy with other things, whereupon Mr. Roosevelt interjected that he hadn't asked Mr. Perkins whether he would take the appointment, but had called up to tell him that the appointment actually had been made.

For the administration expenses of the park commission the legislature had appropriated only $10,000 and Mr. Perkins, who realized that the sum was insufficient, arranged for the commission to meet in his office, and the expenses of administration were applied to the purchase of a quarry company whose operations were detrimental to the natural beauty of the Palisades. The company held its property at $135,000, so Mr. Perkins's next problem was to raise the balance of $125,000.

One of the first men he went to for assistance was Mr. Morgan, whom he expected to contribute at least $25,000. After hearing all that Mr. Perkins had to say, Mr. Morgan made this offer:

"I'll put up the whole sum, $125,000, but on one condition, and that is that you do me a favor."

"I'll be glad to do you any favor, but I can't imagine any favor I can do you," replied Mr. Perkins.

"Well, you can," remarked Mr. Morgan. "You can take that desk beside me as a partner."

Mr. Perkins was reluctant at first, because the New York Life Insurance Company, with which he had been connected for so many years, finally as chairman of the board of directors and as a vice president, was regarded by him as home. Mr. Perkins later explained how Mr. Morgan refused to take him into the firm unless he would sever all connection with the New York Life, and when he would not consent to do so Mr. Morgan finally said to him:

"Well, if you won't leave the New York Life, come along and join the firm and see if you can occupy that dual position. . . ."

Mr. Perkins remained with the New York Life Insurance Company after he became a member of the firm of J.P. Morgan & Co. in 1900.

George Walbridge Perkins was born in Chicago on January 31, 1862. His father . . . was long engaged in the shipping industry at Buffalo, but finally went to Chicago, where he was a pioneer in the life insurance field. The elder Perkins founded religious missions where the bodies and souls of men were kept together in the dark days during the Civil War, and undoubtedly such impulses as moved his father in the interest of mankind were inherited by the lad who entered the business in which his father was engaged.

With only a public school education, he began his career as an office boy at $300 a year in the Chicago office of the New York Life. He made rapid progress.

• • •

When Mr. Perkins was third vice president of the company he revolutionized the life insurance business. Up to that time the company had dealt with general agents, who hired their own agents. The general agent alone had a contract with the company, and made his own contracts with his agents, who consequently were not responsible to the company and not known to it. Mr. Perkins abolished the general agencies and made direct contracts with the agents, so that 10,000 men who had hitherto been out of touch with the home office came in close and immediate touch with it. The other companies followed suit.

Aside from the acquisition of business brains, which J.P. Morgan & Co. had made by the inclusion of Mr. Perkins in its membership, there was another quality which he took along and which once caused the practical Andrew Carnegie to remark that he reaped an additional pleasure from his visit to his friend Morgan's office because of Mr. Perkins's charming personality. . . .

As a member of the Morgan firm Mr. Perkins had much to do with most of the great industrial combinations with which the name of J.P. Morgan & Co. was identified. . . . He organized the International Harvester Company and was largely instrumental in building up the United States Steel Corporation.

• • •

[His political philosophy is set forth in the following quotations.]

"During the 20 years I spent with New York Life, I was identified with a branch of the work that brought me in the closest kind of contact with men of all classes. It was the same thing in Wall Street. I did not come to the firm of J.P. Morgan & Co. purely as a banker. My work with that firm was largely one of industrial organization.

"In the course of the experience it was borne in on me very forcibly that the principal problems with which we are confronted in the industrial and economic world today are problems of men rather that money. . . . The first has been comparatively neglected. And yet it is the most important of the three.

• • •

"The solution of the problem affecting the regulation and control of the relations between the human factors essential in our industrial and corporation life—the employers, the wage-earners and consumers—so as to insure absolutely fair dealings among the three, is one of the principal tasks set before the enlightened statesmanship of the present day and the future. It involves a moral question of the firm magnitude as well as a practical one.

"I want to see those problems solved in a manner that will insure permanency. I realize that the future of this country, its financial and industrial prosperity, and its social welfare hinge on that proposition. I believe that the National Progressive Party in its program holds the correct solution that will make for social and industrial justice, and consequently for social and industrial peace, which must be the corner-stone in our structure of happiness and prosperity as a nation."

At the same time Mr. Perkins described in more intimate detail the reasons which prompted him to turn his back on money making for the activities which occupied the remaining years of his life. He said:

"When a man reaches 40, and when, like me, he has led an active life, if he has any heart at all he naturally will pause and ask himself, 'What is this all about?' And if he has any imagination at all, and looks about him a little, he is likely to ask this further question, 'Where is my work going to lead me?'"

He did the work of a pioneer among business men, among whom he sought to help create a better understanding between capital and labor, and an appreciation of the value of more friendly relations between employers and employees. He became an ardent advocate of profit-sharing before this policy had been adopted by any great corporation, and it was he who urged the plan so strongly in the councils of the United States Steel Corporation that the result is known universally. In support of the plan which permitted employees of the Steel Corporation and the International Harvester Company to purchase stock on installments at less than market value, Mr. Perkins went on this assumption:

"Industrial justice is the most profitable of investments. Justice promotes peace, peace promotes prosperity and the workman's prosperity as necessary to the prosperity of the business man." Mr. Perkins told his friends that he did not have the least idea of going into politics when he severed his connection with the Morgan firm in 1910, his intention being to devote himself wholly to social improvements he had in mind, but he said that he saw in the dawn of the 1912 campaign a new light revealing the connection of politics with the things for which he was to strive. He considered that a Democratic success would not be for the best interests of the people, and he held that the reelection of Taft was an impossibility. Irresistibly he was drawn into the political current, and at Chicago during the convention he was the right-hand man of Colonel Roosevelt.

• • •

Mr. Perkins exerted a directing influence in the organization of the Progressive Party, of whose National Executive Committee he was chosen chairman. He organized the famous National Convention that met in

August and first convinced the Old Guard politicians that the new part
was one with which they had to reckon. The direction of the campaign
which resulted in 4,500,000 votes for Roosevelt was largely in the hands of
Mr. Perkins, and from that time he was one of Colonel Roosevelt's closest
advisers.

James J. Storrow

BERNARD A. WEISBERGER

**James Storrow was Boston's leading financier and a partner of Lee, Higginson and Company, Boston's leading investment banking firm. In the
early 1900s he organized and led a campaign to turn polluted stretches
of the tidal Charles River into the beautiful Charles River Basin (along
which Storrow Drive now passes). In 1910, he became President of General Motors, initiating the corporation's modernization.**

[James Jackson] Storrow . . . was as Bostonian as the Common, the State
House, the Old North Church. He was born in 1864. His mother's ancestors included Oliver H. Perry, one of the naval heroes of the War of 1812.
His grandfather on his father's side, a civil engineer, had taken to wife
Lydia Jackson, whose family was the very marrow of the Bostonian mercantile and manufacturing aristocracy. From his first outcry, Storrow was
ticketed for Signor Papanti's Dancing School, Harvard, a profession, a
home on Beacon Hill. And he was faithful to his genes and his cultivation.
At 21 he had completed a career at Cambridge which lacked academic distinction, but he had been in the correct clubs and he had captained the varsity crew as a senior.

He chose as a career the law, the calling of his father, who had won a
major patent case for Alexander Graham Bell. At the Harvard Law School
he lived like the young Yankee milord that he was, sharing a house with a
small group of fellow students comfortable in their money and position.
They were all waited on by a Scottish couple, and they did not hesitate to
invite to dinner family friends like Professor Charles Eliot Norton, or the
chief justice of the Commonwealth, Oliver Wendall Holmes. On weekends
and vacations, Storrow liked to get away for solitary rural tramps, climbs,

and canoe rides, dressed in cap, tweed knickers, and stout shoes. There was no distinction in his classroom work, but a knack for leadership was emerging. Assigned to coach the undergraduates in the crew, he recruited, on his own, an expert who trained the eight in a new stroke that brought them to the most important finish line of the year, 25 cheering lengths ahead of Yale.

On graduation he clerked for Storey, Thorndike and Hoar, then joined the paternal firm, Fish, Richardson and Storrow. He passed all the expected milestones—marriage, a child, the acquisition of a winter house on Beacon Hill and a country place in Lincoln. The partners assigned to him much of the work with the investment house of Lee, Higginson and Company, a leading client. Frederick Fish told Henry Lee Higginson that Storrow would become Higginson's successor as the first citizen of Boston. After watching the young man for a time, Higginson agreed. In 1900 he invited Storrow in as a partner, and watched approvingly as his new associate climbed the toilsome slopes of civic leadership.

Forward-looking minds in the young century warmed to an array of new ideas that formed a design broadly called Progressivism. One part of Progressivism's pattern was loosely socialistic and talked of restoring government to the people, humanizing the conditions of work, liberating the oppressed, curbing the arrogance of wealth. It was not generally well regarded on Beacon Hill. But another aspect of Progressive belief was that there was virtue in efficiency. It called on voters to modernize, reorganize, purify, and enlarge the tasks of the rusty, patronage-befouled machinery of urban management. That appeal enlisted even "conservative" bankers like Storrow. . . .

At Lee, Higginson, too, he opened windows, let breezes blow Boston dust out of the pigeonholes. When he entered the firm it was 52 years old, and its oldest member, George Cabot Lee, had begun work there the year after Daniel Webster's death. The next senior member, Higginson, was still called "the Colonel," in deference to his service in the Civil War. The partners had made money primarily in securities of western railroads and copper mines, basic Boston investments in the nineteenth century. They had just begun to shift some funds into electrical and communications equipment. Storrow urged and got even larger purchases of municipal and industrial securities; pushed for the opening of branch offices in New York, Chicago and London; created a statistical department and another that specialized in foreign exchange. Under his prodding, the house geared its plans to the scientifically studied functioning of the contemporary world economy.

This was the man who took over General Motors' undisciplined regiments late in 1910. He threw himself into learning the new job with customary energy. For two years, he boarded a train to Detroit almost every Monday afternoon, and returned to New York or Boston only late in the week, in time to struggle to catch up with the rest of his work. He frequented the plants as well as the offices, firing question after question at the production men. Once he made them take a Buick apart and lay out every one of its components on sheets spread over the floor, so that he had a clear mental picture of what it actually took to put an automobile on the road. He was not merely looking for knowledge that would let him evaluate cost sheets with intelligence. He wanted to start organized research programs to replace the rule-of-thumb methods carried over from the industry's fumbling infancy. . . .

Storrow also nursed a strong suspicion of one-man rule. His distrust rose from the same impulse that led to battles against "the boss" in City Hall. He became a forceful spokesman for administrative decentralization. As he once told a group in an exposition of his management philosophy, "I have always tried to work out a division of responsibility from the top to the bottom." As the head of a large organization, he was responsible for overall profits. But his first step was, he said, "to get some men under me who are responsible for the profit and loss of the different departments or units. If I can get into these men a lively sense and keen interest in the game, there is nothing for me to do at the top." . . . In practice, that meant giving a long leash to the heads of operating companies. Storrow let them keep independent bank balances to register their scores, and on at least one occasion when the central office needed money badly, he reported, "We went out and borrowed several million dollars rather than interfere with the pride and joy of some of our managers in the balances that they had succeeded in building up for their companies." But the expectation in return was for teamwork above all. His managers were not to compete with other General Motors divisions, and to share information and resources fully. Each year he had a statement read to them like a proclamation to the troops; it ended: "We are of the opinion that there is no permanent place or advancement in this organization for the man who is not imbued with the spirit of helpful cooperation.". . .

Storrow was in luck in finding, within a year and a half, two men who could carry out his conceptions with dedication and brilliance . . . Charles Nash and Walter Chrysler.

Nash had been superintendent of Durant-Dort operations during the early years of General Motors, but was anxious to move into the vacuum of leadership at Buick caused by Durant's absorption in the holding company's affairs. At the time of the bankers' assumption of power, "Billy" [Durant] obliged him by submitting his name to Storrow for the post. The problematical mating between the Harvard lawyer and the bound boy from Illinois turned out to be a match that delighted both parties. They met on the common ground of their abhorrence of waste, their diligence, their orderliness. The economizing talents that had lifted Nash from the bottom were soon at work, slashing inventories, squeezing extra productivity out of the facilities, and compressing costs. Storrow relished the spectacle of Nash at the head of columns of black-ink figures marching up out of Buick's valley of debt. He liked the man personally, too, and it is likely that the friendship was deepened on hiking and sporting weekends at Lincoln, where Storrow would bring executives to size them up outside their offices. Nash, on his side, penetrated Storrow's New England reserve to find an extraordinary man. A great many men felt that Mr. Storrow was of the "banker" type—rather cold-blooded—which was entirely contrary to his real makeup. . . . If he found he was wrong in his diagnosis of any problem, he did not hesitate to immediately acknowledge that he was wrong and place the credit where it belonged—to the man that was right. . . .

In mid-1912 Storrow nominated Nash to become the president of General Motors. "I picked him to be head," he summarized later. . . . "In five years he turned a wreck into a concern having $25,000,000 in the bank.". . . As he wished, there was nothing for him, at the summit, to do.

Edward H. Harriman

────

JOHN KOBLER

Edward H. Harriman, possessed of a passion for railroading, created a fortune as a financier and a railroad rebuilder. Always competitive, when he was refused permission to build a house in an exclusive location he bought the hilltop overlooking the enclave and erected a great stone mansion from which he could forever look down on those who had snubbed him. Raising the Union Pacific to premier status was a personal and special quest.

In 1862, an act of Congress created the Union Pacific and the Central Pacific Railroad companies in order to connect the West Coast with the Eastern states by the nation's first transcontinental line. The government granted to the companies 25,000 square miles in alternate sections along the designated route and a subsidy of bonds with which to raise construction capital. The Union Pacific started laying track westward from Omaha, Nebraska, the Central Pacific eastward from Sacramento, California. On May 10, 1869, Leland Stanford, former governor of California and president of the Central Pacific, drove a gold spike that joined the two lines at Promontory, Utah. Disaster soon followed. A multitude of evils—profiteering, the rapacity of robber barons like Jay Gould, general mismanagement—threw the Union Pacific into bankruptcy. It owed the government $45 million. More than half its trackage had become unusable. "A draggled creature of the market-place that every philandering speculator had his will of," wrote a pair of biographical collaborators, quoting an unidentified source and adding: "In the degradation to which it had sunk few were willing to make an honest railroad out of it." To J. P. Morgan, who had abandoned an attempt to salvage the wreck, the Union Pacific was "two streaks of iron rust across the plains."

Jacob Schiff, whom Morgan contemptuously referred to as "that foreigner," thought differently. With the immense migratory movement westward and the fast-growing need for transport to convey building materials and goods of every description into virgin territory, the benighted railroad, Schiff concluded, could be revived at a great profit, given congressional support and capital to acquire bonds. No investment house, however, would attempt such a venture without first satisfying itself that the mighty Morgan had no designs of his own upon the Union Pacific. Who would compete against the country's most powerful banker? Schiff suspected the hand of Morgan behind a series of mysterious impediments. There were inexplicable congressional postponements, an unfriendly press, foreign clients who shrank from ratifying contracts already agreed upon. Was Morgan behind it all? Schiff would have confronted him in any event before proceeding. Now it was imperative, and he betook himself to Morgan's Wall Street sanctum.

The old colossus, seated at his rolltop desk before a blazing coal fire, chomping on a huge black Havana cigar, dismissed Schiff's suspicions. He wanted no part of the dilapidated railroad, he assured him, but added: "It's that little fellow Harriman, and you want to look out for him."

Edward Henry Harriman, a "two-dollar broker," as Morgan described him, was not a personable figure. Spindly, pallid, and stooped, prey to a succession of diseases, his eyes rheumy, his nose leaky, he wore a soup-strainer mustache that added no charm to his appearance. In business dealings, as in personal relations, he was cold, ruthless, ill-mannered. His gruff, growly voice was so low that it obliged the listener to lean closer. But behind the repellant exterior was a mind quick, sharp, and prescient.

Descended from English immigrants, the son of a New Jersey Episcopal clergyman, he quit Trinity School in New York City at the age of 14 to work as a Wall Street office boy. By his twenty-first year his nose for money had won him enough to buy a seat on the stock exchange for $3,000. In 1879 he married Mary Williamson Averell, the daughter of a banker who headed a small railroad company. They had a son, William Averell Harriman, future ambassador to the USSR and to Great Britain, governor of New York, and President John F. Kennedy's special roving emissary. Through his father-in-law, E. H. Harriman acquired a lifelong passion for railroading. In 1883 he became vice president of the prospering Illinois Central, and the dominant voice in its management.

Schiff summoned "that little fellow" and said, "Mr. Harriman, my associates and I, as you doubtless know, are trying to reorganize the Union Pacific. For a long time we have been making good progress; but now we are meeting everywhere with opposition, and I understand that this opposition is being directed by you. What have you to say about it?"

"I am the man," Harriman admitted.

"But why are you doing it?"

"Because I intend to reorganize the Union Pacific myself."

Schiff smiled skeptically. "How do you propose to do it, Mr. Harriman? Most of the securities of the company are in our possession. What means have you of reorganizing the Union Pacific?"

"The Illinois Central ought to have that road," Harriman insisted, "and we are going to take charge of the reorganization. We have the best credit in the country. I am going to issue one million dollars in 3 percent bonds of the Illinois Central Railroad Company and I am going to get close to par for them. You, at the best, can't get money for less than 4½ percent. In that respect I am stronger than you are."

Flabbergasted by such arrogance, Schiff replied dryly, "You'll have a good time doing it, Mr. Harriman, but meanwhile, what is your price?"

"There is no price. I am determined to get possession of the road."

Were there no conditions on which they could base a collaborative effort?

"If you'll make me chairman of the executive committee of the reorganized road, I'll consider the expediency of joining forces with you."

"Out of the question," said Schiff. The chairman had already been chosen.

"Very well, Mr. Schiff," said Harriman. "Go ahead and see what you can do. Good day."

The obstructions resumed until Schiff came up with an alternative offer. "If you will cooperate with us," he promised Harriman, "I'll see that you are made a director of the reorganized company and a member of the executive committee. Then, if you prove to be the strongest man in that committee, you'll probably get the chairmanship in the end."

"All right," said Harriman, who had no doubt that he would prove the strongest. "I'm with you."

Before the year ended Harriman was voted chairman. No sooner elected than he set forth on an inspection tour of the entire Union Pacific line. Riding an observation car by daylight, he scrutinized every mile of track, noting rusty ties, eroded rails, loose bolts. In subsequent tours he stopped at every major depot to interrogate officials (whom he astounded with his technical knowledge), to interview shippers, to assess the characters of the men in charge.

Delays en route irritated him. When he asked the reason for them, a division superintendent explained: "Engine taking water, sir."

"Why not make the feed pipe bigger?" Harriman barked.

"Can't be done, sir. The engine wouldn't take any larger feed pipe."

"Then we'll get some bigger engines."

He did not hesitate to direct such improvements on his own responsibility. Without waiting for the executive committee's approbation, he ordered the sides and roofs of old boxcars removed so as to use what remained for flat cars. As one of many economizing measures, he resolved to withdraw most of the light rolling stock and to put a ceiling of $10 each on the cost of repairing any of those remaining. Toward the end of his first inspection tour he telegraphed the committee in New York demanding authority to purchase some $25 million worth of new equipment. He got it.

Kahn [Otto Kahn, second to Schiff at Kuhn, Loeb & Co.] followed Harriman's operations with awe and admiration. Unaffected by the railroader's disagreeable personality, he respected his intellect and approached him as an eager student approaches an inspirational teacher. They became friends as well as investment collaborators.

Mary A. Harriman

ARCHIBALD MACLEISH

Mary Averell Harriman, the wife of railroader E. H. Harriman and the mother of Averell Harriman, was of such competence and sagacity that her husband on his death entrusted her with sole control of one of America's great fortunes. This revealing glimpse is from a 1931 essay entitled "The Most Interesting Line in *Who's Who*."

Mrs. Edward H. Harriman was in 1913, and remains in 1931, an extraordinary woman. But since her eminence consists in the possession to a very high degree of those qualities which it is polite but unwise to assume all human beings to possess in one degree or another, she has never been the object of spectacular journalistic attention. She is, that is to say, a woman of intelligence and character. She herself, and not some other woman acting with her authority, brought up her children—and brought them up free of the contagion of toadyism which, in the houses of the rich, enters with the green groceries, climbs the back stairs with the ice water, and goes to Yale with the eldest son. And she herself, and not some image of herself, acted as her husband's wife. One close friend of Mr. Harriman's believed that she alone had Mr. Harriman's confidence.

The support of a woman of Mrs. Harriman's nature would be and was something more than mere acquiescence. She has had, all her life, a will of her own. The contemporary rumors which attributed the Harriman-Fisk fight on the board of the Illinois Central to the social resentment of Mrs. Harriman as directed toward Mrs. Fisk were tributes rather to Mrs. Harriman's reputation for vigor than to the candor of their originators. And when her husband died, her sense of responsibility and her determination to do her duty herself were marvelously apparent. She ordered offices for the estate to be installed uptown, and for three days out of every seven she kept business hours. She asked and received the advice of such friends of her husband as Mr. Charles A. Peabody and Judge Robert S. Lovett, for many years general counsel for the Harriman roads. But she neither asked nor received more than their advice. The decisions she made herself. And they were very frequently her own and no one's else. When it is considered that she was controlling one of the most important reservoirs of power in American transportation, some comprehension of Mrs. Harriman's ability and her character is gained. Most striking and challenging evidence of her preeminence can be read in one line of her brief biography in *Who's Who:* "Sole heir upon death of husband to estate appraised at about $100,000,000, of which is manager." When Edward H. Harriman, whom his worst enemies (and there were many claimants to that distinction) never accused of sentimentality, left his entire estate and the entire responsibility for the execution of his will to one person, and that person a woman, he was paying her such a compliment as none of the famous women of chivalrous antiquity ever received. The industrial age has also its favors.

Amadeo P. Giannini

GARY HECTOR

Amadeo Peter (A. P.) Giannini founded the Bank of America—as the Bank of Italy—as a means of protest in 1904. Within 40 years it was the nation's largest bank and had redefined the way banking was done in America. Giannini had begun work in the family's produce business at age 12 and retired at age 31, only to have his father-in-law's death oblige him to look after his real estate and other interests. These included a seat on the board of San Francisco's first Italian-owned bank, Columbus Savings, from which Giannini quit in disgust to build an empire of his own.

Giannini stood six feet two inches tall, weighed more than 240 pounds, had a booming voice, and a near-photographic memory for names and faces. He entered business at the age of 12, buying and selling fruit on San Francisco's docks, and didn't become a banker until he was over 30. When he did, he brought an unorthodox style to the profession. He advertised for customers, a practice his fellow bankers thought vulgar. He worked long hours, rising early, hitting the streets in time to solicit business from merchants, shopkeepers, workingmen. He coveted customers that other bankers wouldn't touch, the small businessmen and the working stiffs, many of them immigrants who could barely speak English.

In 1930, Giannini told Congress, "The little fellow is the best customer that a bank can have, because he is with you. He starts in with you and stays to the end. Whereas the big fellow is only with you so long as he can get something out of you; and when he cannot, he is not for you anymore."

Giannini despised most bankers, didn't trust big corporations or Wall Street, and worried constantly—often with justification—that his enemies were hatching plots against him.

He built the first statewide branch banking system in America. He diversified into insurance, investment banking, and mortgage banking. Fifty years before it became fashionable, Giannini was building a financial department store, a single, nationwide chain that would offer loans, investments, and insurance under one roof. He bought banks throughout the western United States, preparing for a march across the nation (a march that Congress would thwart with legislation passed in the 1930s and the 1950s).

Giannini championed nationwide banking. He sensed that it was inevitable that banks would operate coast to coast, just as department stores and drug stores did. As he told Congress in 1930, "It is coming gentlemen, and there is nothing that you can do to stop it."

Giannini was quotable, accessible, and independent, with a common touch that success never changed. He told the press that it was a constant battle for him not to build a large personal fortune. "Too much money spoils people, it always has, it always will," he said. At his death, Giannini's personal net worth totaled under $500,000, less than he had when he founded what is now BankAmerica. He could easily have amassed a fortune to rival that of the robber barons, but he chose not to. Under his contract with the company, he earned 5 percent of the company's annual profits—in some years nearly $2 million. He drew enough to live well, often traveling to Europe, but gave most of the rest away.

Giannini also built well. By the time of his death, in 1949, his family ran one of the largest financial empires in the world, for his son Mario was president of Transamerica, the holding company that owned Bank of America. The vestiges of that empire remain today in four companies: BankAmerica Corp., until 1980 the nation's largest commercial banking company; Transamerica Corp., one of the nation's largest insurance companies; First Interstate Bancorporation, the nation's seventh largest bank holding company; and Citicorp, the nation's largest bank holding company, in which the Gianninis were once the major single shareholders. These four companies in 1988 controlled over $400 billion in assets with stock worth more than $15 billion.

The shadow that A. P. Giannini cast still hovers over BankAmerica. Almost 40 years after his death, employees seek inspiration from him as they try to solve problems. A 118-page collection of quotations from A. P. circulates throughout the bank. The company quotes him faithfully in its publications, and, each May, celebrates his birthday with a ceremony that includes placing fresh flowers on the bust of A. P. in the lobby of the BankAmerica world headquarters building. . . .

When A. P. Giannini joined the board of Columbus Savings, he began urging the directors to expand rapidly by making loans to small businesses. A. P. had traveled throughout California and he knew that farmers, merchants, and workers needed money, not merely in North Beach, but outside as well. Scatena & Co. had, on occasion, acted as a banker to many of its clients, buying farmers' crops in advance, in effect making interest-free loans. So A. P. knew from experience they could be trusted to repay their debts.

But the management of Columbus Savings, which listened to Isaias W. Hellman, president of Nevada National Bank, saw no reason to change policy. Used to winning most battles, Giannini fought back. He tried to pack the board. Failing in that, he pushed for a vote on his policy recommendations—which he lost.

About this time A. P. discovered a banking practice common at the turn of the century. One of the Columbus directors was accepting commissions for arranging loans through the bank. In addition, he was selling fire insurance to bank customers and pocketing the premiums. Outraged by what he thought was theft, A. P. confronted the board, arguing that the director was taking money that should have gone to the shareholders of the bank. When he demanded that the board fire the offending party, the board refused.

This was too much for Giannini, who stormed off the board, taking several other directors with him. Furious at being rebuffed, Giannini visited an old friend, James J. Fagan, an executive at the Crocker-Woolworth Bank. A. P. knew Fagan well enough to call him "Giacomo" (Italian for James). "Giacomo, I'm going to start my own bank," A. P. said. "Tell me how to do it." Reminiscing later, Giannini admitted, "I might never have gone into the banking game if I hadn't got so damn mad at those Columbus directors."

A. P. found a home for his bank in the middle of Little Italy, when the owner of a saloon decided to retire. He acquired the lease and for just over $5,000 converted the saloon into the headquarters of his bank, which he named, somewhat grandly, the Bank of Italy. It opened on October 17, 1904, with A. P. taking the job of vice-president, without salary.

Then A. P. Giannini, one of the city's most successful fruit merchants, with no experience as a banker, began banking his own way. He knocked on the doors to find customers, rising early to solicit business on the docks and in the markets. He made loans of as little as $25 to workers who had no collateral except the calluses on their hands. He advertised in newspapers, passed out fliers. Other bankers complained that A. P.'s advertising was undignified, to which he replied, "How can people know what a bank can and will do for them unless they're told?"

Giannini stumped not only for depositors and borrowers, but for stockholders. He raised $300,000 from local businessmen by selling stock for $100 a share. By the time the bank opened, it had 160 shareholders, dominated by local businessmen who knew North Beach.

From the beginning, Giannini's bank was successful. By the end of 12 months it had $1 million in assets, and, one year later, almost $1.9 million. By the standards of the city, it was still a tiny, unknown commercial bank in the Italian section—but Giannini was about to change that.

On April 18, 1906, just a little after 5:00 A.M., A. P.'s house, Seven Oaks, in San Mateo, a suburb just south of San Francisco, shook with the reverberations of the worst earthquake in San Francisco's history. A. P. dressed quickly and headed for the commuter train. He hopped aboard and made his way north to within a few miles of the city, where the train stopped. Giannini could see smoke rising from downtown San Francisco, but didn't realize yet that the quake had broken gas mains and the city was in flames.

Whole sections of San Francisco lay in ruins. Worst hit was the area south of Market Street, which had been built on landfill. Whole blocks had been leveled. City Hall was in ruins, the roof of the Empire Theater had caved in. Although the business district still stood, it was in the path of the fire, which had started in the section south of Market and was spreading rapidly.

Giannini walked the last few miles to his bank. When he arrived, at around noon, the Bank of Italy was open for business. Two of his officers, Armando Pedrini, the assistant cashier, and Ettore Avenali, a clerk, had withdrawn the bank's gold, notes, and securities as usual from the Crocker Bank's vault (where they were stored each night) and were ready to serve the bank's customers.

But by now the fire was within a few blocks of the Bank of Italy headquarters. Giannini hurried to Scatena & Co. and grabbed two produce wagons, onto which he and his assistants loaded the bank's gold and other cash, heaping crates of oranges over it all to hide the valuables. They piled the bank's papers and records on top, but had no room for its new adding machine, which was left in the safe.

The city was in a state of anarchy. Gangs of thugs roamed the streets, breaking into stores and looting homes. At other, larger banks, employees stuffed papers and valuables into fireproof safes. Refugees streamed out of the city, paying high prices for wagons or for ferries across the bay.

The roads were so crowded that it took all night to drive the 18 miles to San Mateo. At Seven Oaks A. P. hid the bank's cash and gold in an opening under the fireplace.

Without sleep, he returned to San Francisco to assess the damage. The fire had destroyed much of the downtown business section, including Bank of Italy's headquarters and most of North Beach. About one third of the city, nearly 2,600 acres, was in ashes or rubble, with five hundred dead and damage estimated as high as $500 million.

A. P. attended an emergency meeting of business and city leaders near the waterfront. The merchants and bankers were desperate. Many had lost everything in the fire. Some had their records and cash stored in vaults that would be too hot to open for days, if not weeks. One banker proposed a moratorium of six months on all lending, admitting that it would be weeks before his bank could get its vault open.

Giannini decided this was incredibly wrongheaded. Normally quiet in such meetings, he rose to speak.

"Gentlemen, you are making a vital mistake. If you keep your banks closed until November, you might as well never open them, for there will be no city left. The time for doing business is right now.

"Tomorrow morning I am putting a desk on Washington Street wharf with a Bank of Italy sign over it. Any man who wants to rebuild San Francisco can come there and get as much cash as he needs to do it. I advise all of you bankers to beg, borrow or steal a desk and follow my example."

The next morning the bank opened for business, setting a plank across two barrels at one of the city's busiest piers. A. P. urged his customers to pull their money out of their mattresses, then lent them what they needed to start over. North Beach, devastated by the fire, was the first to rebuild. Hundreds of local residents saw their dreams restored from ashes by money from Giannini's bank. Their families would remember and remain loyal to the bank for generations.

Jesse H. Jones

BASCOM N. TIMMONS

Jesse Jones, the remarkably effective head of the Reconstruction Finance Corporation, made a major contribution to the nation's war against the Depression. He did it by combining daring in lending, imagination in application of the law, and skill in managing the politicians, particularly Franklin D. Roosevelt. Even Senator Robert A. Taft became a believer. This admiring sketch tells about Jones' adventures when FDR set out to get farm commodity prices up.

Jones had early recognized that unsound banks, the dilemma of the railroads, and sulking prices of farm products were the trinity of economic culprits plaguing the country and standing in the path of its recovery. Banks and railroads were giving him quite enough problems. He had expected no part in the agriculture program.

Suddenly, on October 17, 1933, the Commodity Credit Corporation burst upon the Washington scene. It was the first of the RFC's special-purpose children, conceived to bolster the precarious instability of particular industries. CCC was incorporated, like all its later sisters, under the laws of Delaware, and domiciled with RFC. With its birth Jones was in the farm-commodity loan business.

President Franklin D. Roosevelt was deeply worried over the farm situation in that autumn of 1933. So were men wiser in the field of the national

From *Jesse H. Jones: The Man and the Statesman* by Bascom N. Timmons, © 1956 by Bascom N. Timmons. Reprinted by permission of Henry Holt and Company, LLC.

economy than he. There had been the plowing under of every third row of cotton as a panacea for Dixie's despair; the experiment of the killing of the 6,000,000 little pigs as a solution of the corn-and-hog problem of the Midwest, and the various other dubious Henry Wallace stratagems. But there was still the painful fact that the price of farm commodities was at a disastrously low level.

The prospect was especially wan for cotton, the South's principal money crop. There was a tremendous hang-over of the unmarketed yield of other years; and the forecasts were for a bumper new crop.

One day, when pickers were just entering the fields of the Southland in full force, Oscar Johnston, a big Mississippi planter, regarded as one of the nation's leading authorities on cotton, went to the White House to tell the President that ruin faced him and all the growers.

"We'll see what Jones can do about it," Roosevelt said. He called Jones and asked him to come to the White House.

Jones had not taken his chair in the President's office before Roosevelt said, "Jess, Oscar says cotton is selling at nine cents a pound, and may go lower if we don't do something to support the market. Cotton ought to be worth ten cents."

"All right," Jones said, "we will make it worth ten cents."

"How can you do it, and how soon?" Roosevelt asked.

"We will offer to lend ten cents a pound anywhere in the cotton-growing section," Jones replied.

"Yes, but the law says you can lend only on 'full and adequate' security."

"Certainly; I know that. I also know that cotton is worth ten cents a pound; and, if all our loans are as well secured as loans on cotton will be at ten cents, we'll be mighty lucky."

"Who decides what 'full and adequate' is?" Roosevelt asked.

"Our board," Jones replied. "Our loans to banks and railroads have always been made on what we regard as full and adequate security, and I think we will get our money back. I think cotton is worth more than ten cents a pound, even though it is selling at nine; and there will be no loss to the government."

Jones returned to his office, called in Stanley Reed, his general counsel, and together they studied the problem. Reed agreed that the ten-cent cotton loans could be made.

"If we lend on cotton, we are going to have to lend on corn, wheat, potatoes, tobacco, peanuts, butter, and a lot of other things. So we had just as well prepare," Jones said.

Thus the Commodity Credit Corporation was set up, and in the six years of its life under RFC it made loans to farmers that topped the government's help to railroads, and was second only to the amount dispensed to banks and other financial institutions. Years afterward Jones was to say:

"I feel that the Commodity Credit Corporation, as much as and maybe more than any government agency, saved the country from disaster. The money it advanced enabled the farmers to market their crops in an orderly manner. We raised the price of farm products. We took some losses; but there were more gains than losses, and we came out ahead on the books."

The Commodity Credit Corporation brought to Jones an association which was no contribution to his happiness. President Roosevelt felt that the Secretary of Agriculture should be included on the CCC Board of Directors. Theoretically, of course, this was perfectly sound practice; and so, at the President's request, Jones made Henry Wallace a member of the board of directors of CCC, along with several RFC men, Jones continuing to dictate its management and policies. Jones' opinion of Wallace at the time was low; it never ascended.

Jones, as was his custom, provided a device to keep RFC loans on cotton as few as possible. He had believed as proved to be the case, that the offer to lend ten cents a pound, with no recourse on the borrower, would quickly establish the value of that commodity. It was arranged that the farmer who wished to borrow on his crop could go to the most convenient bank or warehouse and there pledge his cotton as security for a Commodity Credit loan at 4 percent interest.

A lending bank could present the farmer's note to the nearest RFC agency and get its face value in cash plus 4 percent interest. As an incentive to the bank to carry the note, there was the provision that the originating country bank could keep 3 percent and send the remaining 1 percent to Commodity Credit, which stood ready to take over the note at any time.

An enormous crop of 13,100,000 bales was picked in the autumn of 1933. However, Jones' plan of guaranteed private-bank loans at ten cents a pound resulted in only $103,000,000 dollars' worth of cotton being pledged for these CCC loans. But in later years the management of the cotton loans came to require great skill.

The Jones cotton-loan plan worked so well in its first year that President Roosevelt, with his usual cavalier approach to serious economic problems, ordered an increase to twelve cents a pound on the 1934 crop. This 20 percent increase in the loan resulted in 1,198,000 separate loans to farmers on approximately 4,500,000 bales; and in the spring of 1935 producers were sending their cotton to twelve-cent loan warehouses instead of to the market.

Jones thought the twelve-cent pegging price went too far, and protested against it. An adroit plan was finally formulated by Jones, under which any farmer might claim the cotton that he had warehoused with the government, for the average price of 10 "spot" cotton markets on the previous day, less 25 points, or $1.25 per bale. This offer would be carried out whether or not the price at which the farmer took his cotton out of the loan would pay his note; and there would be no further recourse on the farmer. The move resulted in 2,000,000 bales of government cotton coming into market in 120 days, on a rising market.

As the program continued, Commodity Credit had almost unlimited discretion in handling its cotton for three years. But, at the time the enormous 19,000,000-bale 1937 crop came in, Congress had amended the Agricultural Adjustment Act to make it mandatory that loans be made on cotton, wheat, and corn whenever the three commodities reached a price fixed by the Secretary of Agriculture.

The result might have been foreseen. Soon Commodity Credit had on hand 11,000,000 bales of cotton, with a market value of $90,000,000 dollars less than the loans. The Jones plan had combined resourcefulness, imagination, and sound judgment. President Roosevelt, under Wallace's influence, had substituted economic charlatanism.

Cotton had taken all the money that CCC had in its till by the time wheat and corn farmers began clamoring for loans in 1938. Congress was not in session and Roosevelt was not in Washington. Jones was in a difficult spot. He could not secure enabling legislation to make wheat and corn loans until Congress came back in January. So he asked Stanley Reed, his general counsel, if he could have RFC buy $150,000,000 dollars in cotton-farmers' notes from the CCC to give the latter agency money to lend on corn and wheat.

Counsel Reed reported back to Jones that he could not do it. Jones wanted to know why. Reed replied, "There is no provision in the law for it."

Jones then wanted to know what would be the penalty if he took the action without authority from Congress. "Can they hang me if I do it?" he asked.

"No," Reed replied.

"How long is the jail term?" Jones pursued.

"There is none," Reed informed him.

"What can they do to me?"

"They can fire you," Reed said.

"Is that all?" Jones asked. Reed assured him that it was.

"Well, the ox is in the ditch, and it's up to us to get him out," Jones said. "I will have RFC buy from Commodity Credit Corporation $150,000,000 dollars' worth of farmers' notes secured by cotton. This will give us the money to lend on corn and wheat." The RFC had ample borrowing authority.

When Congress came back into session in January 1939, Jones went before the Senate Banking and Currency Committee, asking for a billion-dollar increase in borrowing authority for loans on cotton, corn, and wheat, and perhaps some other farm products. He told the committee what he had had to do to be able to make loans on corn and wheat the previous year.

Robert A. Taft, who had been elected to the Senate for the first time the previous fall, had been made a member of the Banking and Currency Committee. He questioned Jones rather critically about the method used to get money for the corn and wheat loans. Finally he said, "Mr. Jones, you have violated the law."

"No, Senator, I have not violated the law," Jones replied. "I have construed the law and administered it according to my best judgment under the circumstances; and if you think the increases I have asked should not be voted, vote against them. What I did was what I felt sure Congress would have authorized me to do had it been in session. I felt that it was my responsibility to meet the situation, and did, always having something to go home to when my services are no longer required."

That ended the matter. Taft joined in voting for the billion dollars Jones asked.

Charles E. Merrill

EDWIN J. PERKINS

Charlie Merrill both conceived and inspired Merrill Lynch's growth as a financial services organization. Along the way, he educated the investing public with a steady flow of research and "straight talk" advice, started the first in-house training program, converted Wall Street from an insiders' business to a truly public business, founded a trust that gave more than $100 million to charity, built Safeway Stores, and earned this comment from Martin Mayer: "He is the first authentically great man produced by the financial market in 150 years."

Charles Edward Merrill, a cofounder of Merrill Lynch & Company in 1915, was one of the most dynamic and innovative leaders in the twentieth-century financial services sector. During World War II, his reinvigorated enterprise became the nation's foremost stock brokerage firm and one of the most active investment banking houses. The internal reforms that he publicly advocated and successfully implemented at Merrill Lynch & Company after 1940 had a major and continuing impact on the business practices and ethical procedures of every Wall Street firm. In the brokerage field, Merrill had no peer in American history.

Born on October 19, 1885, he was the eldest of three children and the only son, of a physician and drugstore proprietor in Green Cove Springs, Florida. . . .

As an undergraduate at Amherst College in Massachusetts from 1904 to 1906, he sold clothing and waited on tables and participated in sports.

Excerpted from *The Encyclopedia of American Business History & Biography: Banking and Finance, 1913–1989*, edited by Larry E. Schweikart. 1990 (Facts On File, NY), pp. 283–289.

After leaving Amherst without graduating, Merrill spent the summer months working on West Palm Beach's *Tropical Sun* as reporter, editor, and occasional typesetter. He later recalled the job as "the best training I ever had; I learned human nature." That fall he enrolled in law school at the University of Michigan, but legal training had little appeal, and he did not return for a second year. He spent the summer of 1907 playing baseball for a Class D minor league team in Mississippi.

After the baseball season ended, Merrill, then twenty-two, went to New York City. His first position was in the city office of Patchogue Plymouth Mills, a textile firm that operated its main factory in Patchogue, New York. He rose to the position of credit manager and assistant to the president. "My two years there," he later remarked, "turned out to be the equivalent of a university course in general, and credit, finance, cost accounting, and administration, in particular." Soon after arriving in New York, Merrill met Edmund Lynch while both men were exercising regularly at the 23rd Street YMCA. A Johns Hopkins graduate, Lynch at the time sold soda fountain equipment. The two young men became fast friends. . . .

In September 1909 Merrill got his first job with a Wall Street firm. George H. Burr & Company, a commercial paper house, performed financial services for Burr's textile firm, and its owner had become aware of Merrill's abilities. Burr wanted to expand into handling corporate bonds, and he hired Merrill to head the newly created bond department. Merrill in turn hired his friend Lynch to work in sales. Merrill's main plan for attracting new customers was to rely on direct mail solicitations, and he concentrated on the dissemination of accurate, informative circulars devoid as much as possible of misleading statements and overblown optimism. In the early twentieth century any newspaper advertising that appealed blatantly for new accounts was still considered taboo by the most prestigious and high-minded securities firms.

An emphasis on straightforward dealing appears to have been one of Merrill's hallmarks from the outset. In an article entitled "Mr. Average Investor," published in the November 1991 issue of *Leslie's Illustrated Weekly,* he stressed the importance of knowing a customer's financial, requirements before suggesting an investment vehicle. He lamented the industry norm, which consisted of promoting any security in which a given brokerage house had a direct financial stake and the tendency to place too much emphasis on opportunities for short-term, speculative gains. Merrill also discussed the advantage of attracting a broad clientele: "Having thousands of customers scattered throughout the United States is infinitely preferable to being dependent upon the fluctuating buying power of smaller and perhaps on the whole wealthier group of investors in any one section." In another article he wrote, "The customer may not always be right but he *has* rights."

For the next half century, Merrill remained at the forefront of the movement to make honesty and integrity the bywords of the securities industry. In addition, he led in the movement to enlarge the customer base of securities firms to include millions of middle-class investors. Over the long run, he believed, truthfulness and full disclosure would benefit all parties involved in the routine trading of stocks and bonds—not just the public who were the major buyers and sellers, but sales personnel hoping to retain accounts over the long run as well.

Merrill made Burr's bond department a quick success, and the firm soon ventured into underwriting equities. In 1912, Burr sponsored an offering of $2 million in preferred stock plus 10,000 shares of common stock for the Kresge chain stores. That transaction launched Merrill's long association with chain stores, then a fresh and innovative concept in retailing; it was an involvement that continued, almost uninterrupted, over the next 40 years.

Dissatisfied with his compensation at Burr & Company, Merrill became sales manager of Eastman, Dillon & Company in 1913 but resigned within a year to establish his own small securities firm, Charles E. Merrill & Company, in January 1914. He persuaded Lynch to join the business before the year ended, and was twelve months later, in October 1915, the partnership was retitled Merrill, Lynch & Company. . . . The pair made a perfect team. An associate later remarked," Merrill could imagine the possibilities; Lynch imagined what might go wrong in a malevolent world."

The firm's initial underwritings in 1915 included the securities for two chain stores—McCrory Stores and Kresge, with the latter's account won away from Merrill's former employer. Indeed, the partners made the emerging chain store industry their specialty. The timing was opportune since the public had started to cultivate an appetite for stocks of enterprises beyond the traditionally narrow circle of railroads and heaving manufacturing. When the partnership originated, the fighting in Europe had already begun, and after the United States entered World War I in 1917, Merrill, now thirty-two, volunteered for service. He became a combat flight instructor for the air division of the army but never left the United States.

Following the end of the war in November 1918, the partnership had poised itself for the stock market boom of the 1920s. Millions of Americans had acquired the investing habit as a result of their regular purchase of U.S. war bonds, and they were now prepared to venture into corporate securities. The partners' strategy of catering to a broad spectrum of middle-class investors fit perfectly with new trends within the financial services sector. Merrill aimed to overturn two popular images about the character of employees in the typical Wall Street firm—that they were either elitist stuff shirts or sleazy, get-rich-quick speculators.

As in the past, Merrill stressed a flow of accurate information, simple honesty, and reliable service for clients of moderate means. . . .

In its underwriting activities, Merrill Lynch continued to concentrate on the expanding chain store sector. About half of its underwritings in the postwar decade included retailers, including J. C. Penney, National Tea, and two former clients, Kresge and McCrory. The firm also made several venture capital acquisitions in the 1920s. One acquisition was Pathè Exchange, the U.S. subsidiary of the early French filmmaker Pathè Freres, in 1921. The American unit was famous for its "Perils of Pauline" serials and its regular newsreels. When the partners learned that future success in the motion picture industry required a huge investment in a nationwide chain of theaters, they sold out to Cecil B deMille and Joseph Kennedy. . . .

With the cash from the sale of the movie company, the partners acquired Safeway Stores, a southern California food chain, in1926. For the next two decades Merrill remained an active participant in overseeing the development and expansion of Safeway. In 1929 he formed another food chain under the name MacMarr Stores, starting out with nearly 40 retail outlets. From his association with Safeway and other chain stores, Merrill had an opportunity to become familiar with the business principles behind the mass marketing of goods at high volume and low margins; eventually he got into the perfect position to transfer those ides to the securities field.

As the stock market rose to spectacular heights in the late 1920s, Merrill became increasingly alarmed. In a letter addressed to all the firm's customers on March 21, 1928, a date well over a year before the great crash, Merrill warned: "Now is the time to get out of debt. We do not urge that you sell securities indiscriminately, but we do advise in no uncertain terms that you take advantage of present high prices and put your own financial house in order." Early in 1929 he finally persuaded Lynch, who remained more upbeat about market trends, to reduce the firm's own exposure to the possibility of a sharp decline in equity prices.

When the crash came in October 1929, Merrill's reputation as a forecaster of market trends soared. Customers who had heeded his advice avoided the worst consequences of the debacle on Wall Street. Merrill's conservatism and prudence had paid off for his associates and customers with the good sense to listen to his warnings about stock market excesses. Unfortunately, the firm could not profit from its enhanced public reputation over most the next decade because brokerage and investment banking were two fields that contracted sharply in the 1930s.

The outlook for Wall Street firms, given the reduced volume of trading, was so uncertain that the partners decided to transfer all their brokerage business to E. A. Pierce & Company, an established firm with branches connected by private telegraph wires throughout the United States, including the West Coast states. Jointly Merrill and Lynch invested about $5 million of their own capital in the merged firm, while Pierce and his partners put up another $10 million. . . . In 1931 he arranged the absorption of the

MacMarr chain, with 1,300 stores, by Safeway Stores, which had twice that many outlets. The new Safeway, with almost 4,000 stores, became the nation's third largest chain. . . . Merrill emerged as the enlarged Safeway's largest stockholder. . . .

Merrill made an assessment of the outlook for E. A. Pierce & Company. The securities industry still languished in the doldrums, and the prospects for the Pierce network of offices across the nation still did not seem very favorable. Operating losses systematically depleted the firm's capital. As a result Merrill transferred his monies. . . out of the partnership equity account and converted the balance outstanding into a strictly interest-bearing account in November 1938.

Despite the generally bleak outlook on Wall Street at the close of the 1930s, a series of meetings in the last few months of 1939 rekindled Merrill's interest in reentering the brokerage and investment banking fields. . . . Merrill finally agreed to a realignment of the existing partnership based on his assumption of managerial control. . . .

In one of his first acts as senior partner, Merrill had a small pamphlet prepared for the guidance of employees, which outlined, in no uncertain terms, the basic policies of the firm. At the heart of the document appeared the commandment: "The interests of our customers MUST come first." In advertising brochures prepared for the public at large Merrill promised to devote substantial resources to investigating thoroughly the securities recommended by sales personnel, to ban trading by partners and employees on the basis of advance information, and to give customers, not insiders, priority in filling orders for securities underwritten by Merrill Lynch. By the end of 1940 the firm has 50,000 accounts, and about 12,000 of them had opened within the previous 12 months.

Over the next decade and a half Merrill Lynch introduced a host of innovative policies. Starting in 1940 the firm voluntarily published an annual report, the first ever by a private firm on Wall Street. The initial report featured little to crow about, however. Trading volume on the New York Stock Exchange had dropped 20 percent in 1940, and the firm, despite massive cost cutting, recorded losses totaling more than $300,000. It was an inauspicious beginning.

The next year trading on the Big Board fell off even more. One of the firms that developed serious financial problems in 1941 was Fenner & Beane, the nation's second largest brokerage firm with more than 50 offices in cities across the country. Within a few days the firms arranged a merger, and the newly organized Merrill Lynch, Pierce, Fenner & Beane claimed representation in 92 cities from coast to coast. The organizational network was in place, but the public still held back from broad participation in the stock market. Due in large part to underwriting commissions on new securities issues for retail food chains, the firm reported net profits of $459,000 in 1941. The tide had finally turned.

Robert Moses

HERBERT KAUFMAN

Robert Moses never held an electoral office and was decisively defeated
on the only occasion he tried for one. Nevertheless, he dominated New
York City politics and public finance for more than 30 years and, almost on his own say-so, built more public works than any other American—ever. These excerpts from a review of a 1974 biography reveal his
methods. The biographer, Robert A. Caro, while admitting that Moses
was a city-shaping giant, also portrayed him as being arrogant, bully-
ing, vain, law-violating, inhumane, bigoted, scheming, ruthless, vindictive, imperious, dictatorial, and egomaniacal.

The "why" of it, according to Caro, was Moses' insatiable lust for power.
Where did it come from, that "susceptibility to the infection of power"?
Its origins "lay not in Albany but in family—in heredity or upbringing or
some combination of the two. He was 'Bella Moses' son. . . . " Caro suggests it can be discerned in his undergraduate days at Yale (class of 1909),
but it was tempered by a rather conventional municipal reformer's ideal-
ism until he began to learn the lessons of practical politics in the administration of Al Smith. From his mentor he acquired in 1924 his first real
seat of power as president of the Long Island Park Commission, which automatically made him a member of the State Council of Parks, whose
other members promptly elected him chairman. The exercise of power so
gratified him that his appetite was whetted forever—initially for what he
could do with it, but ultimately, Caro suggests, for the sheer pleasure of
possessing it, wielding it, flaunting it. He was greedy for it, obsessed with
it, and corrupted by it, and his passion for it drove him to the astonishing
and controversial list of construction products that are his monument and
his legacy. But it was also to be his downfall as he overreached himself, accumulated enemies, and finally alienated his essential supporters. As Caro
describes him, he never was afflicted by self-doubt; his confidence in
himself permitted him to use his power to the limit, and his successes in
the use of power built his self-confidence. The power drive as a self-
reinforcing spiral.

• • •

Caro's explanation of the "how" of Moses' ascendancy is of a different
order. The amateur psychologizing yields to professional reportage.

Reprinted by permission of *Political Science Quarterly*, 90 (1975): 521–538.

To be sure, much of the explanation turns on personal attributes of the subject—his quickness of mind, his imagination, his breadth of vision, and his incredible energy. It took relays of secretaries and engineers to keep up with him; he drove them and himself mercilessly, and ideas poured from his fertile brain in a seemingly endless torrent.

But it is the inventory of his strategies that is the fascinating core of the story. Caro's list is long; Moses was most resourceful. But the methods can be grouped for convenience into six categories.

The first is *move quickly and vigorously*. Moses did not engage in polemics over broad principles and general plans; he went into every fray with blueprints in hand, ready to start building the moment he was in a position to take the first step. Indeed, he sometimes had his work crews poised to go into action instantly; once, in 1936, [Mayor Fiorello] La Guardia actually called out the police to stop the demolition of a ferry slip by his own Parks commissioner while the ferries using it were still plying the East River. . . . Such was his speed that when a lawyer for a group trying to save the old Aquarium in Battery Park proposed on a Friday to get an injunction on Monday prohibiting Moses from demolishing the historic structure, he was told by one who knew Moses' techniques, "'Are you crazy? There won't be anything left of this . . . Monday morning. He'll demolish it over the weekend.'" . . . He believed if he could drive the first stake on any project, no matter how large the enterprise, the project could not be blocked, and he acted on that belief with great success. . . .

The second strategy was to *supervise personally*. Moses was not one to sit in an office pushing paper. He went out into the field himself, making suggestions, giving orders, evaluating performance, and formulating new plans. Caro thinks that this accounts for the high morale, the loyalty, and the productivity of his staff, and for the excellence of his projects' designs. By the mid-1930s, however, he was so overextended that he was at the point of exhaustion, and he could no longer give his undertakings the personal attention and thought that he gave them earlier. . . . And his empire was to grow further in the years ahead. That, says Caro, is when deterioration of the quality of the work, arbitrary use of authority, and indifference to the people reached alarming proportions. Nevertheless, his personal intervention in the early stages set the tone for his whole organization and laid the groundwork for his later victories.

Third, he was a master at *discovering or imbedding in law seemingly innocuous provisions that added to his power*. Among the most effective of these were clauses that made the powers of the Triborough Bridge and Tunnel Authority part of the contract between the Authority and its bondholders. This accorded them the protection of the Constitution of the United States, which prohibits the impairment of contractual obligations by the states. Presumably, therefore, the state government that established the Authority could not terminate it except with the agreement of both the Authority and its bondholders, and since the Authority could continue indefinitely to issue bonds, up to the limit of its statutory authority, as older issues matured, it could survive forever, regardless of what the state wanted. . . . Whether or not the state is quite as helpless as this description makes it sound, Moses certainly gained enormous leverage from the arrangement.

He realized the potential for power in obscure legal provisions early in his career. It was in the course of the campaign for reorganizing state administration under Al Smith that he first perceived opportunities of which he was subsequently able to take advantage. And when the Town Board of Babylon sought to prevent the cession of its ocean beach to the state so that Moses could build Jones Beach, Moses bludgeoned the board into cooperating by threatening to reveal a technicality he had happened on: years earlier, the state legislature had failed to pass a bill giving the town rights over bay bottoms everyone assumed it had. The bay bottoms were more important to the town than the beach was because many fishermen made their living from them. In the end, Moses got his beach and the town got its missing rights, but he probably would have lost the fight had he not come across that small detail.

From then on, he always looked at the fine print other people overlooked. A good deal of [the] time, he drafted it himself. His opponents usually found out about the implications when it was too late. Thus, for example, the local law establishing the position of city construction coordinator, a law Moses wrote and a position that only he would ever occupy, included a phrase allowing that official to "represent the city in its relations with cooperating state and federal agencies." For two decades, Moses was able to use it to make himself sole broker between the city and higher governments, and thus to control the funds that flowed from them. And Caro insists he did not hesitate to misrepresent to the city the terms and conditions of those grants. . . .

In this way, he got sole control of the revenues from his Authorities, virtual control over grants-in-aid to the city, immunity from interference, and invulnerability to removal. He thus became an autonomous force in the politics of the metropolis.

His fourth strategy was the superb execution of *an imperial style of public life and administration*. . . . He entertained officially on a lavish scale, more often the host than the guest, and kept kitchen staffs standing by daily at three of his offices "so that, wherever he might be, he could serve lunch to invited guests.". . . His car roared through the toll booths of his facilities that even the governor's vehicle was compelled to pass around so as not to disturb the treadle count. A boat was constantly at his disposal. His staff, according to Caro, fawned on him. His style was positively regal.

Above all, he acknowledged no one as his superior. In fact, he treated few as equals. For most, he showed only condescension, expecting their homage—and usually getting it. Mayors, governors, cabinet officers, and even presidents of the United States received no deference from him; on the contrary, if they did not accede to his demands, he made his disrespect unmistakably (and sometimes publicly) clear to them.

Nor did he regard rules as made for him. For other people, perhaps, but not, says Caro, for him—least as far as he was concerned:

> Robert Moses must have known—he proved it by his actions—that he could with far more impunity than any private citizen, defy the law. He gloried in the knowledge; he boasted and bragged about it. For the rest of his life, when a friend, an enemy—or one of his own lawyers—would protest that something he was doing or was proposing to do was illegal, Moses would throw back his head and say, with a broad grin, a touch of exaggeration and much more than a touch of bravado: *"Nothing I have ever done has been tinged with legality."*. . .

Like a Byzantine ruler, he had his men in agencies everywhere (the "Moses Men," Caro calls them), including, allegedly, members of mayors' and governors' staffs and city and state legislators secretly on his payroll. . . . He summoned fellow commissioners, supposedly his coequals, from the theater or even from their beds when he wanted action. . . . Caro declares he lied to destroy the reputations of any who stood in his way. . . . He was a master of insult, and he even threatened, and occasionally resorted to violence against, his adversaries. . . .

So whether people loved him or hated him, they feared him. His subordinates were cowed, and most of his opponents and critics crumbled in his presence. He played the part of an emperor so well that few dared to stand up to him.

His fifth strategy was *public relations*. For years, he was a hero to the city's newspapers, which, dazzled by the scale and number of his works, magnified and projected his image with astonishing unanimity and frequency; rivers of praise and adulation cascaded over him. . . . Late in his career, the media would turn against him, but at his height, he had them all with him. Indeed, again and again, Caro comments on the failure of the press to raise questions, to investigate, to expose the defects and improprieties of the Moses empire. In many respects, Moses owed much of his strength to his popularity with the press; newspapers and magazines helped make him what he was by both their breathless encomiums and their docile acceptance of the myth they helped to create.

He knew it, too. In 1934, when he was the Republican candidate for governor of New York in the only electoral race he ever entered, alienation of the press was one of the mistakes he made in a campaign distinguished by the number of mistakes he made and groups he offended; he was swamped. Although he would continue to have run-ins with newspapermen from time to time even when he was generally on good terms with them, for the most part he managed to keep them behind him from then on until his final decline began in the 1960s.

Part of his success may be ascribed to the natural impressiveness of construction projects. The results are tangible; they lend themselves to spectacular ceremonial openings; they can be photographed and visited. Social programs—education, public health, welfare, police, for example—are less inherently visible and dramatic even when they are of high quality.

Part of his success was due to his record as a reformer and an anti-Tammany crusader (despite his long and intimate association with the Democrats). Although he condemned most reformers for their alleged impracticality, the reform mantle benefited him greatly.

Another part of his public relations success was the result of his own carefully prepared flow of brochures, releases, and documents describing and acclaiming the accomplishments of his many organizations.

But nothing was more important than his cultivation of the publishers and editors of the mass media as well as the reporters. He lavished attention on them and became close friends with many of them, and at one stage was therefore able to induce the *Herald Tribune* not only to suppress a critical series of stories by an investigative reporter, but to force the reporter to apologize to him personally for writing it. . . .

Moses had been warned by Al Smith that popularity is too slender a reed on which to rely very long in public life. Caro contends he therefore made himself invulnerable to public control. He did so, however, by using his popularity while it was high to establish his nearly impregnable power base. His popularity was one of the weapons he used to make himself independent of popular support! Few dared do battle with him even before he achieved seemingly total security; consequently, fewer still could stop him after he achieved it.

But his most important strategy—the one on which all the others ultimately came to rest—was *patronage*. He had billions to spend. He controlled contracts for construction, for services, for supplies, for interest on loans. Banks were eager for the deposits of his agencies. Investment houses profited from the marketing of his bonds. He had jobs to fill, and the salary scales of the top posts in his public authorities were a good deal higher than those in the city and state public service. No Civil Service Commission hampered him in these appointments and removals, and no city or state budget officers rode herd on him. No political party in the area, not even in Tweed's day, had so much unhampered discretion over so many benefits as Moses did—or used it so freely.

He could not only reward his friends; he could punish his enemies as well. The punishment might be petty—deletion from the list of invitees to his entertainments, for instance—or brutal—he fired his longtime favorite aide and 30-year personal friend instantly for pointing out financial problems with the 1964–1965 World's Fair, which Moses headed. . . . What he gave, he could take away and give to someone else. If he could build, he could also raze. According to Caro, he seemed to take pleasure in hurting people, and this helped him achieve his aims. . . .

Consequently, when he needed them, he could mobilize "contractors, architects, engineers, lawyers, bank presidents, presidents of bonding, title-insurance and building-material-supply companies, union leaders.". . . They turned out like loyal troops at his command.

Nobody ever suggested that any of these immense resources ever went into his personal accounts; when he finally was deposed, he was far from a rich man. "Money honest" is the epithet some, including Caro, applied to him. He used his patronage for political purposes, not for lining his own pockets. For those purposes, it paid off handsomely.

Ultimately, even all these strategies were not enough to protect him against Nelson Rockefeller, who, as governor, had plans of his own into which Moses did not fit. Of course, Moses was 80 years old when he was ousted; perhaps he had slipped a little. Moreover, his public image had acquired some tarnish in the later years. At any rate, whatever the reason, even Moses' time ran out.

But for four decades, his strategies served him well. They enabled him to satisfy the power hunger that drove him all his life and made him, in Caro's view, the chief shaper of the urban scene in the United States.

MOVERS, SHAKERS, AND SCOUNDRELS

John Law

John Law, a renegade Scottish financier and speculator, was also Controller-General of French finance in the early eighteenth century. There, he introduced paper money, is said to have invented inflation, and certainly created one of the grandest, most extraordinary financial debacles ever recorded, subsequently known as the *Mississippi Bubble*. A man briefly possessed of virtually unlimited wealth, he died in poverty after leaving France in disgrace and under a false name.

[John Law was born in Edinburgh in 1671 into a rich family of bankers educated in that city] and was early remarkable for his proficiency in arithmetic and algebra. He grew up a handsome, accomplished, and foppish young man of dissipated habits, and a great gambler. In April 1694 he killed Edward Wilson [in a duel about a lady] and being convicted of murder, was sentenced to death. The capital sentence was commuted to one of imprisonment on the ground that the offence was one of manslaughter only; but against this decision an "appeal of murder" was brought by a relative of his victim. While the appeal was pending, Law escaped from prison and took refuge on the Continent.

For a time Law is said to have acted as secretary to the British resident in Holland, and to have devoted much attention to finance, especially to the working of the bank of Amsterdam.

At the close of 1700, he was in Scotland, then in a state of collapse, due to the failure of the Darien scheme. Early in 1701, he issued anonymously at Edinburgh his "Proposals and Reasons for Constituting a Council of Trade in Scotland," which was to abolish the farming of the revenue and to simplify taxation. The revenue raised and administered by it was to furnish a fund from which advances should be made for the encouragement of national industries, or the council might undertake certain needful branches of production neglected by private enterprise, abolish trade monopolies, free raw materials from import duties, and set the unemployed to work. In 1709 was published, also anonymously, at Edinburgh, Law's second pamphlet, "Money and Trade considered, with a Proposal for Supplying the Nation with Money." Law starts here with the assertion that the trade of a country depends on its possession of a supply of money equal in quantity to the demand for it in all departments of industry. Law maintained that paper-money, as yet unknown in Scotland, was not only in itself a much

Excerpted from *The Dictionary of National Biography*, Oxford University Press, Vol. XI, 1963, pp. 671–675. Reprinted by permission of the Oxford University Press.

more convenient currency than specie, with which the country was scant-
ily supplied, but could be easily and safely issued in quantities adequate to
the demand if it represented not gold and silver, but non-metallic objects
possessing real value, especially land. By such an issue the rate of interest
would fall, and production of all kinds would flourish. In the year of the
publication of this pamphlet he appears to have submitted to the Scottish
parliament a scheme for the establishment of a state bank, which was to
issue paper-money on the security of land. . . . His scheme was rejected by
the parliament, not on economic grounds, but because it was "so contrived
that in process of time it" would have "brought all the estates of the kingdom to depend on the government.". . .

In February 1715 Lord Stair . . . suggested that Law might be useful in
devising some scheme for paying off the national debt of England, and described him as "a man of very good sense and who has a head for calcula-
tions of all kinds to an extent beyond anybody."

After the death of Louis XIV . . . [in] 1715, Law plied the Duke of
Orleans, on becoming regent, with proposals for the establishment of a
state bank. The regent was favourable to them, but the opposition of his
advisers and of experts procured their rejection. He, however, allowed Law
and some associates to found a bank of their own, the first of any kind, apparently, founded in France. . . . It was speedily successful. Law was able to
try his pet scheme of a paper-currency under circumstances peculiarly
favourable. The metallic currency of France was then subject, at the
caprice of the government, to frequent alterations of value. Law made his
notes payable on demand in coin of the same standard and weight as at the
date of issue. Having thus a fixed value they were preferred to the fluctuating French coinage, and rose to a premium. Their reputation and that of
the bank was increased when, . . . [in] 1717, a decree ordered them to be
accepted in payment of taxes. His paper-money being thus preferred to
specie, Law freely advanced money on loan at a low rate of interest, and the
immediate result was an expansion of French industry of all kinds. "If,"
says Thiers, "Law had confined himself to this establishment, he would be
considered one of the benefactors of the country and the creator of a superb system of credit.". . . But Law now had in view a scheme of colonisa-
tion by means of a company, which he hoped would rival or surpass the
East India Company of England, and he persuaded the regent to make over
to him and his associates Louisiana, which at that time included the vast
territory drained by the Mississippi, the Ohio, and the Missouri. From the
first-named river Law's enterprise became known as "The Mississippi
Scheme," but . . . was also called "The System." The decree incorporating
the Compagnie d'Occident, with sovereign rights over Louisiana, was issued in August 1717. The parliament of Paris was indignant at the conces-
sions of banking privileges and territory to a foreigner and a protestant. Its
opposition reached a crisis when in August 1718 it was rumoured in Paris

that the parliament intended to arrest Law, try him in three hours, and have him hanged forthwith. . . . The regent met the parliamentary resistance in December 1718 by converting the Banque Générale into the Banque Royale, the notes of which were guaranteed by the king. Law was nominated its director-general, but he was unable to prevent the regent from freely increasing the issue of paper-money in order to satisfy his extravagant personal expenditure.

Law meanwhile was enlarging the responsibilities of his Western Company. In August 1718 it acquired the monopoly of tobacco, and in December the trading rights, ships, and merchandise of the Company of Senegal. In March 1719 it absorbed the East India and China companies, and thence-forward assumed the designation of the Compagnie des Indes. In the following June the African Company came under its authority, and thus the whole of the non-European trade of France was in its hands. In July of the same year the mint was handed over to Law's company, and he could manipulate the coinage as he pleased. In August the company undertook to pay off the bulk of the national debt of the kingdom, and became practically the sole creditor of the state. . . . As a fiscal administrator Law appears in a very favourable light. He repealed or reduced taxes which pressed directly, and he abolished offices the emoluments attached to which pressed indirectly, on commodities in general use, and the price of the necessaries of life was reduced by 40 percent. Rural taxation was so adjusted that the peasant could improve the cultivation of the soil without fear of losing the honestly earned increment. Free trade in cereals and other articles of food between the provinces of France was established. . . .

Law promised high dividends to the shareholders of his great company, and the public expected that its enormous enterprises would ultimately yield fabulous profits. Its issues of new shares were accompanied by fresh issues of paper-money from the bank, for which the stock of the company offered a means of investment. "The System" reached its acme in the winter of 1719–20. Multitudes of provincials and foreigners flocked to Paris eager to become "Mississippians." The scene of operations was a narrow street called Quincampoix, where houses that previously yielded 40 percent a year now brought in over 800 percent per month. Enormous fortunes were made in a few hours by speculators belonging to all classes. . . . The highest in the land courted Law in the hope of a promise to be allowed to participate in each new issue of shares. The market price of shares originally issued at five hundred livres reached ten thousand livres, and when on 1 January 1720 a dividend of 40 percent was declared, the price rose to eighteen thousand livres. On 5 January 1720, having as a needful preliminary abjured protestantism and been admitted into the Roman catholic church, Law was appointed controller-general of the finances. According to Lord Stair, then British ambassador in Paris, Law boasted that he would raise France to a greater height than ever before on the ruins of England and Holland, that he could destroy English trade and credit, and break the Bank of England and the English East India Company whenever he pleased. Stair resented his language, and from a friend became an enemy of Law. To appease Law, early in 1720 Stair was recalled by his government.

On 23 February 1720 the Company of the Indies was united to the Royal Bank, and "The System" was completed. But a reaction had already set in. The successful speculators in the shares of the company had begun to realise their gains, and to drain the bank of coin in exchange for their paper-money. The specie thus obtained was partly hoarded, partly exported. To check this movement Law had recourse, during the earlier months of 1720, to violent measures, enforced by royal decrees. The value of the metallic currency was made to fluctuate. Payments in specie for any but limited amounts were forbidden. The possession of more than five hundred livres in specie was punished by confiscation and a heavy fine, and domiciliary visits were paid to insure the enforced transmission of specie to the mint. Informers of infractions of this order were handsomely rewarded. Holders of paper-money began to realise by purchasing plate and jewellery, but this traffic was prohibited. Investments in the purchase of commodities was the last expedient tried, and it increased the already enormous prices due to a super-abundant paper currency, which were paralysing trade and industry and exciting popular discontent. It has been much disputed whether the final decree which precipitated the downfall of "The System" was planned by Law or by Law's enemies in the councils of the regent. . . . On 21 May 1720 a decree was issued directing the gradual reduction of the value of the bank-note until it reached one-half. This flagrant repudiation of the state's obligations caused a panic, which was not checked by the withdrawal of the decree on the 27th, since at the same time the bank suspended cash payments. On the 27th Law was relieved of the controller-generalship, yet was soon appointed by the regent intendant-general of commerce and director of the ruined bank. But "The System" had fallen with a crash. In the popular commotion which followed, Law's house in Paris was attacked and himself insulted. His enemies in the regent's councils gained the upper hand, and he had to leave the country. He had invested the bulk of his fortune in the purchase of estates in France. They and whatever other property he left behind him were confiscated. . . .

Law was a handsome man of polished and agreeable manners, and of much conversational talent. Saint-Simon, who knew him intimately, pronounced him "innocent of greed and knavery," and described him as "a mild, good, respectful man whom fortune had not spoilt." Some of the chief French historians of his times speak of him provingly as a precursor of modern state-socialism, and most of them agree that "The System," however ruinous to individuals, gave a great impetus to the industry and enterprise of France, exhausted as it had been by Louis XIV's wars. According to Voltaire, . . . who was an eye-witness of its collapse, "a system altogether chimerical produced a commerce that was genuine and revivified the East India Company, founded by the great Colbert, and ruined by war. In short, if many private fortunes were destroyed, the nation became more opulent and more commercial."

Gerson Bleichröder

FRITZ STERN

Gerson Bleichröder was both a private and a public banker to Otto von Bismarck, first Chancellor of the German Empire. He capitalized on the extraordinary opportunity this represented with both skill and persistence. The Rothschilds were his models and coveted associates, but he was a self-made man who did his own work.

For Bleichröder, the growing intimacy with Bismarck was invaluable. To be Bismarck's banker and confidant—and to be known as such—certified Bleichröder's special status. But there were also certain immediate, practical advantages that Bleichröder drew from this close relationship. Like the Rothschilds, like any financier, Bleichröder put a special premium on being abreast of major developments, on knowing a few hours or days ahead of his competitors the likely climate of the market. Because of his double role as Bismarck's investor and adviser, Bleichröder had ample reason for supplying the chancellor with a steady stream of news about the political economy of Europe. In conversation or correspondence Bismarck would have to offer some comment of his own, some confirmation or denial of a report. In short, by transmitting news to Bismarck, Bleichröder was also continually soliciting news from him. And for Bleichröder to know the thoughts or the disposition of the most influential actor on Europe's stage was of incalculable importance. Both men were perfectly candid about this aspect of their relationship. At the end of 1869, for example, Bleichröder counseled Bismarck not to sell his securities, but hedged: "If, however, Your Excellency should expect troubles in the Near Eastern question or other political complications, then I would indeed sell all Your Excellency's securities.". . . Bismarck was equally candid; he once defined his relationship with Bleichröder to Lord Odo

Excerpted from *Gold and Iron: Bismarck, Bleichröder, and the Building of the German Empire*, by Fritz Stern. © 1979 by Fritz Stern. Reprinted by permission from Vintage Books, a division of Random House, Inc.

Russell, the British ambassador in Berlin in the 1870s, when Russell had been instructed to find out whether the British government should consider Bleichröder as a well-informed source. Bismarck said: "Are you aware of the fact that Bleichröder administers my private fortune? If so, do you believe that I would mislead him?". . .

Gradually something more than a mere business relationship ripened. Bleichröder must not only have been efficient and successful, as well as pleasingly subservient and solicitous; he must have been congenial as well, for their relations deepened in these years and even Johanna formed personal ties to him. Some of the Bismarck clan—Otto's cousin and collaborator, Bismarck-Bohlen, for example—used Bleichröder because Bismarck referred all financial matters to him. . . .

Bleichröder's rise after 1866 illustrates dramatically the interlocking nature of Germany's new order. It was Bleichröder's simultaneous success in different realms—in the banking world, in Bismarck's world, in the world of European finance and of the Rothschilds, in the tightly ordered world of the Prussian court—that gave him his preeminence. He helped to bring these worlds closer together, and his success in one realm reinforced his claim in another. Money begets more than money; it begets influence and some—limited—forms of power. But for Bleichröder, as for European financiers generally, wealth was not enough; in a traditional-hierarchical society, it was status and public acceptance that mattered. Bleichröder's spreading importance symbolized the triumph of capitalism itself, and yet Bleichröder's story also demonstrates the limits and travails entailed in that triumph.

After 1866 Bleichröder's intimacy with Bismarck was a celebrated fact of social and political life. He was known as a man of shrewd judgment, integrity, and prudence, blessed with a Midas touch. If anything, popular imagination already began to exaggerate Bleichröder's influence. He was rightly reputed to be the best-informed man in Berlin, precisely because he lived and worked in so many diverse realms. He had friends, clients, creatures everywhere, visibly and invisibly. He spun his web of contacts. He had much to offer and needed much in return. He had influence sometimes, political power never. And for every rung of the ladder, he had to fight or jockey. The power of capitalists is a common theme; the precariousness of their success in some societies is often ignored. . . .

The Rothschilds remained Bleichröder's models and most coveted associates. Baron James [Rothschild] retained his special place, although Bleichröder was also in constant touch with the London and Frankfurt Houses. They often collaborated, and in addition, Bleichröder plied Baron James with confidential news that emanated from "the good source."

He also plied him with presents. In 1864 Baron James must have mentioned some particular antique he coveted, and Bleichröder at once sent it as a gift. "I am very partial to this sort of antique," wrote Baron James in reply, "because otherwise, I confess, my dear Herr Bleichröder, that I would not have accepted it because the piece is really too valuable. I hardly dare to give you any further orders to buy things for me, otherwise I would ask you now to keep an eye out for old paintings or other antiques there because the war against the poor Danes probably has brought many beautiful and interesting pieces on the market. . . . "

In 1867 the two men met at Wildbad, and in the same year Bleichröder presented Baron James with an option for a rare collection of paintings, including Cranachs and Breughels, which had very nearly gone to Prince Orlov. . . . Bleichröder's efforts to please Baron James remained, but the old subservience gradually diminished. In 1868 Baron James died, and Bleichröder hastened to his funeral. James, a legendary figure who came to believe in his own legend, had already been the patron of Gerson's father, and it seemed natural for the son to preserve feelings of deference, even subservience, toward this older man. With Baron James's son and successor, Baron Alphonse, the relations became less burdened with Bleichröder's own modest beginnings. Bleichröder's growing independence—and his basking in Prussia's glory—annoyed the Rothschilds at times. . . .

Like the Rothschilds, Bleichröder wanted all governmental business, however small, provided the terms were favorable. Even routine transactions yielded commissions and some profit. Bleichröder grew richer and richer in the late 1860s. A certain kind of power accrued to him as well: his resources allowed him to bestow or withhold various forms of help to governments, companies, and individuals. Not all money was equal: Bleichröder's money had a special cachet and hence was especially valuable. He could in effect decide the fate of a person or a charity or even a company. But there was a rub to it all: he was also dependent on the good will of governments and of the socially prominent. This dependence hobbled his power. Hence his was an endless pursuit of wealth and prominence, carried on indefatigably and quite deliberately. Every profit, every title, every friend, helped to establish or maintain Bleichröder's place in the world. There was no fixed goal, there was hardly time for a contented look backwards to realize how far, how immeasurably far, he had traveled.

Wealth was not enough, nor was its pursuit an end in itself for Bleichröder. Wealth was a necessary but not a sufficient condition for his becoming an accepted part of the governing elite of Germany. Wealth without social distinction was but a flawed achievement. . . .

For centuries, grateful governments had eased the passage of the rich into the kingdom of man by distributing formal signs of recognition: titles and medals. The Prussian government systematically exploited its subjects' hunger for decoration. The politically reliable were rewarded, the dissident would go bare. The rich could expedite their rise—some would say, buy it—by making large gifts to communal charity. Such purposeful charity was a kind of voluntary tax. The state meticulously scrutinized Bleichröder's qualifications on all these points . . . . On New Year's Day 1866, Bleichröder was accorded the title Geheimer Kommerzienrat, a further, rare distinction which meant that in the future he would be addressed as "Herr Geheimrat." Before the award, the Berlin police scrutinized Bleichröder's record, and the chief wrote a long report, supporting the new title. He explained that the integrity of Gerson's father had led the Rothschilds to appoint him their deputy in Berlin; Gerson had continued in that role but had achieved "greater independence." The House of Bleichröder "is now regarded as the greatest banking house in Berlin."

Jay Cooke

ALBERT BIGELOW PAINE

Jay Cooke's energy and innovative selling techniques were crucial to the success of the Federal government's financing of the Civil War. Described here, after his firm had become the nation's leading financial institution, is its over-expansion and subsequent failure in 1873. This precipitated a panic and, ultimately, caused the New York Stock Exchange to close its doors for the first time ever, "to save the Street from utter ruin."

With the beginning of the seventies the nation's prospects were not particularly bright. The business boom that had followed the close of the Civil War had reached the point that booms generally reach when there is too much enthusiasm and credit for the supply of available cash. It was a time of general inflation, and the day approached when not only the bonds that the great corporations had floated—and were still gaily floating—but also a panic, would be coming due. . . .

Jay Cooke was a fine, handsome man, very religious, and of undoubted genius. But he was also an enthusiast, and if not a visionary he at least had visions that were set in advance of his time and capabilities. Buoyed by his successful government financing, full of confidence and dreams he now turned his attention to railroads.

It was a period of railroad construction. Corporations capitalized at many millions were everywhere forming; steel arms were reaching out in

Excerpted from *George Fisher Baker* by Albert Bigelow Paine. G.P. Putnam's Sons, 1920, pp. 86–95.

every direction to embrace the continent. The Union Pacific, completed in 1869, had connected the oceans, and it was Cooke's conviction that another great link was needed to the northward—a connection between Duluth and Puget Sound. This was the Northern Pacific railroad, incorporated in 1864, but still far from completed. Jay Cooke determined to finish it and make it one of the great properties of the world.

With all the enthusiasm and glowing eagerness which he had put into the promotion of the government securities, he now organized his Northern Pacific campaign. He even adopted the same style of bonds—the 7–30's—and he offered them in glowing terms that took on an added luster from the halo of his great personal prestige. Cooke meant to deceive nobody, but his imagination ran away with him. Nothing was too extravagant for him to believe of his new property, or to claim for it. All the land along the line of the Northern Pacific to him was fertile land. The temperature was always mild, almost semi-tropical. As for health, it was impossible for anyone to die in that golden climate. Some of the newspapers jokingly referred to "Cooke's banana route," for, from his prospectuses, one might almost infer that this culture was possible along his right of way. The bonds sold, of course, largely for a time, then less readily. Too many railroad bonds were being floated; too little money was available for all the schemes. The public was already burdened with securities, some of which were beginning to have a doubtful look. Cooke, however, had no qualms. He foresaw only a magnificent railway system, with profits to pay all bonds, and dividends for happy stockholders. He meant his road to be the best in the land, in its appointments and management. . . .

Jay Cooke, with optimistic outlook, always expected a betterment of credit conditions. When Northern Pacific bonds began to go slowly, and his hard-headed partners counseled against further expansion, he assured them that matters were doing very well, indeed—that they need have no fears for the future. . . .

By the summer of 1872 Northern Pacific bonds were going very slowly indeed, and the interest on those already placed was not easy to pay. Cooke & Company were obliged to raise funds wherever they could find them, and on whatever acceptable securities they could muster. . . . A presidential campaign—Greeley against Grant—was in progress, and every day the affairs of the country grew more unsettled. The credit of Cooke & Company became fearfully strained.

In August (1872) the finances of the Northern Pacific suffered at least a partial collapse. But the great firm of Jay Cooke & Company did not fail. Cooke himself believed that with the end of political uncertainties there would be a general improvement of conditions. This was not the case. Promotion and speculation had gone too far. The country was financially unsound. In April 1873, call money rose to over 200 percent, and in some instances as high as 1 percent a day was paid. Then followed another disaster—the Crédit Mobilier exposure in Washington, a railroad scandal which involved some of the foremost men of the nation. . . . Public confidence was shaken to its depths. Railroad legislation that might have benefited legitimate enterprises could not now be obtained. To Jay Cooke's New York partners and creditors it became clear that only a miracle could avert the crash.

It came—the crash, not the miracle—in September. Early that month the money market went wild, due to the gold operations of Jay Gould, who attempted to duplicate his [earlier] Black Friday [gold-cornering] success. Cooke & Company, called upon for large sums, were unable to respond. For their great mass of railway collateral there were no takers. They were in desperate straits.

On the morning of September 18, 1873, Jay Cooke, breakfasting with General Grant, at Ogontz, Cooke's country home, near Philadelphia, received telegrams of an alarming nature. He caught a train and hurried to his Philadelphia office. There the worst was confirmed. He had scarcely arrived when a dispatch was handed him, announcing that Mr. Fahnestock, upon the advice of prominent bankers—creditors of course—had closed the New York office. The end had come. His eyes streaming with tears Jay Cooke ordered the closing of the Philadelphia office, as well. The most dramatic figure in finance, the knight of a hundred splendid victories, had met defeat. The man who had saved the nation's credit could not save his own.

In his fine [biography] of Cooke, Ellis Paxson Oberholtzer writes:

The ensuing excitement is not easily described. "A financial thunderbolt," said the New York *Tribune*. . . . "No one could have been more surprised," said the Philadelphia *Inquirer*, "if snow had fallen amid the sunshine of a summer noon. The news spread like fire on one of the Northern Pacific's own prairies. The building at Wall and Nassau Street, in New York, was surrounded by a crowd of men, women, and children, who were gesticulating wildly. They crowded into the basement, peered into the windows, and insultingly accosted the partners and clerks if they ventured out of the building."

When the suspension was announced in the New York Stock Exchange a brief silence ensured. There was "an uproar," said a journalistic eyewitness, "such as has scarcely filled the Exchange since it was built. Messengers fled every way with the story of ruin, and down came stocks all along the line."

The Exchange in fact became pandemonium. Stocks tumbled from five to fifty points in as many minutes and it became impossible to execute orders. Other suspensions were quickly announced—that of E. W.

Clark & Company, and others of less importance during the afternoon. In Philadelphia a force of police was required to keep the mob from breaking into Cooke & Company's banking house. Similar scenes prevailed in Washington.

The next day was another Black Friday. The great firm of Fisk & Hatch (not Jim Fisk), second only to Cooke & Company in importance, closed its doors early in the forenoon. The collapse of this firm was quickly followed by at least a dozen others, and by as many more in Philadelphia.

The third day opened darkly. Two large trust companies, the Union and the National, and the Bank of the Commonwealth, closed their doors. Every bank and trust company was regarded with suspicion, and runs were general. The Stock Exchange was no longer a place of business—it was bedlam. Twenty-five of its firms failed. The streets leading to it were thronged with frightened, fighting investors who saw their holdings vanishing at a breath. A little after midday the officers of the Exchange closed its doors, for the first time in history, "to save the street from utter ruin," the vice-chairman announced.

At night the Fifth Avenue Hotel became a storm center. There President Grant conferred with the nation's foremost financiers, as to means of relief. It was agreed that the desperate conditions were the result of an expanded business, done on insufficient cash. It required no great wisdom to reach that conclusion.

Jay Gould, Daniel Drew, James Fisk, Cornelius Vanderbilt, and the Erie Road

MAURY KLEIN

The War for the Erie Railroad brought to new heights the skillful machinations of this notorious group of speculators and financial warlords. When it was over, Jay Gould had clearly won and, in his early 30s, established himself as a force to be reckoned with. This story, in addition to introducing Jay Gould and Jim Fisk (about whom more later), captures the character of the various principals and of the nature of the recurring contests for control of America's railroads.

The Erie Railroad had a checkered history long before it felt [Jay] Gould's touch. Chartered in 1832 as a grand project to connect ocean traffic at New York City with the Great Lakes, it floundered for two decades as a political football among local interests. When the road was finally completed in 1851, it ran from Pierpont to the obscure village of Dunkirk on Lake Erie, without access to Buffalo at one end or New York City at the other. The interplay of local politics had forced the company to occupy a route through southern New York that had poor grades, was expensive to maintain, and could not tap rich sources of traffic in northern Pennsylvania. Botched management obscured whatever prospects the Erie had during the 1850s. The road was in such poor shape that, as Edward Mott observed, it "became notorious for the insecurity of travel upon it." Thirty serious accidents occurred in 1852 alone. A succession of financial blunders saddled the road with a persistent floating debt. By August 1859 Erie stock had plunged from 33 to 8 and the company was in receivership. . . .

The road reorganized as the Erie Railway under the presidency of Nathaniel Marsh, who in two years tripled the road's traffic, acquired a short line to Buffalo, developed the valuable Long Dock facility at Jersey City, gained access to the Pennsylvania coal fields, paid off the floating debt, and reduced the mortgage by several million dollars. The Erie also profited from a large oil traffic through connection with the newly opened Atlantic & Great Western Railroad. It seemed assured of a bright future unless one noticed that prosperity had been achieved through the abnormalities of wartime. In July 1864 Marsh's sudden death removed his restraining influence from a speculator who had been skulking through the Erie's history for a decade.

Daniel Drew started out as a drover running herds of cattle across the Alleghenies to New York. Some said it was he who inspired the phrase "watered stock" by his practice of feeding salt to his steers to make them drink prodigious amounts of water and swell in size. During the 1830s he went into steamboating on the Hudson River, where his People's Line dazzled travelers with its floating palaces. Later he drifted into Wall Street and became the most notorious bear since Jacob Little. . . .

A gaunt, cadaverous figure, coarse and sly of manner, Drew laid traps, switched sides, and betrayed allies until his raids became the stuff of legend. When cornered he did not hesitate to resort to what the Street called "squatting" or dishonoring his contracts and taking refuge behind a lawsuit. His demeanor was pious and austere, the product of his early conversion to Methodism. Although fond of quoting Scripture, he took care to shield his business dealings from the influence of Christian ethics. This habit, coupled with his ruthless depredations in the market, led others to regard him as a hypocrite. "Mr. Drew," noted one observer delicately, "is singularly lacking in popularity.". . .

Drew had been preying on the Erie since 1854, when he became its treasurer and promptly secured a mortgage on all its property by endorsing some of its notes. Through every financial upheaval Drew clung leech-like to his hold on the road. At the same time he milked the stock dry, working it up then down, using his inside position to swell his personal fortune with such brazen success that he became known as the "speculative director.". . .

In 1859 Drew persuaded Cornelius Vanderbilt to come into Erie as a director. The two men had undertaken ventures together since their days as rival steamboat entrepreneurs, and their backgrounds had much in common. Vanderbilt was born in 1794, Drew three years later, both of dirt-poor families. After clawing their way to wealth, neither bothered to glaze his crude, uncouth ways with a veneer of social refinement. Vanderbilt had a brutal, tyrannical streak that showed itself no less to his family than to business rivals, yet he was also subject to outbursts of generosity. His emotions veered from one extreme to the other. He was foul-mouthed, possessed an outlandish sense of humor, and showed a zest for life utterly lacking in Drew. . . .

While Drew in all his rail ventures never rose above the level of speculator, Vanderbilt took hold of them as enterprises. At seventy, his powers undiminished, he launched a new career in railroading devoted to forging a trunk line between New York and Chicago. His strategy was as elemental as it was effective: buy a road, put in honest management, improve its operation, consolidate it with other roads when they can be run together economically, water the stock, and still make it pay dividends. By 1865, after a bitter struggle, he had acquired the Harlem and Hudson River roads and put them in the hands of his son William. He then went after the New York Central, which would complete his line from New York City to Buffalo. Since the chief competitor of this new line would be the Erie, Vanderbilt was eager to have it under his thumb as well. That desire brought him into conflict with the wily Drew. . . .

At the war's end deflation and rate cutting reduced the Erie's earnings sharply and produced a large floating debt just as its competitive position was crumbling into ruins. Besides Vanderbilt's line the Erie was threatened with the loss of its lucrative oil business to the newly opened Pennsylvania Railroad. The Atlantic, its key link to the oil fields, grew disenchanted with the Erie and decided to create its own route to the seaboard. The Erie had incurred heavy obligations to purchase new equipment, much of which now sat idle, and the roadbed was in wretched condition. Amid this sea of woes Drew cruised with lethal skill. He resumed his favorite game of loaning money in exchange for stock, which he then dumped on the market to drive down the price and reap fat profits from his short sales. While Drew filled his purse, the Erie scrounged for cash enough to pay its bills. . . .

Both Drew and the Erie had become thorns in Vanderbilt's side. After finally gaining control of the New York Central in 1867, he decided to capture the Erie and oust Drew from its management. His scheme ran afoul of another group intent on bending the Erie to its purposes. Led by John H. Eldridge, a Boston banker whose venal instincts smacked more of Wall Street than State Street, this faction represented the Boston, Hartford & Erie Railroad, a proposed line between Boston and the Hudson River. Since 1865 Eldridge had been soliciting financial aid from the Erie. Dangling the prospect of a connection to southern New England as bait, he wanted the Erie to guarantee interest on $6 million of the Boston's bonds. Even if the Erie could have afforded the commitment, which it could not, the cost of building the Boston far exceeded its value as a feeder. Nevertheless, the Erie board voted in June 1867 to guarantee $4 million of the Boston's bonds, though it attached several conditions to its action. . . .

From this conflict emerged a complex struggle to control the Erie election of 1867. Unhappy with the Erie's offer, Eldridge decided to acquire enough stock to join its board and force its hand. Vanderbilt too was corralling stock for his campaign against Drew, a fact that did not escape Uncle Dan'l's attention. There followed a bizarre three-cornered hat dance in which partners changed so often it was difficult to know who was odd man out. . . .

The scramble for Erie stock revolved largely around the proxy market. Much of the stock belonged to English holders who simply left it in the name of a broker for the sake of convenience. This allowed the brokers, unless otherwise directed, to vote the stock as they saw fit or to sell their proxies to the highest bidder. While Vanderbilt combed the Street for proxies, Drew formed an alliance with Eldridge's agent against their common foe. The agent soon defected to Vanderbilt, leaving Drew to play the part of wallflower.

Vanderbilt's bargain with Eldridge did not take into account the curious bond that had formed between him and Drew over the years. Two days before the election, Drew recognizing that his position was hopeless, went to the Commodore and begged forgiveness. If allowed to keep his seat he promised to mend his ways and serve only Vanderbilt. It was neither the first nor the last time this lachrymose scene would be enacted. Time and again Drew had bamboozled Vanderbilt in some outrageous way and then, brought to bay, had pleaded tearfully for mercy amid a torrent of references to bygone days. The Commodore was far too shrewd to believe that so incorrigible a predator as Drew would actually change his ways. Yet each time he relented, perhaps because he relished the spectacle of watching Drew squirm.

The Boston crowd was flabbergasted at the news but agreed to go along. On October 8, the board was elected and promptly installed Eldridge as president. The next day, however, one of its members resigned and was replaced by Drew, who also reclaimed the office of treasurer. The newspapers buzzed with rumors of an alliance between the two archrivals. In their excited speculations they passed over the board's lesser lights, which the *Herald* dismissed as "a batch of nobodies." One of these nobodies was a broker named James Fisk Jr., a man sufficiently unknown that some papers recorded his name as "Fiske" or "Fish." Another was a broker so obscure that he was listed only as "J. Gould.". . .

It was through Eldridge that Jay [Gould] wangled his place on the Erie board. Eldridge had sent Fisk and lawyer Frederick A. Lane to secure Erie proxies. Apparently [Gould] held enough stock to attract their interest; possibly he held title to a large amount through the brokerage firm he joined sometime during 1867, Smith, Gould & Martin. Whatever his source, a pivotal moment in his career had arrived: for the first time he became an insider. . . .

The quest for Erie proxies had still another fateful consequence for Gould: it introduced him to the man with whom he would form the oddest couple ever to grace Wall Street. Not even the genius of Dickens could have invented two more unlike characters than Jay Gould and Jim Fisk. They were the same age, and there the resemblance ended. Short and rotund, his twinkling eyes spread on a broad face, his reddish-yellow hair fringed with curls and his lip masked by a formidable moustache described by one wag as "the color of a Jersey cow," Fisk looked the part of Falstaff and played it to the hilt. His excesses outmatched Jay's abstemiousness by half again. He loved the best of wine, women, and song, not always in that order. For every occasion he dressed and strutted like a peacock. . . .

Above all Fisk craved the limelight. In all his outrageous antics he sought publicity as a moth seeks the flame with what a biographer called "a love of notoriety so extravagant that he preferred to be insulted than ignored." He started out as a peddler in his native Vermont and graduated to jobbing for the Boston drygoods house of Jordan, Marsh & Company. During the war he ran cotton out of the South to feed his employer's mills, and developed a taste for the good life. At 19 he married Lucy Moore, to whom he remained devoted in his own bizarre way. When Fisk set out to conquer New York in 1864, Lucy stayed behind in Boston. That arrangement allowed Fisk to indulge his taste for "actresses," especially the overripe Josie Mansfield. . . .

On Wall Street Fisk was a whirlwind in both success and failure. He fell in with Drew and opened a brokerage in partnership with William Belden, the son of an old friend of Drew's. Notorious for being a sharpster on the Street and a fast liver off it, Belden's ability fell far short of his extravagant tastes. Board members and curb brokers alike regarded Fisk & Belden as a house of ill repute, partly because they could not separate its bold and risky ventures from Fisk's own splashy displays. . . .

It was easy to dismiss Fisk as a garish, vulgar buffoon, and for some it proved a fatal mistake. Behind the clown's costume loomed a native genius, a cunning, imaginative intellect that made him a formidable presence in business. His boisterous good nature made him easy to ridicule, impossible to dislike, and hard to take seriously. Gould was alert enough not to underestimate his talents; so was an observer who described Fisk as "a shrewd speculator & very careful to take care of No. 1." The Erie provided Fisk a perfect stage for his outsized personality. Within months after landing on its board he assumed the role of ringmaster for the grandest circus ever to play Wall Street. . . .

A rude awakening that the Erie was not his to run came quickly to Vanderbilt. He permitted Drew to manage a pool in Erie stock on behalf of his clique only to discover that Drew was lining his own pockets by secretly working against the pool. In December the Erie board opened negotiations with the Michigan Southern & Northern Indiana for a line to Chicago that threatened to drain much of the New York Central's traffic onto Erie. A fierce, prideful man accustomed to having his own way, Vanderbilt realized the folly of trusting Drew to do his bidding. The only recourse, he concluded grimly, was to buy control of the road. In 1867 the Erie had outstanding about $16.5 million in common and $8.5 million in preferred stock. Vanderbilt began secretly to buy Erie while laying legal snares to prevent the company from increasing its capitalization. In February 1868 his nephew, Frank Work, secured from Judge George G. Barnard, a notorious Tammany Hall wheelhorse who had been elevated to the state supreme court, a series of injunctions against Drew and the Erie board. Without knowing it, Vanderbilt had fired the first salvo in the Great Erie War. . . .

A provision of the General Railroad Act of 1850 prohibited rail companies from increasing their stock but allowed them to issue bonds for construction or equipment and then to convert the bonds into stock. Since Drew had used this "convertible" clause to burn the Commodore in 1866, Vanderbilt knew the danger it posed to his plans. The injunctions asked that Drew be removed as treasurer and that he return 58,000 shares acquired as collateral in 1866. Both Drew and the Erie board were enjoined from selling stock or convertible bonds, but the suit overlooked the executive committee, which had the power to act during the intervals between board meetings. Drew was a member of that committee, as were Eldridge and Gould. Unbeknown to Vanderbilt, Drew allied himself with the two "nobodies," Gould and Fisk, to resist the Commodore's takeover of Erie. Eldridge was willing to follow anyone who promised to give the Boston what it wanted. . . .

Politics never created stranger bedfellows than the trio who united against Vanderbilt. Their step was to have the executive committee authorize an issue of $5 million in bonds for "improvements" on the road. In one meeting the bonds were approved, reported sold to Drew's broker, and the sale ratified. The bonds were then converted into stock and thrown onto the market along with another 10,000 shares manufactured in December 1867 when the Erie board leased the Buffalo, Bradford & Pittsburgh Railroad, converted its bonds to stock, and exchanged the stock for Erie shares. . . .

Suddenly the market was awash with Erie stock. Vanderbilt's brokers, ordered to buy all stock offered, dutifully absorbed the new issues. The price of Erie held firm, yet Drew and his associates kept selling short with a serenity that puzzled the Commodore. At his request Barnard extended his injunctions to include the Bradford shares, the guarantee of Boston bonds, and the Michigan Southern connection. The executive committee blithely ignored these mandates and recruited its own judge. It was a peculiarity of New York's judicial system that all 33 of its supreme court justices enjoyed equal authority throughout the state in certain equity actions. Drew found a judge in Broome County who obligingly stayed all of Barnard's orders and suspended Frank Work from the Erie board. An outraged Vanderbilt launched a new suit in Richard Schell's name staying the stay and forbidding the Erie board to meet or transact business without Work. . . .

There followed a bewildering crossfire of injunctions. While the lawyers traded volleys, the executive committee converted a second $5 million issue of bonds and dumped them on the market. It also created a $500,000 fund for "legal expenses" and an elaborate report justifying the road's urgent need for improvements. Attached to the report were two letters from the superintendent bewailing the road's sorry physical condition even though a year earlier he had reported it "in better condition and better equipped than at any period during the past ten years.". . .

In publishing this report the Erie clique cleverly portrayed themselves as defending the public from Vanderbilt's grasping attempt to erect a railroad monopoly. To cover their action they applied to Judge Gilbert in Brooklyn, an impulsive jurist who astounded everyone by restraining all parties to all other suits from further proceedings and ordering all the Erie directors except Work to discharge their proper duties. A perfect legal stalemate had been achieved. "One magistrate had forbidden them to move, and another magistrate had ordered them not to stand still," observed Charles Francis Adams Jr. "If the Erie board held meetings and transacted business, it violated one injunction; if it abstained from doing so, it violated another.". . .

Meanwhile Vanderbilt's unsuspecting brokers snatched the newly offered bait. Since the shares were dispersed through several brokers, Vanderbilt did not grasp what was happening until fresh certificates bearing Fisk's name began to appear on the street. The light dawned too late; the Commodore had already strained even his immense fortune trying to sustain the price of Erie. Pandemonium shook Wall Street as the stock's quotations reeled back and forth. Drew precipitated a spasm in the money market by withdrawing the nearly $7 million proceeds of stock sales from banks and locking the greenbacks in the Erie safe. If Vanderbilt faltered at this critical hour, his failure would launch a panic of grand proportions. But the old man stuck grimly to his task of buying Erie even though he had to borrow on collateral of falling value. . . .

The Erie clique had little time to savor their triumph. On March 11, word came that Barnard had issued contempt orders and intended to clap them all in the Ludlow Street jail. Alarmed, they packed up files and ledgers, bundled sacks of greenbacks, stuffed their pockets with securities and papers, and dismantled the offices. Drew, Eldridge, and some other directors, along with a few clerks, dashed for the ferry. Three directors stayed behind as rearguard and later bore the brunt of arrest. Fisk and Gould were not among them. They felt bold enough to dine at Delmonico's that evening until news that the law was approaching sent them scurrying to Canal Street. Hiring a small steamer, they plunged into a fog so thick that they cruised in a circle for a time and narrowly escaped being rammed by a ferry. Like poor Eliza in *Uncle Tom's Cabin* they crossed the river, seeking on the Jersey shore freedom from the bloodhounds sniffing at their heels, clutching to their bosoms not an innocent child but $7 million in greenbacks and the corporate majesty of the Erie Railway Company. . . .

In Jersey City they ensconced themselves in Taylor's Hotel near the Erie terminal, quickly dubbed "Fort Taylor" by newspapermen who rushed to view the novel spectacle of a corporation in exile. The ebullient Fisk accommodated them with cigars, liquor, and an endless stream of blather about how the struggle against Vanderbilt's monopoly was "in the interest of the poorer classes especially." Alone among the clique Fisk took readily to his new surroundings. Where Drew was out of his element and Gould missed his family, Fisk gleefully installed Josie Mansfield in the next room and reveled in the attention showered on him. . . .

A state of siege suited neither side. Vanderbilt still shouldered his heavy burden of Erie stock which, if not maintained, might destroy his personal fortune and engulf Wall Street in panic. His lawyers got Judge Barnard to unleash a fresh barrage of injunctions, to which the Erie judge responded in kind, but no damage could be done so long as the target hovered out of range. In Albany the state senate created a committee to investigate the Erie's affairs, a move interpreted by cynics as legislative resentment that the judiciary was hogging the spoils of war. . . .

Meanwhile Fisk and Gould managed surprisingly well at operating the Erie from Fort Taylor. As part of their antimonopoly campaign they opened a rate war with the New York Central even though it meant running the road at a loss. When Jay declared that the Erie had come to stay, the New Jersey legislature gratefully rushed through a bill incorporating the company. Possession of legal status in New Jersey would allow the Erie to issue more stock, a fact Vanderbilt must have found unsettling. The financial community followed these events with dumbfounded amazement. So unprecedented was the situation that even respectable journals did not know which way to turn. . . .

Despite the conferral of legitimacy by New Jersey, the Erie clique could not afford to remain in exile. The railroad did its business in New York and so did its managers who, away from Wall Street, were fish out of water. Drew pined for home and so did Gould; both felt uncomfortable as neighbors to Fisk's private saturnalia. The press castigated them as outlaws fled with their loot. New York law forbade arrests in civil cases on Sundays, which allowed them to return home for that day; otherwise they could not set foot in Manhattan without facing the threat of jail. The impasse could be ended by negotiating a compromise with Vanderbilt or by inducing the legislature to pass a bill legalizing the convertible bond issue. The Erie clique decided to pursue both possibilities.

From the start, Vanderbilt and the press alike had focused their attention on Drew as the Erie ringleader. If that assumption was true at first, it did not long remain so. Once in exile Drew lost all heart for combat; weary and homesick, he undertook in typical fashion to negotiate his own settlement with little regard for his cohorts. Gradually Fisk and Gould emerged as Vanderbilt's true adversaries, a fact the Commodore was slow to grasp. The odd couple made an effective if improbable team, their strengths masked by Fisk's flamboyant style and Gould's quiet, retiring manner. Where Drew was adept at laying an ambush and Fisk knew how to lead a charge, [Gould] alone had the talent for planning a campaign. It was his subtle mind that formulated strategy in the weeks to come.

Sensing that Vanderbilt was not yet ready to compromise, Gould concentrated on Albany. An Erie agent was already trying to obtain a bill by bribing that notorious element of the legislature known as the Black Horse Cavalry. Vanderbilt's agents were also on the scene and apparently employed a more generous fee schedule, for on March 27 the assembly crushed the Erie bill by a vote of 83 to 32. Meanwhile the senate investigative committee was preparing its report. Two members supported the charges against Erie and two opposed them, leaving the decision in the hands of A. C. Mattoon, whose personal research included visits to both the Vanderbilt and Drew camps. With fine impartiality he sold his support to both sides. When the report appeared on April 1, Mattoon was found on the side of those denouncing the Erie even though he had declared the opposite intention only the day before. . . .

By that time [Gould] had already decided to risk a personal visit to Albany. A deal was struck whereby he agreed to appear before Judge Barnard on April 4 provided he was left undisturbed until that date. On March 30 he left Jersey City with a suitcase full of greenbacks and a ready reserve of checkbooks. For three days he wooed legislators with a liberal supply of food, drink, and greenbacks. Vanderbilt's agents set up shop on another floor of the Delavan House, enabling legislators to shuttle back and forth in search of top dollar for their vote. On April 4, [Gould] dutifully went to New York to answer charges. After a lengthy hearing Barnard deferred until the 8th but ordered Gould to remain in the custody of a court officer. When Gould declared his intention of returning to Albany, the officer protested, "You are in my custody."

"But you may go with me," Jay replied blandly. "I will still be in your custody.". . .

Back in Albany [Gould] tried to resurrect the Erie bill. When time came to return to New York, he pleaded illness and asked for a postponement. While the lawyers wrangled, Jay emptied his satchel of greenbacks. "Jay Gould is still at the Delavan House, Albany, with his keeper," noted a bemused reporter. "Many legislative friends are calling on him." Charles Francis Adams, not in the least amused, described Gould as devoting "the tedious hours of convalescence to the task of cultivating a thorough understanding between himself and the members of the legislature.". . .

The inside story of the Albany debacle will never be known. If the rumors that flew and the stories told about the amounts exchanged are even half true, they are enough to satisfy any connoisseur of avarice. Legislators tumbled over each other trying to bid one side against the other. Awed reporters spoke of a trunk filled with thousand-dollar bills, but there was no shortage of exaggeration at Albany. The situation looked anything but promising for passage of a bill nearly identical to the one defeated so resoundingly a few weeks earlier, yet on April 18 the senate passed it by a vote of 18 to 12, with the ubiquitous Mattoon switching sides again. The fight moved to the assembly where, on the eve of what loomed as a desperate battle, Vanderbilt abruptly quit the field. His withdrawal threw the spoilsmen into dismay; in their wrath the assembly turned on Vanderbilt with a vengeance. On April 20 the bill passed by a landslide vote of 101 to 5 and the assembly ransacked its docket for other bills hostile to the Commodore. . . .

The battle of Albany ended with Gould the victor. Despite his prominent role, the press persisted in describing the struggle as one between Drew and Vanderbilt. In the public eye [Gould] was merely Drew's henchman, a misapprehension he made no effort to dispel. Nor would he ever admit how much money he had dispensed. His testimony before an investigating committee was plagued with so many lapses of memory that Adams, his severest critic, was driven to observe:

Mr. Gould [in Albany] underwent a curious psychological metamorphosis and suddenly became the veriest simpleton in money matters. . . . The strange and expensive hallucination lasted until about the middle of April, when Mr. Gould was happily restored to his normal condition of a shrewd, acute, energetic man of business; nor is it known that he has since experienced any relapse into financial idiocy.

James Fisk

As we have seen, Big Jim Fisk flashed into Wall Street in the company of Jay Gould and Daniel Drew. He lived an exaggerated and exaggerating life and died, at age 38, from shots fired in a quarrel over money—and the affections of an actress—by a business associate. His funeral was an 1872 spectacular, featuring full Tammany honors and a 200-piece band.

[James Fisk] was the son of James and Love B. (Ryan) Fisk, of Bennington, and later Brattleboro, Vermont. After scanty schooling, he was successively waiter in a hotel, ticket-seller for the Van Amberg circus, and salesman with his father's "traveling emporium," which he later purchased and operated himself, graciously admitting his father to his employ. A boastful,

Reprinted from *Dictionary of American Biography*, Vol. VI (NY, Charles Scribner & Sons, 1931) with permission from the American Council of Learned Societies.

flashy, genial youth, with endless impudence and push, he was soon aspiring to larger spheres. He branched from peddling into a jobbing business for Jordan & Marsh of Boston, entered their wholesale department in 1860, and managed large war contracts for them on a commission basis. Later he went South to buy cotton in the occupied districts for a Boston syndicate, handled extensive purchases for Northern ports, and England, and became wealthy enough to launch into business for himself. His Boston establishment as dry-goods jobber was badly hit in 1865 by postwar deflation, and a brokerage office in Broad Street, New York, was a failure. But his conceit, swaggering energy, and taste for speculation were undiminished. He recouped his fortunes by acting as agent in the sale of Daniel Drew's Stonington steamboats to a Boston group, returned to New York, and with Drew's support founded in 1866 the brokerage house of Fisk & Belden.

Fisk's rise to fortune was thereafter rapid. Drawn into the "Erie War" between Drew and Vanderbilt, he became a director of the Erie, helped Gould and Drew despoil it, and was an able, self-assertive second in all their schemes. During the battle royal of 1868, when Vanderbilt with the aid of Justice Barnard tried to capture the line, it was he who evaded Barnard's injunction against the issue of more stock by seizing 50,000 ready-signed shares, who used them to break Vanderbilt's attempted corner, thus netting millions for the trio, and who led the famous flight with Gould and Drew to Taylor's Hotel in Jersey City. When Drew and Vanderbilt made peace, Fisk and Gould shared control of the half-wrecked Erie Railroad. They at once embarked on a series of bold and unscrupulous ventures. They increased the Erie stock during the summer in 1868 from $34,265,000 to $57,766,000, where it stood on October 24. Part of the proceeds was used for expansion, the two managers—Fisk as comptroller, Gould as president—leasing other railways, building branches, buying steamboats, rolling-mills, and car shops, and adding new equipment; part was used in reckless speculative forays. They launched a campaign with Drew in the fall of 1868 to make credit tight and raise the price of gold which reacted disastrously upon the nation's business and was felt even in Europe, but which netted them large sums. They also carried out a cornering operation which was so outrageous that Erie stock was stricken from the brokers' board; a raid upon the United States Express Company, whose stock they manipulated at will; and a raid upon the Albany & Susquehanna Railroad which resulted in a pitched battle of gangs of employees near Binghamton. These raids, exasperating public sentiment, culminated in the famous Black Friday attempt to corner the gold market (September 1869), when once more hundreds were ruined and all business suffered a profound shock. The coup disastrously failed, and Fisk flatly repudiated contracts of many millions through his responsible partner Belden. American opinion regarded him and Gould as public enemies, but he flippantly told a

Congressional committee that the money had "gone where the woodbine twineth."

Meanwhile Fisk, now a fat, jovial, brassy voluptuary, was leading a life of half-barbaric prodigality. Buying Pike's Opera House at Twenty-third St. and Eighth Avenue he fitted up costly offices there, at the same time producing dramas and French opera bouffe; he leased the Academy of Music and put on grand opera till the expense chilled him; swaggered as "admiral" of the Fall River and the Bristol lines of steamboats, which he controlled; placed on the Hudson its largest ferryboat, the *James Fisk;* bought a summer garden for a restaurant; kept a stable; and diverted the East by his antics as colonel of the 9th Regiment of the New York militia, a post to which he bought his way in May 1870. His visit with this regiment to Boston on Bunker Hill Day in 1871, when he asked permission to celebrate "divine service" on Boston Common, was one of the best-advertised episodes of his career. His end befitted his flashy life. After keeping numerous mistresses he singled out the actress Josie Mansfield as his favorite, quarreled over her and over business transactions with the dissolute Edward Stokes, was fatally shot by the latter in the Grand Central Hotel on January 6, 1872, and died the next day. A spectacular funeral, with every honor from the Tammany administration and a cortège including the 9th Regiment and a band of 200 pieces, was accompanied by innumerable denunciatory sermons and editorials.

Jay Gould

Jay Gould began to build a railroad finance fortune in Wall Street in 1859, at age 23. He completed it at age 56 with large holdings in Western Union, Missouri Pacific, Union Pacific, and the Wabash, among others. Along the way he attempted several gold corners and participated in many intense railroad-related battles. From these, as in the case of the Erie War—and the Kansas Pacific deal described here—he usually emerged victorious. Despite a reputation for hard dealing, his private life was admirable. This excerpt is from his December 3, 1892, *New York Times* obituary.

It is the Kansas Pacific deal which Wall Street will always believe to be Mr. Gould's greatest stock-market transaction. Mr. Gould, having bought control of Union Pacific in the open market, turned up at a meeting of the

Reprinted from the *New York Times*, December 3, 1892, Sec. 1, Col. 4, p. 2, by permission of the New York Times Company.

company one day and quietly suggested that he thought a new Board of Directors had better be elected.

The board as it was then organized was composed of the blue bloods of Boston. They fairly shivered as they listened to the irreverence of the quiet little man from New York. Mr. Gould asked them, however, not to feel bad over his plan for bouncing them. He was perfectly willing that a few of them should stay.

He was fairly hooted at. Boston didn't believe that he had the control he claimed. The excellent bluebloods of the Back Bay remarked that they'd test the question; they looked with proper disdain upon this newly-rich man from Wall Street.

They were soon satisfied—if not gratified. Mr. Gould had his way.

Then came the Kansas Pacific deal. There had been a traffic contract between the Union Pacific and the Kansas Pacific system. Mr. Gould saw that this was not right. He ended it. The only way the Kansas Pacific could get accommodation from the Union Pacific was on a basis of local rates. Thus, virtually, the Kansas Pacific was bottled up. Its securities went down the Gould toboggan till they were kicking around Wall Street as hardly valuable enough to use for wall paper.

Then came a lightning change. Mr. Gould had been giving more personal attention to the Western railroad situation. He had discovered many surprising things. One was that the Kansas Pacific was really a mighty valuable property. He had become convinced, too, that the old traffic contract was quite proper, and it ought to be renewed. Indeed, in view of what might have seemed like the harsh treatment which the road had been lately receiving, Mr. Gould felt it to be his duty really to allow the Kansas Pacific a few extra advantages, just to make up for what it had suffered.

Wall Street said Mr. Gould was a just man. Kansas Pacific securities went up, and they went up a good deal. One day it was announced that Kansas Pacific stock was about to be exchanged at par for Union Pacific. It certainly seemed as if finally Mr. Gould was making ample atonement for any wrong he had done to Kansas Pacific in the year before.

When Kansas Pacific securities were exchanged and Union Pacific stock issued for them share for share, it did not take Wall Street long to discover that the man who did the exchanging was Mr. Jay Gould. He and his friends had picked up every available share of the stuff when it was dragging on the Wall Street curbstones, apparently not worth a cent and a half a pound. Finance is not always a complicated thing.

James J. Hill and the Northern Pacific

ALBERT BIGELOW PAINE

James J. Hill was a great American railroader and, when it suited him, an occasional business associate of J. Pierpont Morgan. To say that he became deeply engaged in finance at a very high level is to understate the case by a wide margin. An example of the high-stakes games he played is found in this account of the 1901 struggle for control of the Northern Pacific Railroad.

In spite of the general prosperity of 1901, or indeed because of it, the month of May that year saw one of the most violent, even if one of the most brief, panics on record—a panic due to a battle of titans in the world of finance. The Northern Pacific Railroad, that in 1873 had compassed the fall of Jay Cooke & Company and upset the business affairs of the nation, was to come once more into the limelight with an accompaniment of fresh disaster.

The road had been always more or less spectacular. As late as the middle nineties the stock had sold as low as $2.50 a share and during the same period it had sold around $50, gradually advancing until by 1901 it was selling not much below par [100]. That within a period of a week it should jump to $500, $700, and to an extreme of $1000 per share was a bit sensational, however, even for Northern Pacific.

By the summer of 1900, J. Pierpont Morgan and J. J. Hill had become somewhat estranged. Perhaps the feeling between them was hardly so strong as this word would imply, but certainly their financial relations were not entirely amicable. Earlier Mr. Hill had bought Mr. Morgan's Northern Pacific interest—about 300 thousand shares. Mr. Morgan had reorganized the road, and Mr. Hill had taken the stock off his hands, at $16 a share—a good price at the time. Since then it had become a dividend paying investment, with a good market value. For whatever reason, the two men had drifted apart, and in such a case it always fell to George F. Baker to be the mediator. Meeting Mr. Morgan one day, he casually remarked that he felt sure that Mr. Hill would like to be on more intimate terms again. Mr. Morgan in his usual terse way said:

Reprinted from *George Fisher Baker: A Biography* (New York, 1920), Chapter XXV, pp. 196–208, by permission of [Public Domain] G.P. Putnam's Sons.

"Yes, I should think he would."

There was very little more to the interview, except that Mr. Baker added that he thought a meeting would be to the advantage of both men. A few days later he mentioned the matter to Mr. Hill.

"Why can't you and Mr. Morgan come together?" he said, "and have a little talk."

Mr. Hill, always cordial, declared he would be very glad indeed if such a meeting were arranged. Mr. Morgan when sounded on the subject also admitted that such a meeting would be agreeable. Mr. Baker proposed that they come to his Club and all dine together, whereupon Mr. Morgan suggested that they meet and dine on his yacht.

"What is the matter with the *Corsair*," he asked, "where we can have entire privacy."

It was agreed that this would be an ideal arrangement, so they planned to go aboard the *Corsair* that afternoon. This they did and spent the night there, afterwards. . . . There was quite a long discussion before dinner, mainly of generalities, gradually narrowing down to the question of which of the western roads would be the most advantageous to buy, the St. Paul or the Burlington; the said road to be bought jointly for the Great Northern and Northern Pacific—the idea being a great merger of rival railway interests.

Mr. Morgan was enthusiastic over the St. Paul, while Mr. Hill's preference seemed to be the Burlington. The discussion continued—a very friendly discussion—its only object being to reach a decision as to which road would be most advantageous to their plan. In the course of the talk Mr. Hill, who was always an optimist—a man with a vision without being visionary—observed that it would make something over ten millions increase in their annual earnings if they should buy the St. Paul, and it was at length agreed that Mr. Morgan should try to purchase a control in this road. This was about 2 A.M. and presently Mr. Baker and Mr. Hill went for a walk on deck to get a little fresh air before turning in. The *Corsair* was lying off the New York Yacht Club Station in North River, near the foot of 86th Street. The city up there had gone to bed and the Palisades across the river rose high and black against the sky. It was a quiet and beautiful night, and the two men walked up and down, speaking in subdued voices. Finally Mr. Baker said:

"Now J. J. you mustn't let your enthusiasm for your western properties run away with you."

"Why, George, what do you mean?"

"Well, I was thinking of your statement to Mr. Morgan about St. Paul—You know ten millions would be a very large increase in annual earnings."

Hill laughed.

"Why, George," he said, "that's all right. I didn't dare to tell him what I really thought. It will be a great deal more than that."

Mr. Baker also laughed good-naturedly. Like all the railroad king's friends he not only admired but believed in him. Once he said:

"J. J. Hill was a remarkable man. He had the enthusiasm and simple-heartedness of a child, the wisdom and knowledge of a sage, the energy of one of his own locomotives. He would work 36 to 48 hours on end, then eat a big dinner, and go to bed and sleep for 16 hours or so, regardless of demands. If he was sleepless he read Mother Goose's Melodies. He would read them through and then go to sleep. Yet he was the best read man I ever knew. We went out West together once in his private car and it was a great experience. Judge Clark was along, and I remember one day he quoted a verse from the Bible, and Hill promptly quoted the next one. Clark tried it again and again, and each time Hill capped his quotation. We both tried him but he never failed, and it was the same with hymns. . . . Next day we were crossing the Rockies and saw the beautiful formations of stone, and J. J. took up the subject and told us more geology than I ever knew before. . . .

"He had a remarkable memory. He never forgot the smallest incident, and he had the keenest perception of details. When he traveled over a road, his eye never seemed to miss a single item of it. Once when he was about to make a trip over one of his lines, an official who knew him said to a station master: 'Mr. Hill is coming along here today, you had better pick up a little, around the station.'

"'Oh, he'll never notice a little thing like that,' was the answer.

"He won't, eh? Why Jim Hill could see a spike in the grass with the train running 60 miles an hour.". . .

All of which gives us something of Mr. Baker's personal estimate of this unique figure of railway industry. His admiration for J. J. and his deep faith in him made him always ready to finance his undertakings. He was by no means skeptical, therefore, as to the prophecy concerning the proposed combination.

The purchase of the St. Paul, however, fell through—defeated by some other members of the St. Paul board—whereupon it fell to Mr. Hill to buy the Burlington.

At this point a new factor was added to the situation. Matters had progressed quietly enough until one day E. H. Harriman and Jacob H. Schiff, of the firm Kuhn, Loeb & Company became alive to what was in progress, and appeared with a proposition in behalf of the Union Pacific to join in the purchase, an arrangement by which each of the three great roads, the Northern Pacific, the Great Northern, and the Union Pacific would acquire a third interest.

Mr. Hill had been down on the Potomac and was coming to New York to go with Mr. Baker to meet the Burlington directors in Boston. They were to leave by the midnight train, and Mr. Baker inadvertently mentioned in Mr. Harriman's presence that Mr. Hill was coming to dine with him at his home that evening. No reference was made of the Boston trip, but Harriman must have suspected it, for about eight o'clock he arrived with Mr. Schiff at the Baker home. Mr. Hill had brought along Daniel Lamont.

The Harriman–Schiff campaign promptly opened and continued with increasing animation and fervor, not to say violence. Mr. Hill had no particular admiration for the Harriman–Schiff combination, and he promptly declined to give them any interest in the Burlington purchase, whereupon the discussion increased in vigor, becoming at moments almost heated, continuing until the moment when it was necessary to leave the house in order to catch the midnight train. Even then it did not end, for Messrs. Harriman and Schiff accompanied the travelers to the Grand Central, continuing their argument until the train began to move.

Mr. Baker and Mr. Hill arriving in Boston found themselves confronted by a new situation, this time with the directors of the Burlington as to the matter of terms. Mr. Morgan, a few days before, had sailed for Europe, leaving as a parting injunction to Mr. Baker that while he was willing to pay $200 for the Burlington stock, this purchase sum, which would amount to $200,000,000 was to be paid in 4 percent bonds, not cash. This resulted in plenty of discussion, and no definite conclusion was reached until Mr. Hill and Mr. Baker had returned to New York, when Mr. Morgan cabled his consent to a cash payment of $50,000,000, to provide for smaller stockholders who might not care for the bonds. The trade was concluded on this basis, and it seemed now that the matter of the merger could be settled without further difficulties. This was in April 1901.

The Harriman–Schiff forces, however, had just begun to fight. It was noticed presently that there was an unusual activity on the street and that the sales of Northern Pacific were becoming abnormally large. The price did not jump as yet, but it stiffened perceptibly, reached and passed the hundred mark, and continued its upward way.

May 1, 1901, was a day of record sales on the stock exchange. On that day more than three and a quarter million shares of all sorts changed hands. The next day was a close second as to sales, leaving the temperature of Wall Street decidedly feverish. The week closed ominously. Nearly 500 thousand shares of Northern Pacific common and over 50 thousand shares of preferred had changed hands. The price of the stock was not yet excessive—115 being the top, thus far. The cause of the increased demand was unknown. Harriman and Schiff were buying, but so adroitly as not to appear in the transactions. Mr. Baker and Mr. Hill may have had a suspicion of the truth but it certainly was no more than that, until Mr. Schiff now suddenly appeared before Mr. Hill and declared himself openly.

"Mr. Hill," he said, "we have obtained control of the Northern Pacific Railroad, and I have come to offer you the management of it. We will give you an irrevocable power of attorney for 10 years."

Mr. Hill listened quietly and said he would consider the proposition. This interview took place at Mr. Hill's home, and Mr. Schiff had hardly left before the man of railroads started downtown, stopping at Mr. Baker's to apprise him of the new move of the Union Pacific forces, and their bid for his cooperation. A very short time after that they were on their way to Mr. J. P. Morgan's office, where it was agreed with Mr. Bacon (Mr. Morgan himself being still abroad) that they would go into the market and pick up a little Northern Pacific on their own account. This must have been on Saturday, for the *Times* of Monday contained a rumor story of the new big merger of competing railroads. The street confirmed the rumor and the war was on. On that day Northern Pacific common shot up 17½ points, and by three o'clock 175 thousand shares, along with 30 thousand of preferred, had changed hands.

Now the preferred stock was something of a "joker" in the situation—there being a clause in the Northern Pacific charter which provided for its retirement on a basis of cash payment, at par. Its voting tenure was limited. The Baker–Morgan–Hill forces knew of this clause and while they began buying blocks of common stock, they also began cautiously to feed out their preferred. Apparently the other side did not realize this difference, for the preferred was snapped up with the other, and all the prices soared.

On Tuesday the 7th of May, the jump in Northern Pacific was 16 points; on Wednesday there followed another jump of 16½ points for the day, the price closing at 160. There was, however, a heavy falling off in the sales; the supply of stock was getting scarce; another day, and pandemonium reigned.

Mr. Hill, meantime, had wired to friends in England and Canada, who held large blocks of the stock—enough to change the control. Among them were Lord Strathcona, the Barings, and Lord Mount Stephens. His cable conveyed the idea that something was about to happen in Northern Pacific, and asked them to stand by. No immediate reply came from them, and the Morgan member, Mr. Bacon, began to have visions of the English contingent selling out and leaving his faction with nothing but a lot of high-priced shares that would presently slump back to their normal figure. When the stock struck the hundreds and soared through them toward a thousand he was quite naturally impatient for news, and made frequent inquiries. Mr. Hill was cool but finally said, a little impatiently—"Damn it, Bacon, don't worry. My friends will stand without hitching."

The strain, however, was terrific. . . . Thursday, May 9th, was the big day. The floor of the Stock Exchange became like a football field. Youth led the rushes, but age joined them. Northern Pacific rose to 300–500–700—it touched a thousand dollars a share, cash. The most conservative traders lost their heads: the shorts were frantic. Men made fortunes in a few minutes; others lost them. Brokers climbed over one another to buy and sell. For the first time in history the galleries were cleared. The streets outside were crowded with anxious and curious people. Even lower Broadway was thronged. The Waldorf Hotel, the uptown speculation center, was jammed with excited men.

The quest for stock extended throughout the world. The cable sent men scurrying into remote corners of the earth gleaning for shares. Persons of moderate means, who not long before had purchased 100 shares or so, around 80, as an investment, were awakened from their beds and offered a fortune for their holdings. Most of them sold, but a few did not, and among these were Mr. Hill's English friends. They did not sell a share. Lord Strathcona, approached with an offer of $700 a share for all his holdings, regarded his caller mildly and shook his head:

"I really don't know what is going on over there," he said, "but I have had word from Mr. Hill that there is likely to be something doing in Northern Pacific, and not to part with my stock, or be disturbed by any little flurry."

Yet it has been said that the English have a lack of humor. Lord Strathcona owned some 30 thousand shares of Northern Pacific. The "little flurry" would have meant something like a $20 million profit, had he sold. No better example could be found of financial faith and loyalty. But J. J. Hill's friends were like that; they would, as he said, "stand without hitching."

There was still no real public knowledge as to what it was all about. The wildest rumors circulated. Some of the papers declared it to be a war between Morgan and Hill, and other pretended explanations were advanced. The men in the streets did not particularly care, or have time to think; they knew only that they had sold Northern Pacific short and must make good their deliveries; or that they were long on other stocks and must unload or perish. For of course all of the rest of the list had to pay for Northern Pacific's debauch.

The rails suffered most. St. Paul showed a loss of $23\frac{1}{2}$ points for the day. Night came down in ruin for many; call money was at 60 percent, and in poor supply. That night the bankers got together and made up a pool to relieve the money situation. Northern Pacific had closed at 320, but by agreement the shorts were allowed to settle [at] 150. It sold next day up to 175, with the preferred at 169, but cut no special figure. The panic was at an end; the struggle was over.

The entire list recovered. St. Paul got back $17\frac{1}{2}$ of its lost points. The sales of the Northern Pacific for the week was 711,773 shares of common and 88,202 of the preferred. The votes were all in. It was a time to count the returns.

On the morning of the 9th the headlines had reported "STINGING DEFEAT FOR MORGAN," and it is possible that the Morgan forces were at that time in danger; but with the morning of the 10th came, "MORGAN IN CONTROL: KUHN LOEB & COMPANY ADMIT DEFEAT IN N. P. FIGHT." And this, at least, was true. Harriman and Schiff had acquired very large holdings, possibly enough to control, but for the fact of the preferred shares, which the other side proposed to pay off presently, as provided in the charter. A peace pact was in order. The rival factions agreed at length to put all the stock of the Northern Pacific, and the Great Northern (which included the Burlington), into a merger, to be known as the Northern Securities Company, with Mr. Hill as president. This arrangement was completed, but in the end the powers at Washington refused to recognize it, and compelled a dissolution. The Harriman forces now wanted back their original holdings, but by this time conditions had materially changed, and the mingled stocks could not be sorted out again in their exact identity. It was at this point that Mr. Morgan made his famous remark, so often employed since, by others: "It is easy enough to scramble eggs, but it is pretty hard to *un*scramble them."

The Northern Pacific fight was one of the great money battles of history. Like most such battles, it was neither intended nor desired. It developed suddenly and without any special preparation. With the Morgan–Baker–Hill faction, at least, there was no plan as to the campaign, no agreement or writings of any sort, simply an unspoken understanding and trust. Any one of them could have stopped his part of it, at any time. But nobody flinched. They stood, as Mr. Hill expressed it, "without being hitched," and wagered their millions, with only the sky as the limit.

Nelson W. Aldrich

NELSON W. ALDRICH, JR.

Nelson W. Aldrich, a Republican senator from Rhode Island for 30 years (1881–1911), was the Federal Reserve System's principal legislative sponsor. A man who accumulated some $12 million of personal wealth while serving the public interest, he was described as "The Boss of the United States" by Lincoln Steffans. So tenuous was his reputation that the only way Congressional acceptance for the legislation creating the Fed could be obtained was to remove his name from it. Here, his great-grandson reveals the source of this powerful man's power.

Nelson W. Aldrich was raised in East Killingly, Connecticut, just across the line from Rhode Island. His father was a mill hand, indolent and charming, whose name was Anan. His mother was called Abby, and there were times when she could hardly believe that such a man as Anan had

From *Old Money* by Nelson W. Aldrich, Jr. Copyright © 1988 by Nelson W. Aldrich, Jr. Reprinted by permission of Alfred A. Knopf, Inc.

fathered such a boy as Nelson. He was bright, and so much more serious and ambitious than his father. At nine, in 1850, he took some money his mother had given him for the circus and with it bought a little book called *A Tinker's Son, or, I'll Be Somebody Yet.* Later he read Walter Scott—perhaps to learn what a Somebody was in the Old World. His mother told him what Somebodies were in the New World. He was descended from two of them, she said: from John Winthrop, the first governor of Massachusetts, and from Roger Williams, the founder of Rhode Island. What basis she had for making these claims is a little obscure, but Nelson believed them all his life. While the world might suppose young Nelson W. Aldrich to be a nobody, he himself knew otherwise. His blood told him so.

His mother sent him to Greenwich (Rhode Island) Academy, and then he went to Providence to seek his fortune. He began as a clerk in a wholesale grocery business, and he was still a clerk when he left to be a soldier in the Civil War. Four months later he was mustered out, sick, and was back in Providence, a clerk again and more serious than ever. He was going to the Lyceum now, and while he learned much in those instructive halls that would be practically useful to him later—parliamentary rules and tactics, debating, and the like—he also learned a view of life that struck him as a grim and fearful thing. He learned about Charles Darwin's theories and what evolution meant for human society—an intense and relentless struggle for advantage.

There were grounds for hope in this account of the way things were, especially for someone destined, as he felt himself to be, to take his place among his country's once and future founding fathers. But there were also grounds for a terrible anxiety. Engaged to be married (and doubly blessed in his fiancé: she was the wholesale grocer's daughter, and her name was the same as his beloved mother's, Abby), he wrote to his fiancé that he often felt as though he'd been "set adrift upon a sea of doubts and fears." He anticipated "catastrophe." He imagined himself prey to "all conceivable evils." With her—his future haven, his solace even then—he could freely vent his unhappiness. But he could not change it to happiness, or not for long. . . .

By the mid-1870s, he might have called himself happy. His wife had brought him some money and, through the grocery business, a means of making more of it. Soon he also became a director of a small bank. It was not enough: his "ideal creations" seemed no more real than ever. As an American, indeed as an American of high destiny, what he wanted from America was simple enough: "Willingly or forcibly wrested from a selfish world, *Success!* Counted as the mass counts it, by dollars and cents!"

Politics must have been one way; otherwise it is hard to imagine my great-grandfather abandoning, as from the late 1870s he increasingly did, the direct pursuit of dollars and cents. . . .

Many states in the United States have been as undemocratic as Rhode Island in fact, but few states have been so undemocratic in law. The last of the original thirteen states to ratify the federal Constitution, Rhode Island was also one of the last to ratify a constitution of its own. For more than half a century after the nation organized itself in Philadelphia in 1787, the state's politics were conducted under a royal charter given to "The Colony of Rhode Island and the Providence Plantations" by Charles II, amended by a few unwritten provisions. None of the latter touched the suffrage requirement, which remained what it had always been, ownership of land. In 1842, with the adoption of a written state constitution, the vote was extended to owners of personal property (males only, of course), but only if they were native-born. In 1888, voting rights were extended to the foreign-born if they owned property, and to the native-born even if they didn't . . . however . . . the propertyless and the foreign-born could not vote at all "upon any proposition to impose a tax or the expenditure of money."

At the same time, until the very end of my great-grandfather's political career, election to both houses of the General Assembly was governed by rules that assured maximum representation of the small, conservative, and solidly Republican towns and villages, at the expense of the growing, increasingly appetitive, and soon solidly Democratic populations of the cities.

For my great-grandfather, these conditions were almost perfect. One of his "ideal creations" (and I suspect the most cherished) had always been the dream that he might one day find himself, as he put it, "above the reach of circumstance, above the whirlwind of common passion." Not for a long time now has any sane man gone into American politics with a dream like that. But in Rhode Island for about fifteen years on either side of 1900, it seemed a feasible thing to do—at least for a United States senator, a Republican, and a man devoutly disposed to further the interests and foster the values of the leading citizens of his state. For such a man, the laws of politics could provide as sure and permanent a lift above the tumult of circumstance and common passion as the marketplace, with its "unscrupulous laws of business," ever could. . . .

As my great-grandfather saw it, so far as I can tell at this distance, there were only two flaws in the arrangement. One was that he had a large and growing family, refined and imperious tastes, and very little money relative to his needs. This circumstance, as he took his seat in the Senate for the first time in 1881, he probably felt he could someday correct. But the other flaw was not so easily dealt with. This was that the whole constitutional apparatus he counted on to hold him aloft among "the honor'd number" was not really all that dependable. Not only did it have to be shored up by an extraconstitutional political machine but the machine had to be extensively lubricated by bribes.

The best Senator Aldrich could do about his squalid situation was to keep it at a comfortable remove from himself. In Washington, tending to great affairs of state, he let General Brayton, the Republican machine's boss, handle the sordid details of the voters' market.

My forebear's noble disdain for the unattractive machinery that maintained him in office might have been no more than hypocrisy, except for one thing: it went hand in hand with a loathing for those whom the machinery exploited—the poor. Very early in life, there had worked its way into his sensibility an unmistakable fear of and repugnance for those he'd left behind him in his drive for success.

Nelson W. Aldrich was not a great man with the people; he abhorred the people. In 1881, just elected to the Senate, he was cornered by a minion of the New York *Tribune*. The reporter wrote: "He has brilliant dark eyes which he fastens closely upon the person with whom he is conversing. His manners are genial and attractive." All that was true. Strikingly good-looking as a youth, well over six feet tall, with black hair and fine, balanced features, he grew into a man of imposing presence, with a flowing handlebar mustache and an erect posture. He was also intelligent, discreet, and reasonable. He had humor and charm. Just as important, he had an unequaled mastery of the minutiae of the nation's economic business. For thirty years, as chairman of the Senate Finance Committee, he was the principal author of all tariff legislation—the instrument of government economic policy in those days before taxes and the Federal Reserve. Yet for a long time the *Tribune* had said all there was to say, or all that was publicly available to say, about my family founder. "No, don't ask me any questions," the new senator had told the reporter, "let's talk about something else." For the next thirty years, he never gave a public speech outside the Senate, never gave interviews to the press, and seldom even wrote a letter. The conduct of the public's business, in my great-grandfather's view, was none of its business.

The only public whose company the first Nelson W. Aldrich ever sought, whose counsel he considered, or whose interests he chose to advance was the public of the "emerged". . . . Primary among them was the man whom he admired over all others, J. P. Morgan. In Senator Aldrich's view, Morgan's great labor to bring order, reason, and gentlemanly cooperation to the country's chaotic, often ruinous industrial growth was a labor of history.

What history was accomplishing through Morgan was an oligopoly of superior wealth-producing institutions for an oligarchy of patrician men. It was Senator Aldrich's task to help these men and institutions by protecting them from troublesome free-market competition from abroad, and from rivalrous assertions of governmental power at home. He did help them, indispensably. He included them in every step of the painstaking process of legislation, going over every detail of the tariff schedules, any one of which meant millions of dollars gained or lost for an emergent monopoly, or "trust." The last step, steering the bill through Congress, he took himself. In the genre of politics preferred—a politics of private consultation and discreet negotiation, as between men of honor—he was unsurpassed: competitive, delighting, in feint and infighting, but generous in victory and forgiving in defeat. He was a consummate parliamentarian and a calculating student of human nature. "In pursuing personal power," a recent student of his career has written, "few men were more dedicated, and no one had a more sensitive feeling for drawing it from other men's self-interest."

For ten years, he must have thought that his ideal creation had come close to reality. He had power. He was free. There were times when he thought himself safe. He had as well the gratitude of the men and institutions whose interests he protected so paternally. One lobbyist wrote to ask for his portrait: "I should like to frame it where the wool manufacturers can look upon the features of the man who has done more services, in a more effective way, in their behalf, than any other man, living or dead." My forefather was a father of industries, of fortunes and empires without number! He should have been happy.

But then, in 1892, he announced that he would not seek reelection. The weaker reason was that the "disturbances to his peace of mind" back home in Rhode Island were increasing. He was being maintained in office by a mercifully distant but exceedingly unattractive "traffic" in votes.

The stronger reason for his decision had to do with another sort of asset—dollars and cents, the banal stuff with which the vulgar masses count *Success!* The Senator hadn't enough of it. . . . This most reticent of men went so far as to confide in a Rhode Island businessman, Marsden J. Perry, that he was resigning from the Senate because his "independent" income, the income from his equity in the grocery business and the bank, was no more than $3,600 a year. (His salary as a U.S. senator was $5,000).

Whatever his income, his confidence in Perry proved well-placed. The Senator was soon the recipient of a tantalizing offer from a small group of Rhode Island businessmen, Perry among them. Briefly, what the Perry group proposed was to bring some order—that is to say, monopoly—to the rats' nest of independent street-railway companies in Rhode Island. The group needed Senator Aldrich's blessing. The new "trust," eventually called the United Traction and Electric Company (UTE), would require the cooperation of the state legislature to extend the long-term franchises and tax breaks needed for assured profits, and Senator Aldrich, through General Brayton, controlled the state legislature. It would only be fitting, then, and a wonderful answer to my great-grandfather's need for lucrative employment, if, after his retirement, the Senator would assume the presidency of the new company.

What happened next was that one of the monopolies most dependent on Senator Aldrich's paternal concerns, the American Sugar Refining Company, better known as the Sugar Trust, took alarm at the impending loss of its most powerful political patron. Learning of the UTE offer, an agent of the Sugar Trust devised a scheme by which my family founder could share in the equity of the new company without having to give up his Senate seat. The agent agreed to provide my great-grandfather . . . with up to $7 million in cash, the money to be used in the purchase and electrification of four profitable but inefficient horse-drawn trolley companies in and around Providence. The money would be paid back in forty-year, 5 percent bonds issued by UTE.

As the years went by, stock in the company did reasonably well, with the result that Senator Aldrich, having laid out no money of his own (not having any), was soon worth many millions of dollars. At his death, these assets would come to something like $16 million, a magnificent accumulation for a full-time politician in that era. But they did not reach that height without further dubious exertions of his senatorial power. In 1902, the new millionaire was able to acquire some longed-for liquidity with the sale of UTE to the United Gas and Improvement Company, a holding company controlled by the Philadelphia traction magnates W. L. Elkins and P. A. B. Widener. What he didn't take in cash he took in stock; by 1906, when the stock of United Gas and Improvement was languishing and sale was in order, it was arranged through the good offices of Mr. Morgan's bank that Rhode Island's trolley systems would be bought by the New Haven Railroad. This was not fortuitous. For some time, the relationship between Senator Aldrich and the bank had been close to the point of intimacy. A letter from a Morgan partner, Henry P. Davison, strikes the right tone:

> The enclosed refers to the stock of the Bankers Trust Company, of which you have been allotted one hundred shares. You will be called upon for payment of $40,000. . . . It will be a pleasure for me to arrange this for you if you would like to have me do so. I am particularly pleased to have you have this stock, as I believe it will give a good account of itself. It is selling today on the basis of little more than $500 a share. I hope, however, you will see fit to put it away, as it should improve with seasoning. Do not bother to read through the enclosed, unless you desire to do so. Just sign your name and return to me.

With the New Haven Railroad deal, however, my forebear seems to have acted with less nonchalance than this letter implies was his custom. Several years later, when the railroad was tottering (among other reasons because of bad investments), its president was summoned before an investigating committee and asked why he had paid such an unconscionably high price for United Gas and Improvement stock. Charles Mellen shrugged. "I was dealing with Nelson W. Aldrich," he said. "Do you think I got the stock at par?"

This was the sort of thing, quite as much as his patronage of monopoly and the "trusts," that caused my great-grandfather to become one of the most vilified men in America.

William C. Durant

BERNARD A. WEISBERGER

Billy Durant was a "go getter" with imagination, drive, and little or no sense of limits—his organization's or his own. At his best, he was the sort of fellow who could and did begin a venture that would, a few years later, enable him to buy a faltering Buick Motor Company and eventually assemble what became the world's largest and most profitable corporation: General Motors. Here, he is at the very beginning—creating a reality out of an idea.

He was walking down Saginaw Street to keep an appointment, just prior to a board meeting of the water company, and he was in a hurry. No one else seemed to be. The side avenue stretched ahead of him in easygoing autumn fullness. Wagons were parked along its edges, horses switching their tails and occasionally tossing their heads against the bridles that held them fast to the hitching posts. Men came and went from Veit and Perry's harness and leather shop, Ellis's bicycle store, the printing office of the *Wolverine Citizen*, the Bryant House, which was both local hotel and meeting place of the Masonic Lodge and other orders. Above the expanse of two-story-high roofs rose cruciform symbols—the iron cross above St. Paul's, and the many wooden ones formed by the crossbars and poles that carried Flint's recently installed telephone and electric wires. At the major intersection of Kearsley and Saginaw, on opposite corners, stood the First National Bank of Flint and the Genesee County Savings Bank. Church, banks, printing office, hotel, markets—the elements of civilization, suspended in momentary tranquility.

Durant's destiny was at the intersection, too. It was disguised as his friend, John Alger, who worked at Jim Bussey's hardware store. Destiny, in this unlikely manifestation, was waving at him from the seat of a two-wheeled cart, offering him a lift.

Gratefully, he climbed in. The cart was simple, little more than a modified sulky. Its four-foot wheels held between them a simple seat, barely 24 inches wide, a tight fit for two adult bottoms, surrounded by a low iron bar for hanging on. The passenger's and driver's feet rested on a curved, slatted footboard. The whole thing resembled a ferris wheel's chair, brought down to earth. But when Durant had squeezed himself in, and the horse

From *Dream Maker* by Bernard Weisberger. Copyright © 1979 by Bernard A. Weisberger. By permission of Little, Brown & Company, (Inc.).

was . . . in . . . trot, he made a pleasant discovery. The seat swayed easily up and down and side to side, with none of the hard bouncing and shaking that usually went with a ride in a light vehicle.

When they dismounted, Durant made a quick examination, and discovered the secret in a beautifully simple idea. It was all in the mounting of the seat on the springs. They were half-elliptical, curving forward from the rear axle like old-fashioned pistols fastened by their butts. At the top of the "barrels" were horseshoe-shaped stirrups, through which the shafts ran. The seat was fastened by wooden arms to the tops of these stirrups. It rode up and down with the flexing steel, but the stirrups moved freely around the shafts, so that none of their vibration was felt.

Durant was entranced. The cart was slight, graceful-looking, smooth-riding, and, above all, so simple that it was clearly inexpensive to make. It would be an ideal form of individual personal transportation for short distances. In his mind was an idea that he had not yet put into words: the inspired salesman should look for a self-seller, and if he could not find one, *make* one. He saw himself selling the cart to young men of modest means, showing them at how little cost they could be borne swiftly, comfortably on necessary errands, or on the pursuit of legitimate relaxation. And he knew at that moment that the demand he could create for the cart would be so great that no one of lesser clairvoyance than himself could be trusted to take the risks necessary to fill it. He would be manufacturer as well as salesman.

He found out from John Alger that the cart had been made in Coldwater, some 75 miles away. His other affairs pushed aside, he got on the local train the very next day, spent the night at Coldwater's hotel, and on the following morning poked his head inside the door pointed out to him as belonging to the cart "factory" of William Schmedlin and Thomas O'Brien. He was comforted at once by the familiar smell of shavings. He was in the carpenter shop. Around him were unfinished spokes, shafts, and seatboards. From another room in the back he could hear the clanking of hammers. That would be where the blacksmiths were working on bolts, springs, fittings. That was all. There was no office. The plant, he judged quickly, looked as if it might turn out two carts a day.

He found O'Brien, pleasant-faced and fiftyish, among the carpenters. To him he explained softly, quickly, why he was there. He had ridden in their cart, liked it "immediately," thought that it had a "wonderful future." He had very little money, but wanted to buy a small interest in the concern.

O'Brien listened thoughtfully, and answered. They did not need another partner, he was sure, but they might be willing to sell the whole outfit. But Schmedlin ought to be asked. He stepped back into the blacksmiths' room and returned with a young man whom Durant immediately found likable—alert and self-confident, like himself. Perched on a carpenter's bench, he chatted with them awhile, then asked: "If the business is for sale, what is the price?"

They were possibly surprised by the quickness of the question, but obviously required no elaborate accounting to come up with an answer. For $1,500 anyone could take away everything—finished and unfinished carts, lumber and parts on hand, dies and patterns. Schmedlin held the patent on the spring-and-stirrup combination, and wanted a royalty, but Durant said no to that, and got his way. Then he made his proposal, directly and without hesitation or bluff. He did not have the money. Let them all step over to the office of Schmedlin and O'Brien's attorney and draw up a bill of sale and an assignment of patent, and deposit them in the partnership's bank. He would leave for Flint immediately. If the funds were not in the Schmedlin and O'Brien account in five days, the deal was off.

It was agreed. Less than 24 hours later, Durant found himself standing on Saginaw Street again, about to tackle the job of raising $1,500. Whatever savings he might have had before marriage had vanished into his new home and furnishings—had, in fact, been converted into $3,500 in debt. It was a large sum of money for the time and place. Lenders would be very skeptical about advancing more to a young man, even a popular and hardworking one, for a new business venture.

He mulled over the possibilities. There was Josiah Begole, his grandfather's old, friendly competitor. But he frankly lacked the nerve to ask him.

And there was Uncle William, or any other Crapo relative, the most logical choice in one way. But there was an overpowering drawback for the son of William Clark Durant. "If I make a failure of this venture," he thought to himself, "I will never hear the last of it." That decision cut him off, unfortunately, from at least two banks. The Genesee County Savings Bank had been founded by Uncle James, and numbered among its directors cousin Will Orrell. The First National Bank of Flint had recently been headed by Uncle Ferris Hyatt. The same motive that barred approach to the seemingly innumerable husbands and sons of Crapo women also ruled out close friends of the family. At that moment, his connections seemed an absolute disadvantage.

That left the Citizens Bank of Flint, "not as pretentious as the others, but sound as a rock." Its president, Robert J. Whaley, looked the very model of a small-town banker. He had light hair, small ears, close-set eyes behind rimless glasses, and an expression, to judge by later photos, that might merely have been nearsighted but seemed kindly. Durant entered the bank and climbed a flight of steps to Whaley's office, an old-fashioned curiosity shop, furnished in simple pieces and dust. He explained himself quickly and appealingly.

"Do you think it is all right?" asked Whaley.

"I would not be here, Mr. Whaley, if I did not think so."

"Come with me," said Whaley, and he marched him downstairs to the cashier, and ordered that a 90-day note should be made out to Mr. Durant, and the proceeds put in an account for him. In a matter of minutes, he had put Durant on the road to becoming a manufacturer.

Durant walked over to his insurance office, sat down, and meditated on his next steps. His problems were far from solved. He had enough to pay O'Brien and Schmedlin, and another $500 to move the establishment to Flint, but not a cent of working capital.

At that moment, the door opened, and the youthful, moustached face of Josiah Dallas Dort looked in. "Hello, Billy," he said, using the nickname by which Durant was becoming known to close friends outside the family. "I've missed you—where have you been?"

"Over in Coldwater, Dallas. And by the way, I'm in the manufacturing business."

"What are you going to manufacture?"

"Road carts."

Dort's eyes widened. He was both a partner and a clerk in Bussey's store, and he knew exactly what Durant meant.

"Do you mean to say that you've gotten involved in making that road cart of Johnny Alger's?"

"Bought it lock, stock, and barrel, with the patent as well."

Dort weighed the implications of this for a moment; his friend's sudden announcement had set mental wheels of his own whirring. He was 10 months older than Durant, another young businessman with his fortune to make. He came from Inkster, a town just outside of Detroit, and had gone to a nearby school where one of his classmates was a boy, two years younger, from Dearborn, named Henry Ford. He had attended the state's normal school at Ypsilanti, but found commerce a more attractive prospect than teaching. He had made his way eventually to Flint, and to James Bussey, who hired him to manage the hardware store on a salary-plus-profit-sharing basis, which now had four more months to run. He had met "Billy" earlier in the year, and they had hit it off at once.

Dort's ambition to be independent was no less sharp than Durant's. He was ready to jump at the chance to leave the second-class status of employee behind him. He now put to Durant, surprised and grateful, the one question above all that he needed to hear. "Will you sell me a half-interest?" Durant would, in fact, be delighted to do so for $1,000.

Dort immediately ran across the street for a conference with Bussey, and returned full of enthusiasm. Bussey was having a bad year, and was glad to release him from the contract with a $500 cash payoff in settlement of all accounts. The other $500, he told his new partner, would be no problem. He would be on the one o'clock train to Inkster, where his mother lived in what he called the old homestead. "I know she will let me have the money," he said, "if she has to mortgage the farm to make it.". . .

And so, in that simple and speedy way made possible by a town's small-ness and intimacy, an enterprise was begun. The handshake partnership was formalized on September 28, 1886, when the two young men opened an account in the name of the Flint Road Cart Company. From the start it was agreed that Dort would supervise production, and Durant sales and fi-nancing. They were a good team. Durant had exuberance, curiosity, bold-ness, a nose for adventure. Dort was steady and attentive to detail, the perfect ballast when his associate soared high and fast.

Van Sweringen Brothers

DANA THOMAS

The Van Sweringen brothers demonstrated—vigourously and vividly—both the pros and the cons of leverage in the 1920s and 1930s. This ret-rospective story tells how these two "go-getters" parlayed a shoestring into a $3 billion property, lost it and—in an absolutely stunning show of financial ingenuity—got it back again, against all odds.

Oris and James Van Sweringen [were] Cleveland real estate operators . . . who . . . kept the headlines boiling with their exploits.

The brothers were a curious pair. Oris was two years older than James, but they lived and worked as though they were Siamese twins. Both were unmarried. They occupied the same house, slept side-by-side in twin beds. Observed one social historian, "They were almost like two halves of a sin-gle personality." . . .

The brothers got into railroading when their interest was aroused in the New York, Chicago, and St. Louis Railroad, popularly called the "Nickel Plate," which had rights of way through Cleveland. Controlled by the New York Central, it was a desirable property, and the Van Sweringens heard reports that the Central might be agreeable to selling it. They put in a bid and got a controlling interest in the Nickel Plate stock for $8.5 mil-lion. Actually, the Van Sweringens didn't have $8.5 million to buy the property, but this trifle did not prevent them from acquiring it. They ob-tained a $2 million loan from bankers, using as collateral the stock they were *going to buy*, and this $2 million they handed over to the New York

Central. For the remaining $6.5 million, they persuaded the Central to ac-
cept promissory notes that would come due in ten years. In short, the Van
Sweringens acquired ownership of the Nickel Plate without putting up a
penny of their own.

However, there was the little matter of the $2 million which they had
borrowed and which had to be repaid to the banks. So they formed a corporation, the Nickel Plate Securities Corporation, and handed over to it
the Nickel Plate stock which they had just acquired. The new company assumed the $2 million debt and the obligations on the $6.5 million worth of
notes that were still outstanding. The Van Sweringens and several associates then purchased a block of preferred stock in the new corporation for
$1 million (the brothers put up $500,000 of the money, which they managed to obtain from banks), and they obtained an additional million by
peddling an equal amount of preferred stock to the public. As a result, they
scraped together the $2 million to pay off the previous loan that was due
the banks. The Van Sweringens took up all the common as well as 50 percent of the preferred stock, and since the common alone had voting rights,
they owned the Nickel Plate Securities Corporation lock, stock and barrel,
which in its turn tightly controlled the Nickel Plate Railroad. In short, for
a $500,000 cash investment, most of which they had borrowed from the
banks, they had themselves a railroad whose mileage was ultimately
greater than all of England and the Netherlands combined, with shipping
subsidiaries, dairy properties, trucking firms, mining properties, fruit or-
chards, transportation terminals, retail outlets, office buildings—a complex worth a total of $3 billion in paper holdings.

Using the same techniques, the Van Sweringens bought railroad after
railroad. In each case they commenced with a small payment, usually borrowed from the banks, to take them over the hurdle of the initial haz-
ardous stages of the financing. Then they met their indebtedness to the
banks by unloading huge amounts of stock, bereft of any voting power, to
the public. To annex a railroad, a hotel, a department store, they would
conjure up yet another holding company. To amplify their leverage and
dodge or whittle down taxes, they would sometimes launch several holding
companies as the media through which to purchase a single railroad. Actually, one method was used to build the labyrinthine empire. One holding
company would sometimes be employed to control the stock of a second
holding company. Or in a switch of tactics, the stock of a holding company
would be controlled by a railroad. At the apex of the pyramid, tying the
vast system into a single instrument for their personal control, they organized the premier holding company of all, the Allegheny Corporation.

The aim of the Van Sweringens was nothing less than to develop a
railroad complex that would provide transcontinental passage of passenger and freight in a single system—something never before achieved,
though often attempted, by American financiers. And the brothers might

have succeeded in extending their holdings indefinitely if the Depression had not hit them. In the 1930s, finding themselves overextended, they turned to Wall Street for urgently needed capital; and to obtain loans amounting to $48 million from the Morgan syndicate, the brothers were forced to pledge virtually their entire holdings. By 1935 the Depression was still at its height, and they had not been able to bail themselves out of their financial difficulties. On May 1, 1935, they defaulted and the Morgan interests took over.

When the Morgan group foreclosed, it found itself in possession of properties with a paper value of $3 billion, which had depreciated to virtually nothing. The Allegheny Corporation, which was the key holding company controlling the system, was insolvent. The Morgans had only two choices. They could try to rehabilitate the empire or dispose of it at the best possible price. They decided on the latter course. For one thing, the American press was in an uproar over the shoddy doings of the Van Sweringens. The details of how they had picked other people's pockets on such a colossal scale had become the subject of bitter editorials and head-shaking all over the land. The Morgans decided it would not be fitting for bankers to try to operate such tarnished holdings. And since they did not believe they could get rid of them through the ordinary channels of investment, they took the unusual step of trying to auction them off.

Over the years there have been some rather bizarre means of distributing stock. There are securities that tumble so low no buyer can be found for them on any of the exchanges or through any conventional channels of trading. In such cases, the last resort is to unload them just like sticks of furniture under the hammer of the auctioneer.

A top specialist for over a hundred years in auctioning stocks was Adrian H. Muller & Son, of 18 Vesey Street, New York. . . .

It was to Adrian Muller that the Morgan emissaries came with an invitation to put the Van Sweringen railroad empire on the block. Miss Helen Collins, the brisk, businesslike woman who managed Adrian Muller, didn't flicker an eyelash when she was sounded out on this bizarre offer. . . .

The nation's press buzzed with rumors. Wall Street veterans and financial men all over the country were fascinated with the possibilities of this staggering rummage sale. People everywhere speculated over what bidders would show up and try to grab for peanuts this $3 billion railroad property with its maze of subsidiary corporations. It was known that anybody desiring to bid would have to deposit money with the Morgan group as a guarantee of good faith, but not even Miss Collins was given the names of the would-be purchasers until just before the auction began.

It was scheduled to be held on September 30, at three-thirty in the afternoon. An hour beforehand the crowd began to line up at the door of Adrian Muller. Armed bank guards arrived to provide security against possible rioters.

Shortly before three, the bidders themselves strode in. . . . The Morgans were present purely in a protective capacity, to bid, if necessary, simply to keep the securities from going at a ridiculously cheap price. They were accompanied by an array of lawyers, headed by Frederick Schwartz, a slim, auburn-haired individual who walked up to the auctioneer's platform, presented his credentials as a bidder and handed over a bundle of portfolios containing the Van Sweringen securities. . . .

In a few minutes, a second group of bidders entered and took their seats across the aisle from the Morgan group. The financial writers in the crowd perked up, recognizing three men—Colonel Leonard P. Ayres . . . who was a leading Midwest banker and an executive of the Cleveland Trust Co.; George Tomlinson, an industrialist whose face appeared frequently in the financial pages of Midwest newspapers; and George A. Ball, the multimillionaire owner of a canning jar factory. The financial analysts plunged into lively speculation as to whether Messieurs Ayres, Ball and Tomlinson were planning to bid on their own as individuals or were acting as the front for somebody who represented the real power. . . .

Finally . . . the clock reached half past three, and Miss Collins' assistant, a Mr. Kingston, stood up to open the auction.

Suddenly, people sitting in the rear of the room were astir. A short, rotund individual with metallic gray hair slipped in and took his seat in the back. Several newsmen could hardly believe what they saw. But there was no doubt of it. This was Oris P. Van Sweringen, the older of the brothers, whose default was the reason for the auction.

What was he doing at Adrian Muller's? It wasn't possible that he had come to try to win back his property. Quite apart from the arrogance involved, there were serious legal difficulties. The Van Sweringens could not bid for property they had welched on through a repudiation of their debts. Moreover, they were flat broke and they owed the banks $40 million.

The reporters, along with the Morgan group, who had spotted Van Sweringen, were nonplussed. . . .

It was three-thirty. The bell of St. Paul's Church tolled out across the way when Mr. Kingston opened the proceedings. The properties were to be auctioned off in four major packages, but the key offering was the one that included a heavy proportion of the securities of the Allegheny Corporation, in which the control of the empire was vested. This package contained a block of 456,000 shares of Allegheny bonds, 34,000 shares of preferred stock and 2,640,000 shares of common that represented voting control of Allegheny.

Mr. Kingston began by holding up a parcel of the less important securities. "What am I bid?"

Immediately Mr. Schwartz was on his feet. He put in a protective rock-bottom bid for the Morgans. Colonel Ayres speaking for the Midwestern bidders, responded from the other side of the room with an offer that was a little higher. Several other minor packages were offered; and the same routine was followed. The Morgan people sang out a bid, Ayres upped it. And when no one else spoke, the auctioneer's hammer closed out the sale.

Finally, the key package containing the controlling shares of Allegheny was reached. Kingston grasped the bundle, and held it up.

"What am I bid?" Fred Schwartz for the Morgan group sang out, "Two million, eight hundred and two thousand, one hundred and one dollars."

Colonel Ayres countered, "Two million, eight hundred and three thousand dollars."

"Who else do I hear? Do I hear another bid?"

No one responded. The hammer struck the stand. The deal was closed.

The reporters crowded around Colonel Ayres and ferreted out an amazing story. The real victors were the Van Sweringen brothers. The Ayres-Ball group had been bidding on their behalf and through a legal facade had enabled the brothers to buy back their property on a shoestring.

Several weeks before the auction, Oris Van Sweringen, in a desperate attempt to win back control, had sought out George A. Ball, the wealthy Cleveland manufacturer, and pleaded with him to bid for the securities. . . . Van Sweringen succeeded in inducing Ball, a man in his seventies, to form a holding company, the Midamerica, and to dip into its treasury to raise $3 million to bid for the property. Moreover, Ball was talked into offering the brothers an option for 55 percent of the railroad's stock, once it had been repurchased, to last for ten years (for which the brothers would pay a mere $8,250 of their own money) on the understanding that within this period they would settle all their debts with their creditors. In other words, the Van Sweringens were handed back 23,000 miles of railroads, a network of coal mines, office buildings, streetcar railways, suburban real estate developments, trucking companies, a department store, a hotel and the Allegheny holding corporation for the princely sum of $8,250.

Oris Van Sweringen was confronted by reporters before he could slip away through the door. But he was too overwhelmed with emotion to make a formal statement. Over and over again he nodded his head and muttered, "I would have rather paid the bill." He was referring to the fact that even with the proceeds of the auction, the Morgan interests were over $40 million out of pocket as a result of the brothers' default on their loans. . . .

Fate continued to play slyly with the Van Sweringens. Years of financial aggravation and hounding by creditors had broken them. Ninety days after winning back the property, James Van Sweringen died; the next year his older brother, Oris, followed him. And George Ball was left with a mountain of headaches.

Charles Ponzi

JOHN TRAIN

Charles Ponzi was a deft practitioner of that special type of deliberate, premeditated fraud best described as, well, a "Ponzi scheme." And it didn't end with the collapse of his first big-time scam in Boston; when he got out on parole there, he went to Florida under an assumed name and was jailed again, this time for real estate fraud, returned to do more time in a Massachusetts prison, and was finally deported.

A proper ambition of every young American of ability and zeal is to give his name to something big: to become eponymous. . . .

Italian-born as Bianchi, later Ponzi, he started in Montreal around 1907 near the bottom of the ladder of iniquity as a modest con man in a firm that helped his fellow Italians arrange their remittances back to loved ones in Napoli and Palermo. Many of us have had occasion to find out what an eternity international money transfers can take. The banks collect interest on the idle balances, so they are happy for the transaction to drag out. In this narrow area of finance Bianchi/Ponzi was a *petit maître:* his transfers were conducted at so stately a pace that many have not arrived to this day, three-quarters of a century later.

Then there was the rubber-check imbroglio. A year later the Canadian authorities, apparently misunderstanding some technical detail, actually stuck Bianchi/Ponzi in prison for forging signatures on a series of checks. On his reemergence into the light of day our hero resolved to lead a new life. Not to go straight, of course, but to do things differently . . . better. Shaking from his boots the dust of Montreal—and its courts and its jails—he headed south, to Boston, town of the bean and the cod. But the path to success is arduous. Before he could devise his big coup Bianchi/Ponzi, now rechristened Charles Ponzi, tried washing dishes . . . hard on the hands and dull; running his in-laws' agricultural produce business. . . bankruptcy; clerking in an import-expert firm . . . tiresome and complicated.

While promoting a loose-leaf periodical for people in the import-export trade he wrote to acquaintances abroad, and in August 1919 received an answer from Italy. Inside the envelope nestled an International Postal Reply Coupon, redeemable in stamps. As Ponzi peered gloomily at the little square of printed paper he noticed a curiosity. The coupon had in fact been bought in Spain. Because International Postal Reply Coupons were redeemable at fixed rates of exchange negotiated by participating governments, while currencies themselves can fluctuate wildly, this coupon had cost Ponzi's correspondent only one-sixth as much to buy in Spain as it was worth in stamps of the United States.

Well! Many of us have been struck by falling apples, but only Newton, rubbing the spot and glaring upward, derived the law of gravity. Just so, numberless correspondents must have noticed the Postal Reply Coupon anomaly, but only Charles Ponzi, on that August day in 1919, saw in it the possibility of vast profits . . . fraudulent, naturally.

Why couldn't you march into the post offices of some benighted land whose currency had collapsed, acquire stacks—bales, indeed—of these coupons for next to nothing, and thereafter, presenting them for redemption in a strong-currency country, make an immediate, huge profit, in stamps? After that, one would need only to wholesale the stamps, perhaps to business firms at a slight discount. The thing was a gold mine!

The first step was to form a firm, a sound, solid firm. A sound, solid name suggested itself: The Securities and Exchange Company. Then, experienced, reliable officers and employees. As president and, indeed, the entire staff, who better than Charles Ponzi himself? A splendid start!

The deal offered by The Securities and Exchange Company was irresistible. You handed over your cash, the SEC worked its wonders with the coupons, and after 90 days you got back your original stake plus a profit of 40 percent. Very satisfactory, . . . particularly compared to the then prevailing interest rate of 5 percent or so.

The SEC's "prospectus" percolated around Boston in the early weeks of 1920, and investors started to trickle in from here and there, the way a few gulls and then more and more materialize when you toss some scraps out on the water. The initial investors were not turned out in black suits with ample waistcoats anchored by gold watch chains; rather, coming mostly from Boston's North End, they were the same simple immigrants that Ponzi understood and had victimized in the past. A number of policemen, themselves rather simple souls in financial matters, signed up as customers.

Soon word got about, and the inflow of cash picked up. It became a torrent in February, when the SEC lifted its rate on 90-day notes to 100 percent, and began offering a 50 percent return on 45-day notes. Now the money began to pour in so fast that President Ponzi scarcely knew what to do with it all. Six clerks stacked piles of banknotes in closets until they scraped the ceiling. Wastebaskets did duty as coffers for greenbacks. A second office was acquired, and soon overflowed with money like the first. Crowds filled the street, waiting to turn over their savings for SEC paper. Periodically they were treated to glimpses of the Midas himself, rolling up in his cream-colored Locomobile, complete with Japanese chauffeur. Ponzi—all five feet three inches of him—became a vision of opulence, his dapper raiment perfected by a malacca cane and a gold-tipped cigarette holder.

As the financial Niagara continued to pour, Ponzi acquired a quarter-share of the Hanover Trust Company. After that he took over J. R. Poole & Co., the import-export company where he had once been employed. He talked of opening branch offices . . . 20, 30. Also a chain of movie houses, a group of affiliated banks, even a steamship line.

The Boston papers were strangely silent on these exciting prospects. Finally, on July 26, the Boston *Post* broke silence. It ran an article claiming the whole thing was impossible: there weren't enough International Postal Reply Coupons sold to Ponzi to be doing what he claimed.

Some of the investors got the wind up. A number hastened to the SEC's offices in School Street to demand money for their notes. As fast as they appeared they were issued Hanover Trust checks paying them off in full, with interest. Ponzi appeared in person to pooh-pooh the problem. Observers were permitted a glimpse of a certified check for a million dollars languidly peeking from one pocket. The newspaper story was irrelevant, Ponzi assured the crowd. In reality he had quite a different method of multiplying the money, a wonderful method he had to keep secret for a time, for the sole use of The Securities and Exchange Company: the Postal Reply Coupon business was a decoy. The crowd was impressed, and the confrontation passed off satisfactorily. By the end of the day the SEC had accepted another $200 thousand.

Then came trouble. The D.A. stepped in. Ponzi must desist from taking in new funds, pending an audit of the books. There was a run on the SEC. Policemen had to push people back into line. Several women collapsed. Some noteholders who irrupted through a glass door were lacerated by shards. The president appeared undismayed. His clerks went on writing Hanover Bank checks as fast as notes were presented. A Ponzi Alliance Organization promised support. Ponzi announced that he would use his profits to "do good for the people," and was cheered in the streets.

A week later the *Post* let fly again. This time it was an article by Ponzi's former publicity man, one William H. McMasters, who opined that Ponzi was "as crooked as a winding staircase" and in debt to the tune of some $4 million. Furthermore, asked McMasters, if the SEC's scheme really made its investors 50 percent in 45 days, why did Ponzi himself put his own money in 5 percent bank deposits? And why had he scuttled out of the office one day to a store to take advantage of an offer of a free pair of shoes?

New crowds of agitated noteholders surged to School Street, to be soothed by more hundreds of thousands' worth of Hanover checks. More cheerful and confident than ever, Ponzi announced a $100 million worldwide investment syndicate. Declaring that he was being persecuted at the behest of the big bankers, he filed a $5 million suit against the *Post*. He and his wife were cheered in their box in the theater.

August, though, was bad. The Massachusetts State Banking Commission closed down that helpful institution, the Hanover Trust. And the *Post* sniffed out Ponzi's earlier career in Montreal, the aliases, the disappearing transfers, the bum-check rap, the stretch in the pen. There was even a Canadian mug shot, minus the gold-tipped cigarette holder.

Then the auditors revealed that the whole operation was an absurdity. After token transactions of merely $30, Ponzi had never used the International Postal Reply Coupon idea at all. He simply paid off earlier investors with funds received from later ones. There was no network of international correspondents. The SEC was at least $3 million in the red.

The roof fell in. Using the mails to defraud, conspiracy, grand larceny, bankruptcy, civil suits. Once again, Ponzi was hustled to the slammer. But the legal uproar continued unabated, and his time behind bars was enlivened by constant expeditions to court to testify at one hearing or another.

Let out on parole after three and a half years, Ponzi was rearrested, jumped bail, fled to Florida under an alias, and was sentenced to jail there for real estate fraud: he was promising 200 percent profit in 60 days. He again jumped bail, was recaptured, and disappeared into a Massachusetts jail for seven years. On emerging, he was deported to Italy, got a job at Alitalia in Rio de Janeiro, was sacked when Alitalia closed down there during World War II, ran an unsuccessful boardinghouse, taught English, and finally died in a Rio charity ward.

Samuel Insull

STEWART H. HOLBROOK

Samuel Insull was a Horatio Alger-type success as a daring executive in the burgeoning electric power industry. Then, he discovered the "magic of finance." In a subsequent calamity of heroic proportions, investors lost more than $750,000,000 when his utility empire pyramid collapsed in 1929–1930. It was then, and for a long time after, the largest financial failure on record and had a direct connection to passage of the Securities Exchange Act of 1934, which now regulates the issuance of securities, outlaws the kind of holding companies Insull promoted, and governs the workings of our stock exchanges. Even so, three governmental attempts to convict Insull on criminal charges resulted in successive verdicts of "Not Guilty."

Among the American colossi of money Samuel Insull was unique in two respects. His was the greatest failure of them all, greater even than Jay Cooke's; and he was a native of England. Born in 1859 in a grubby part of London, his father was an obscure nonconformist preacher which, in England, is to say that he was a man of little standing and of even less means. Sam's mother aided in the family livelihood by operating Insull's Temperance Hotel. Hotels that were not pubs were notoriously meager in cash return, yet the Insulls' income permitted young Sam to attend a good private school and he seems to have made excellent use of his time there.

At 14 he became a junior clerk for a firm of auctioneers. He learned shorthand and how to run the newfangled typewriting machines. Four years later opportunity knocked when a Colonel Gourard engaged him as secretary. Gourard was the London representative of Thomas Alva Edison, the American inventor and all-around wizard with electricity. Insull's quick intelligence impressed everyone connected with Edison's English interests. In 1881, aged 21, Insull arrived in the United States with the promise of a job with the chief himself. He became Edison's private secretary, and was soon much more than that; he was Edison's most trusted adviser; and a few years more he was general manager of most of the Edison enterprises.

One of these concerns was a small outfit at Schenectady, New York, the Edison General Electric Company. It was having troubles. Its output was slow and irregular. It was losing money steadily. Edison told Insull to

From *The Age of Moguls*, Stewart H. Holbrook. © 1953 by Stewart H. Holbrook. Reprinted by permission of Doubleday, a division of Random House, Inc.

go up there and run it. "Whatever you do, Sam," as Insull liked to tell the story, "either make a brilliant success of it or a brilliant failure. Do something!"

Sammy did something. When he took over, the plant employed 200 men. When he left, less than a decade later, it had 6,000 employees, Insull was in charge of both manufacture and sales, and his salary had risen to $36,000 a year. He was at this time, said one who knew him, a rugged, thickset Briton of the traditional rare roast-beef type, who radiated self-assurance and had "an iron jaw beneath a cushion of fresh, pink skin."

Fresh and pink, and assured, he arrived in Chicago in 1892, ready to head another small and dubious company. This was the infant Chicago Edison. He accepted the presidency at $12,000, a third of what he had been getting at Schenectady. He borrowed $250,000 from Marshall Field with which to buy himself a good hunk of stock in the new enterprise.

The Columbian Exposition of 1893 was to be the greatest demonstration to date of the wonders of illumination by electricity. Insull's little company helped to make the fairgrounds brilliant. Another was the small Commonwealth Electric Company. Insull convinced Commonwealth that the two concerns could grow faster and make more money if he, Insull, headed them both. He was promptly made president of Commonwealth, and ran both firms until 1907, when he consolidated them as Commonwealth Edison. Insull, of course, was president.

He had long since learned the methods by which legislators and assorted politicians are to be charmed, and proved it in 1907 by getting from the city of Chicago a 40-year exclusive franchise "to distribute electric power within the present or future limits of the municipality."

Insull had not overlooked the country surrounding Chicago. In the late nineties he began buying small electric properties in five counties, combining them into the Public Service Company of Northern Illinois. They were acquired in the usual manner, through issues of stocks and bonds, and the swapping thereof, a sort of legal legerdemain at which the young Briton was a master.

He was even better as an operator. Nothing in the mechanical line quite suited him. He wanted bigger energy for his many plants and longer transmission for their power. At about this time there arrived in the United States a sample of a new machine called a compound steam turbine. It had been invented by an Englishman, Sir Charles Algernon Parsons, but that wasn't why Insull wanted one; he knew that a Parsons turbine had already driven a ship faster than ever a ship had moved before. What would a Parsons turbine of enormous horsepower do for the generation of electric power? Insull had one built and it was a wonder of the time.

In 1903, on Chicago's Fisk Street, Sam Insull watched while his Parsons-type turbine produced 5,000 kilowatts. Nothing like it had been dreamed of, nor was the great day forgotten. A quarter of a century later, power men from all over the Midwest gathered at the Fisk Street station to place a tablet honoring its part in bringing light into dark places.

"This turbine," wrote Chicago historian Henry Justin Smith, "unknown to the crowd, had performed an immense feat. Before it, transmission reached only about 2,500 feet. With it, transmission became comparatively without bounds." It is remembered, too, that because Insull's directors showed reluctance to underwrite the cost of the turbine, he guaranteed the cost from his own pocket. Within a year the company had installed another big turbine of the same sort. So far as the Midwest was concerned, the two machines on Chicago's Fisk Street were the Adam and Eve. Turbines multiplied and grew in size—to 20,000 kilowatts, to 50,000 kilowatts, then doubled and tripled.

The great abilities of this assured young Englishman were quite apparent to other Chicago industrialists, including the discouraged officials of the Peoples Gas, Light & Coke Company. They needed help. The firm was a million dollars behind in taxes. There was no money to replace antiquated equipment. Bills for supplies were long overdue. Receivership was being contemplated when Insull went in as chairman of the board. He formed a separate By-Products Corporation, financed by sale of its stock; then proceeded to make and sell gas to the parent company cheaper than had been the case. Obligations were met. Peoples Gas was now a solvent and flourishing utility.

Was this man an Aladdin with lamp in his hand? The boss men of Chicago's battered traction companies believed so. They came to Insull with their difficulties, which were numerous. Insull took over. He combined the several shabby and conflicting and competing lines. He borrowed money, put out a bond issue. He got new equipment to improve the surface lines. He extended the elevated and suburban runs and restored the whole to comparative health, even though like much else in the city they continued to be graft-ridden.

Insull accepted graft as a condition of living in Chicago. Then and later he and his colleagues were always ready to aid whatever political party was in power. He was careful only that whoever was the dominating personality of the public utilities commission should enjoy the Insull generosity. Insull was also freehanded with all things described as "good causes" and no list of patrons of the arts, sciences, or charities was complete without Samuel Insull's name down for a fat contribution.

At suburban Libertyville, Insull established an estate, dressed in knickerbockers, and became a transplanted English squire, growing a sweeping mustache that turned white early and added a distinguished note to this mellow and affable country gentleman. Affable, that is, in his social life. In business he remained ruthless and dictatorial, and "his will seemed to dominate the affairs of Chicago."

Taking heed, long before most of his fellow power men, of the rising opposition to private utility companies, Insull began selling stock in his companies to employees and customers. These people, he thought, would create a bulwark against the mounting sentiment for municipal and government ownerships. Even more remarkable was Insull's attitude about "government interference," remarking publicly that if there was anything wrong about his business, he wanted to know it. He was generally courteous to critics. And once at least he said that if public regulation of private utilities failed, then public ownership would follow. But he did not want public ownership.

In 1912 Insull entered the phase of his career by which he is remembered, none too tenderly, 40 years later. To raise more money with which to expand his operating concerns, he formed Middle West Utilities, the first of his many holding companies. The growth of this concern over the next 20 years, remarks Francis X. Busch, was astonishing, for it came to serve "over 1,800,000 customers in some 3,500 communities in 39 states."

Although the several parts of Middle West Utilities were separately managed, all were directed by Insull himself. He was working harder than ever before, reaching his office before eight after the long drive from his suburban estate. He was dreaming bigger than ever. The time was the twenties, a period for monstrous dreams, a time for the whelping of stock-selling companies, of holding companies, the era when the common man was to become a minor capitalist, even though he carried a dinner pail to work.

This lush period could not have happened earlier than it did. It had to await the appearance of a vast congregation of speculators, or at least investors. The congregation developed in no small part because the years of World War I had created, through Liberty Bonds, a whole new class of investors, people who had never before owned a bond or a share of stock in anything. By the mid-twenties the demand for speculative opportunities had become great. Gifted men, among whom was Sam Insull, rose to the occasion. Within a brief time there appeared wonders like Giannini's Bancitaly Corporation, the pyramid of the Van Sweringens' railroad system, and Sidney Z. Mitchell's mountainous Electric Bond & Share Company. These were primarily stock-selling outfits.

So was Insull's newest creation, which he chose to call Utility Securities Company. This was merely a starter of what became known for a while as the Insull empire and later as the Insull bubble, or the Insull bust. It was an illusion composed of all of the concerns already mentioned as Insull properties, while piled on top were things like Insull Utility Investments, Inc.; Insull, Son & Company; Insull, Son & Company, Ltd. (England); Corporation Securities Company of Chicago; and Corporation Syndicates, Inc.

The relation to each other of these and of still other and minor Insull mirages need not be mentioned here. Owen D. Young, the corporation lawyer, covered the matter in a couple of sentences. It is "impossible," he said after delving into the Insull disaster, "for any man however able really to grasp the real situation [of that vast structure] . . . it was so set up that you could not possibly get an accounting system which would not mislead even the officers themselves . . ."

During the wild seven years of the twenties, it didn't matter. Americans would buy any stock just as they'd try a swig of any bottle plainly labeled whiskey. American business, so the prophets cried in the market places, was headed for new frontiers and a destiny undreamed of. It would carry with it to affluence all who possessed the wit to buy shares—shares in almost anything offered by these new and generous masters of capital who were inviting the man in the street, and even the street cleaner, along with the barber, the store clerk, the housewife, to join them in this golden opportunity.

Of these new-type masters of capital, surely the most potent was Sam Insull. In eight months of 1929, stock in Insull Utility Investments went from $30 to $147 a share. His other paper enterprises were almost as glittering, and the sun-crowned king of this incredible age was living regally up to his station. He scattered largess. On Wacker Drive he promoted and helped to finance the $20-million Chicago Opera House, and in it installed the Civic Opera Company, which he financed—briefly. It was believed that Insull's wealth far exceeded the fortunes of Chicago's earlier capitalists like Field, Pullman, and Armour. A local newspaperman said it was worth a million dollars to any man to be seen chatting with Sam Insull in front of the Continental Bank.

In January of 1929 there was no one to look over the edge of the cliff and note how far it was down to the bottom of the canyon. . . .

Insull's collection of paper corporations had long since entered the regions of unreality. The system on which he had erected the structure depended on continuous growth, or rather a continuous sale of shares. He must have something with which to pay dividends. Money to pay them had to come from new issues of stock. Simple enough. But continuous sale was imperative.

Insull could not retrench. He could only go on, and on he went, showing profits, paying dividends, and selling stock. His brokers stimulated matters in the usual manner by buying and selling Insull stocks to each other. As late as 1931 Insull's brokers, Halsey, Stuart & Company, were managing to peddle shares in Insull securities, chiefly to small investors who would be more likely than the big fellows to hold on to them.

There is good evidence that Insull himself still believed devoutly in each and every part of his monstrous pyramid of what one dislikes to call "properties" and thus abuse one of the most worthy and highly respected words in our language. He borrowed wherever he could, using stock as collateral. It was of no use. The current of liquidation was not to be dammed—not even by the five million dollars Insull borrowed on his own personal account from the National City Bank of New York and turned into the empty coffers of his Corporation Securities Company; or by another million dollars borrowed from General Electric which he used to reduce the National

City Bank loan; or by the half-million-dollar life insurance policy he turned in; or yet by the remnants of his own holdings in stocks and his four-thousand-acre estate. All of his personal property and that of his wife were turned over voluntarily to his creditors. . . .

Samuel Insull avoided personal bankruptcy by turning over to creditors his stocks, his estate, and his life insurance. But the Insull empire had gone to pieces, and in April—it was now 1932—the man with the black hood called at the Insull offices. "Does this mean receivership?" asked the old man. (He had turned 73.) He was told that it did. "I wish my time on earth had already come," he said. He was old, he was ill, he was mortally discouraged, yet somewhere in his tired and shrinking body remained a piece of the man's almost infinite energy; and because of this, Americans and the world at large were to be treated to a dandy cops-and-robbers chase on an international scale.

The saga of Insull the fugitive began quietly enough on June 14, 1932, two months after the receivership was announced. He and Mrs. Insull, with no protest from any quarter and with no great notice, sailed from Quebec for Europe.

In September the investigators of Insull's affairs got busy. It looked to them as if the losses to investors in Middle West Securities alone would run to more than $700 million. Add $85 million loss to shareholders in Corporation Securities.

The investigators also reported certain "irregularities," to use the genteel euphemism employed in the bankers' trade to cover almost any conceivable crime. A "crossloaning" of collateral had taken place between Insull companies. Illegal preferences had been given to favored creditors. Millions of dollars had been removed from assets to pay "questionable" brokers' fees. Insull's inner-sanctum crowd had operated a secret syndicate list by which big profits had been secretly paid to some sixteen hundred favored participants. Relatives and friends of Insull were found in bulk on company pay rolls. . . .

On September 25, Chicago papers reported that the federal Department of Justice had begun a full-scale investigation of the Insull companies.

On October 4, a Cook County (Chicago) grand jury returned indictments against Samuel Insull and his brother, Martin Insull, charging embezzlement from two of the Insull companies.

The investigations continued, resulting in two more indictments. One charged Samuel Insull and 16 others, including his son, Samuel Insull Jr., and Harold L. Stuart, of Halsey, Stuart & Company, with using the mails to defraud. The other said that the Insulls, father and son, and Stuart, had illegally transferred Insull securities with intent to defeat the National Bankruptcy Act.

It was now June 1, 1933. And where were the three Insulls? Martin, Sam's brother, it appeared, had taken up residence in Canada. Sam Jr., remained in Chicago. The old man, somebody suddenly recalled, was somewhere abroad. Over the cables went the news of the indictments, and in Paris an American newspaperman reported Sam Insull Sr., and wife to be living in an obscure hotel there. But when called upon, the old man denied his identity and promptly dropped out of sight.

But there was no hiding place. A news dispatch from Athens said Sam Insull and wife had taken residence there. . . .

Demands for arrest and extradition of Insull were made on the Greek government by the United States. Greece stood stoutly on its rights and refused to comply. The bickering continued by cable, while the Insulls remained unmolested and rather popular in Athens. But on December 5, 1933, the Greeks suddenly ordered Insull to leave the country on or before January 1. By fast work of Insull's Greek attorneys, who pleaded the old man's illness, the order of expulsion was extended to March 15. On that day police were sent to put Insull on a ship. They could not find him, not in Athens or elsewhere in Greece. . . .

His secret departure from Greece piqued the Greek government, which immediately set afoot an inquiry. All vessels that had recently sailed from Greek ports were radioed to report a list of their passengers. Promptly came back a wireless from the captain of the small tramp steamer *Maiotis*, bound for Egypt: Mr. Insull was a passenger; his papers were perfectly in order; he had left without notifying authorities simply to avoid publicity. The ship had been chartered by "an English friend of the refugee."

The *Maiotis* was ordered to return immediately to Piraeus, the port of Athens. It did so. Both the ship's and Insull's papers were found to be in order, and after a brief detention, the *Maiotis* and its full complement of passengers set forth again.

The flight and chase now took front-page position as one of the wide world's favorite news stories. The press flashed daily rumors of wireless negotiations between the refugee and several Mediterranean and other countries, asking permission to land and establish residence. These included French Somaliland, Ethiopia, Yugoslavia, Albania, Rumania, and Turkey. . . .

For several more days the *Maiotis*, now the best known vessel afloat, remained hidden in the ocean mists. Then, on March 28, she put into Istanbul for provisions. The United States ambassador, on direct orders from the State Department, demanded of the Turkish government that it arrest Insull forthwith. It complied. Insull was taken from the ship and placed in Istanbul's house of detention.

The old man was still fighting. Attorneys, probably engaged by the same "English friend" who had chartered the ship, appealed the Turkish court's order. Bickering began. Meanwhile, Insull remained in custody, attended by a valet whom he paid twelve cents a day, as the press took pains to report, and spent the time writing letters and reading novels. He appeared in surprisingly good spirits.

Turkish officials held that no appeal could be made. On April 11, 1934, American's most celebrated refugee was transferred, "under heavy guard," to the American Export liner SS *Exilona*, bound for New York City. The great chase was over.

Arrived at New York, Insull was put aboard a Chicago-bound train. Next day he entered Cook County Jail as prisoner. . . .

The case of the *United States of America v. Samuel Insull et al.*, for using the mails to defraud, came on for trial, as *Bench and Bar* quaintly put it, October 2, 1934. We need not go into it, other than to cite it as one of the most complicated of record. . . .

What the poor jury made of . . . [the] evidence was a cruel disappointment to the mass of Insull investors. Almost two months later, when everything had been said that either defense or prosecution could think of, the jury retired and in a little more than two hours returned with a verdict of not guilty for all of the defendants.

Then, in the following March, Sam Insull and his brother, Martin Insull, were put on trial for embezzlement of a mere $66,000 from Middle West Securities Company. The trial was brief. The jury said the defendants were not guilty.

As June 1935 came in, the federal government made one more attempt to fasten criminal guilt on Insull, his son, and Harold L. Stuart. The charge was that these three had, in contemplation of bankruptcy proceedings, illegally transferred certain property with intent to prefer selected creditors and defeat the purpose of the National Bankruptcy Act. The court held that the proof offered by the government was not very good and directed the jury to return a verdict of not guilty.

The old man's troubles in the criminal courts were over, though civil litigation continued to harass him until shortly before his death, which came July 16, 1938, in his seventy-ninth year.

Ivar Kreuger

JOHN TRAIN

Ivar Kreuger built a world-class empire and a world-class financial reputation. Unfortunately, he was also a world-class crook whose incredibly complicated deceptions, once discovered, destroyed him. It also destroyed Boston's leading investment bank, Lee, Higgenson & Co., and generated more than $1 billion in claims against Kreuger's bankrupt estate.

Unlikely as it seems, there was a period in the mid-1920s when a single man made two-thirds of all the matches in the world; that is, he controlled the two hundred-odd factories that made them, in some 35 countries. He held a legally enforced monopoly in 15 countries, a de facto monopoly in 9 others, and dominated the market in at least 10 more.

In the Middle Ages and thereafter European rulers often raised money by selling monopoly rights to certain manufacturers or mercantile activities; even into our own time many governments maintain state monopolies on tobacco; matches and tobacco go hand in hand, of course. These monopolies require careful policing, including undercover operations. In the heyday of the Kreuger dominance, Peru fielded armies of *agents provocateurs* who would pester prosperous-looking individuals on the streets of Lima, preferably foreigners, for a light. If the victim produced a non-monopoly match, or even a cigarette lighter, he was liable for a stiff fine—several thousand dollars in our money—of which half went to the informant: no small sum in Peru in those days.

But how did Ivar Kreuger ever reach this extraordinary position? In the first place, making matches was as characteristic an industry in timber-covered Sweden as winemaking in France. The principle of the safety match had been developed in Sweden, and by the late nineteenth century there was a proliferation of match factories. Kreuger's father ran three of them. Exports almost tripled from 1870 to 1900, and had doubled again by World War I.

As a child Ivar Kreuger manifested three of the traits for which he later became celebrated: memory for detail, zeal in concocting nefarious designs, and megalomania. He could recite sermons almost verbatim after returning from church; he would steal examination questions from his school principal's office and retail them to his classmates; and once, passing the Royal Palace, he announced, "I'm going to have one like it one day."

After receiving a university degree in engineering, young Kreuger in 1899 took ship to America, and then set forth on a voyage of several years to Cuba and Mexico, working as a construction engineer. He was one of 11 engineers on a bridge project near Vera Cruz, Mexico; all but two died of yellow fever. Once more in the United States, he was employed by various firms, notably the George A. Fuller Construction Company, and then went to South Africa to work on the Carlton Hotel in Johannesburg.

Returning to Sweden in 1907, he started his own construction firm, Kreuger & Toll, said to be the first in Sweden to guarantee customers against either delays or cost overruns. They received a number of major commissions, including the Stockholm City Hall—the *Stadhus*—and the Olympic Stadium. In time it spread into other European countries and diversified into banking and films. Greta Garbo's first screen appearance was in a Kreuger-backed production. The next move was back into matches. By 1915 ten companies had been assembled under his banner as United Swedish Match Factories. World War I interrupted Sweden's supply of phosphorus and potash; by securing better sources, Kreuger was able to outmaneuver and overcome his chief competitor, Jönköping-Vulcan; the two enterprises were merged as Svenska Tändsticks A.B.—the Swedish Match Company.

Sure enough, Sweden's leading architect was commissioned to build a splendid edifice of marble and bronze to house the new company . . . not far from the Royal Palace. Kreuger had achieved one of his ambitions. The citizens of Stockholm soon began calling it the Match Palace. Kreuger himself, inevitably, became known as the Match King (Tändsticks Küngen).

His own office in the Palace was notable for its Gobelins tapestries, wood-paneled walls, and fine antiques. A smaller, sound-proofed, completely private office had a red light over the door: when it was lit, the King could not be disturbed for any reason whatever. He was thinking. Reverently known as the Silence Room, it contained sleeping and washing facilities. Kreuger occasionally spent the night there.

Kreuger's conquest of the world match market proceeded forcefully, often by guile. Belgium was conquered by having a certain Sven Huldt prevail upon a number of other producers to group together under him in order to gain the strength to resist Kreuger. That objective achieved, Huldt promptly sold out to Swedish Match. Kreuger was more than willing to buy the services of agents of influence to persuade his victims to yield gracefully.

But what about the countries with government match monopolies? Governments get themselves into financial straits, and someone with cash can be confident of his welcome. Kreuger would arrange for a loan to a needy country, tied to his taking over the national match monopoly. Turkey,

Yugoslavia, Guatemala, Equador, and Peru were penetrated in this way. Millions went to Latvia and Estonia, to Rumania, Hungary, and Greece. For lending 75 million francs to France, he received the country's highest decoration. A newspaper editorial pronounced him "Olympian."

By this time the Match King was one of the most famous figures on the international business scene. In addition to Stockholm, he had residences in Paris and New York. He arranged for Lee, Higginson, a small but eminent Boston firm, investment bankers for General Motors and AT&T, to underwrite an initial securities offering of $21.8 million in stock and $15 million in debentures for his American company, International Match Corporation. Eventually Kreuger raised a total of $145 million in the United States. On the way over on the *Berengaria* to close the Lee, Higginson deal, Kreuger created something of a stir by booking the ship's commercial radio transmitter and receiver exclusively, around the clock, for the entire voyage, so that nobody else could send or receive messages. When the vessel docked, one of the reporters meeting it asked Kreuger if he had a light. Rather than pulling out the box he always carried, the Match King, smiling faintly, replied, "Sorry, gentlemen, I never seem to have one with me." The reporters ate it up.

This low-key manner was typical of Kreuger. He was a modest, pale, formal man, never flamboyant or domineering. On one occasion he arrived for a gay garden party on Long Island dressed entirely in black, complete with black bowler hat, like an undertaker. He even marched onto the court in this lugubrious outfit and played tennis!

In the heady days of the late 1920s, with stocks hitting new highs every day, Kreuger appeared to have an infallible golden touch. But in fact he was doing some perilous things. One of his favorite devices was an extensive use of off-the-books conduits. Roughly 400 were formed, often based in Liechtenstein and other jurisdictions with minimal controls, and funds were whirled around among them in a way that only Kreuger himself could keep straight. Even though the directors of Kreuger's corporations were generally puppets, the conduit companies' transactions were not reported to them or to the parent company's auditors. Even Kreuger's personal assistant, Kristor Littorin, knew "no more than the lift boy at Match Palace," in the words of a later investigator. The Match King wanted no prime minister, no privy council. An admirer of Napoleon, who held no councils of war, he liked to quote an observation of the emperor that "one first-class brain is enough for an army." International Match paid an absolutely regular 11 percent cash dividend; the world was inclined to take the rest on faith. This permitted Kreuger to funnel $16 million of the first Lee, Higginson underwriting, for instance, not directly into the match business but to Continental Investment Corporation of Vaduz, 80 percent of whose capitalization consisted of Kreuger's "personal guarantee." Why this arrangement? If anyone asked, Kreuger would calmly recite facts, names, and figures until the questioner was overwhelmed—but never give it in writing. Sometimes he would link a stock issue with a rumored new monopoly, to be secured by a loan to the host country. In 1924, for instance, he told his board that Spain had agreed to pay 16 percent interest on a loan of 124 million pesetas—more than enough to cover the 11 percent dividend and make a handsome profit. But the only other person who saw the actual loan agreement thought it seemed fake: the date was a curiously casual "January 1925." In July there was a similarly dubious loan to Poland.

In the great crash of 1929 and the early 1930s, the Match King seemed to repose serenely on a financial rock. Just two days after Black Thursday, Kreuger signed an agreement to lend $125 million to Germany. "Securities in companies like International Match which operate on sound foundations will always be good," he intoned. President Herbert Hoover received him regularly at the White House to discuss the economic situation and what to do about it.

But back in Boston they weren't quite so sure. Lee, Higginson sent Donald Durant, who looked after the International Match account, to Stockholm to sniff around. Kreuger gave his usual prodigious recitation of financial and industrial data, and to clinch matters held a splendid ball, attended by the flower of the nobility and the diplomatic corps; or so it seemed. It later emerged that many of the guests were hired for the occasion. An eminent International Match director, Percy Rockefeller, came to see for himself. His seance with the King in the Match Palace impressed him hugely. Kreuger's telephone rang at various times during their talk. Kreuger would say, "I am always available to talk to Mr. Baldwin. Good morning, Prime Minister! How good of you to telephone." Calls were put through from Premier Poincaré of France and, of all people, Joseph Stalin. Mr. Rockefeller, scarcely a neophyte, since he was on 60 other boards, was agog. "He is on the most intimate terms with the head of European governments," he reported back to his awed fellow directors. "Gentlemen, we are fortunate indeed to be associated with Ivar Kreuger." Alas, later investigations revealed that these cozy dialogues were just stage business conducted via a dummy telephone.

In 1931 Kreuger attracted notice by *over*paying his U.S. taxes by $150,000 . . . cheaper and more convincing than a conventional advertising campaign to assert his solvency. But as the Depression deepened, the wonderful structure began to come unstuck. Even matches, solid, basic business that they are, made less money, and of course Kreuger had to come up with huge amounts of cash, not only for the famous 11 percent dividend but for the loans to governments that were the basis of his monopolies. With the stock and bond markets collapsing, the money had to come from banks, and the banks were feeling sick themselves. Kreuger was reduced to desperate expedients, borrowing several times on the same security, even faking the collateral. He would give a bank manager a stack of banknotes and request a deposit receipt for, say, 100 million francs. If, when finally counted later in the day, the amount proved to be much less, Kreuger would apologize for the confusion and accept a receipt for the smaller amount, but in the interim the 100 million franc receipt would have done its work in another quarter. One of his most outrageous frauds was personally forging $143 million in Italian obligations. The job was so slapdash that the same signature—that of Director of Finances Giovanni Boselli—was rendered in several different styles.

The noose tightened. With the banks running dry and skepticism growing it became ever harder for the once omnipotent Match King to raise the immense sums required to keep the machine going as earlier creditors had to be paid off. A relatively small problem finally did it. Kreuger owned an interest in L.M. Ericsson, a leading Swedish telephone equipment company; ITT had expressed interest in buying his holdings for $11 million. Then ITT backed out. Something snapped. "*Jag minus inte längre, jag blir galen*," groaned the failing King: "I can't think anymore; I'm going crazy." He had a small stroke, became vague and listless. Since there was nobody else who understood his fantastic construction well enough to prop it up, it had to fall with its master. On March 12, 1932, Kreuger shot himself. A Price, Waterhouse audit revealed that both Kreuger & Toll and International Match were bankrupt.

Arsene Pujo

Arsene Pujo is not now a familiar name. When, however, as Chairman of the House Committee on Banking and Currency, he conducted the Pujo investigative hearings in 1912 and commanded the testimony of the leading figures in American finance, it was known across the country. His Committee's 1913 report identified a concentration of financial power in the United States, and led to enactment of a currency reform bill and the Clayton Anti-Trust Act. He died in 1939.

Although Mr. Pujo had been living in retirement at his Lake Charles home for the last 20 years, there was a time, in the early years of the century, when his name was a household word throughout America. This was because of an investigation by him as chairman of the powerful

Excerpted from the *New York Times*, December 31, 1939.

House Committee on Banking and Currency of the Sixty-second Congress. The investigation was held in 1912.

The Pujo Committee called the notable bankers of the day as witnesses, among them J. Pierpont Morgan, James A. Stillman and George F. Baker, all of whom have since died.

• • •

While the committee found no trust in the sense of a deliberate agreement to control the nation's wealth, it reported that there was a "well-defined identity and community of interest between a few leaders of finance which has resulted in a great and rapidly growing concentration of the control of credit and money in the hands of a few men, of which J.P. Morgan & Co. are the recognized leaders."

The committee came into being after a speech by Samuel Untermyer in which the New York lawyer charged that America was dominated by a "money trust." Representative Pujo took up the cry which resulted in the inquiry, and Mr. Untermyer became counsel for the committee. This was the first important investigation of its kind.

• • •

Mr. Pujo was born on a plantation on the banks of the Calcasieu River at Lake Charles on December 16, 1861. He was the son of Paul and Eloise M. Le Bleu Pujo. After attending public and private schools, he studied law privately before being admitted to the bar in 1886. His first political office was as a member of the Louisiana Constitutional Convention in 1898.

Four years later he was elected to the Fifty-eighth Congress. He remained a Representative until President Taft, backed by an opinion of Attorney General Wickersham, forbade the Controller to give the committee any more data on currency, whereupon the investigation was dissolved. A year earlier Representative Pujo was unsuccessful as a candidate for the Democratic nomination for Senator from Louisiana.

After returning to private life, Mr. Pujo . . . practiced law one flight up on the Main Street of Lake Charles. During the world war he was in charge of the selective-service draft board for the western part of Louisiana.

Ferdinand Pecora

Ferdinand Pecora, a native of Sicily and a noted prosecuting attorney, served as an original member of the SEC, ran for Mayor of New York, and was for many years a Justice on the New York State Supreme Court. He was best known for leading the U.S. Senate's investigation of Wall Street and the practices of American finance after the Crash.

Ferdinand Pecora, the former New York State Supreme Court Justice who rose to national fame for his investigation of Wall Street following the crash of 1929, died yesterday. . . . He was 89 years old. . . .

The Justice had retired from private law practice two years ago after a long and distinguished career in public service.

He continued his interest in public affairs in recent years. In 1966 he was one of a group of lawyers, members of Congress and former judges who joined to fight the Association of the Bar of the City of New York over the referendum to kill the Police Department's Civilian Complaint Review Board.

Mr. Pecora was nominated for Mayor by the Democratic and Liberal parties in September 1950.

• • •

At the time of his nomination, Mr. Pecora was a Justice of the Supreme Court, to which he was appointed by Governor Herbert H. Lehman in January 1935. He was elected to the post the next fall, and reelected, with the endorsement of all parties, in 1949.

Previously he had been, for many years, one of the city's leading prosecuting officials. The reputation he had won in New York took him for a time to Washington, to conduct one of the most successful Congressional investigations.

This was the Senate inquiry into the practices of American finance before the 1929 stock market crash, and the years that followed. In that investigation, during which a circus press agent photographed a midget seated in the lap of the great J. P. Morgan, a parade of financial giants passed before the committee, and were subjected to Mr. Pecora's examination. . . .

The conditions revealed led to clamor for widespread reform, and the New Deal administration passed the Securities and Exchange Commission Act. President Franklin D. Roosevelt appointed Mr. Pecora a member of

From *New York Times*, December 8, 1971.

the original SEC, but he resigned, after serving for six months, to accept Governor Lehman's appointment to the Supreme Court.

A byproduct of the justice's experiences with the SEC and the Senate investigation was a book entitled, *Wall Street Under Oath*, published in 1939.

• • •

Mr. Pecora was born in Nicosla, Sicily, on January 6, 1882, the first child of a poor couple, Louis and Rose Messina Pecora, who had six other children. The father, a shoemaker, brought his family to this country when Ferdinand was five. They settled in the Chelsea section of New York, in the neighborhood of St. Peter's Protestant Episcopal Church, and Ferdinand was confirmed there as a communicant.

At one stage, when he was 15, he planned to enter the Episcopal ministry. He enrolled at St. Stephen's College, but the family needed his financial help, and he decided to become a lawyer instead. He worked his way through City College and New York Law School, being graduated from the latter in 1906.

Admitted to the New York bar in 1911, he was appointed an assistant district attorney of New York County seven years later, serving until 1922. He was chief assistant district attorney from 1922 to 1930, when he resigned to enter the private law practice.

• • •

Mr. Pecora, a bit under average height, was affable and soft-spoken, slender, with graying hair and a dignified manner. He was "an easy man to talk to," a reporter who interviewed him many times said.

Albert H. Wiggin

FERDINAND PECORA

Perhaps no more vivid images in U.S. market history exist than those evoked by the record of the post-1929 Congressional hearings that threw an unblinking bright light of disclosure on Wall Street and its high-level insiders. There had been Crashes before. There had been Panics and Depressions before. But, never had the public been so massively involved before—and it was furious and not in a forgiving mood. Skulduggery is one thing; cynical, systematic, and continuous exploitation is something else again. The agent for redress appeared in the person of Ferdinand Pecora, the Senate Committee's examining counsel, who poked and probed in a manner carefully calculated to draw a maximum of self-incriminating admissions from the parade of Wall Street personalities ordered to appear before him. Mr. Pecora subsequently wrote a book about this experience, from which the next two pieces have been excerpted. Although Charles E. Mitchell was the Committee's first witness, his story follows that of Albert H. Wiggin here, to permit a second, even more pungent excoriation of Mr. Mitchell to immediately follow Mr. Pecora's description of this former pillar of the banking community.

Albert Wiggin was the chief executive of Chase National Bank, America's largest, when the Crash came. He was first employed by the Bank in 1904 and left it only on being forced to resign in 1932 at the peak of his dominance. What triggered his departure were the rather awful secrets about his operations in the stock of his Bank that Mr. Pecora brought to light. So great was the popular disapproval brought on by Mr. Wiggin's testimony that he felt obliged to renounce the annual pension of some $100,000 bestowed on him by the Bank in grateful recognition of his many years of faithful service.

"My pride in the Chase National Bank," wrote Albert H. Wiggin in his letter of resignation of December 21, 1932, "is the supreme satisfaction of my business life."

And there was much in the record to justify that pride. Mr. Wiggin in the course of the years had earned for himself a position as one of the very biggest and most important financiers in the United States at the very zenith of its business prosperity. . . .

When Mr. Wiggin first joined the bank in 1904, for example, it had 20 stockholders. When the Senate Committee investigated its affairs in October and November 1933, it had no less than 89,000 stockholders. In

Excerpted from Ferdinand Pecora, *Wall Street Under Oath* (A.M. Kelley Publishers). © Copyright 1939 by Ferdinand Pecora.

1904, it had a capital of $1,000,000, a surplus of $1,000,000, and deposits of $54,000,000. In 1930, following its merger with the Equitable Trust Company, it attained a capital of $148,000,000, a surplus of $148,000,000, and deposits of over two billion dollars. "It was at that time," testified Mr. Wiggin, "the largest bank in the world; and it is today one of the largest banks in the world, and the largest bank in the United States. And its ramifications are many. It is known in every town in the country, and in a great deal of the rest of the world." . . .

During all of this great development in size and power, Wiggin stood at the head of the institution, which he dominated. . . .

At one time Mr. Wiggin was the bank's largest stockholder. At all times it was admittedly under his general direction. When he became associated with the bank in 1904, he was vice-president. In 1911, he became president. In 1918, he became chairman of the board of directors. In 1930, due to the merger with the Rockefeller-controlled Equitable Trust Company, the ultimate control of the Chase Bank passed to the Rockefellers; John D. Rockefeller, Jr., became its largest stockholder, and Mr. Winthrop W. Aldrich, his brother-in-law, became president of the bank.

The bank became known, in the parlance of Wall Street, as the "Rockefeller Bank." But Mr. Wiggin still remained the active head and guiding spirit, with the exalted title of Chairman of the Governing Board—an inner "superboard" outranking the mere rank-and-file members of the board of directors proper.

The reputations of the bank and of Mr. Wiggin were as high and spotless as the bank was great and powerful. Mr. Wiggin's prestige and influence were, in fact, international. When a man was needed to represent American interests in connection with more than half a billion dollars of frozen German credits, he was the one selected. He was a member of the board of directors of [many] important corporations—no less than 59 in all. He was a director and member of the executive committee of the Federal Reserve Bank of New York. He enjoyed the distinction of being one of the favored few on a Morgan "preferred list.". . .

Even the various National Banking Examiners in 1928–1930, found it appropriate to remark that "the national banking system has a great standard bearer in the Chase National Bank," and characterized Mr. Wiggin who "dominates the policies of this institution," as "the most popular banker in Wall Street."

Surely, all this was enough, and more than enough, to inspire Mr. Wiggin's pardonable pride and "supreme satisfaction" in the record of the bank under his direction. Yet, despite the bank's enormous prestige, and despite Mr. Wiggin's pride in its history, the Senate Committee's investigation revealed that this "great standard bearer," behind its imposing facade of unassailable might and rectitude, was not a whit better than the National City Bank itself.

The earlier examination of the latter institution had certainly proved a shocking disclosure of low standards in high places. But it soon became apparent that the National City had no monopoly on improper banking practices; that, indeed, it was a question whether the Chase Bank did not actually exceed the National City, not only in the amount of its resources, but in the magnitude of its errors as well. . . .

Mr. Wiggin's personality on the witness stand was in striking contrast to Mr. Mitchell's. There was about him nothing of the latter's aggressive supersalesmanship. At rare intervals, he permitted a strain of sharp humor to color his testimony. But, in general, his answers were terse, succinct and directly to the point, with seldom an unnecessary word. Calm, shrewd, and cynical, he would admit that which could not possibly be denied, and even then, with what must strike an observer as superabundant caution. Unlike many of the leading figures who testified before the committee, he disdained to express more than perfunctory regret, and while he acknowledged certain past errors in judgment, he was not inclined to recognize any pressing necessity for radical change. He was most decidedly a die-hard.

Mr. Wiggin's conservatism was, indeed, too much for his own colleagues in the Chase Bank. The hearings presented at times the highly interesting spectacle of a head-on collision in opinion between the redoubtable Mr. Wiggin—for over a quarter of a century the guiding genius of the bank— and Mr. Aldrich, the representative of the new management and the new banking ethics. Mr. Aldrich, who had succeeded Mr. Wiggin as chairman of the governing board, differed violently with his predecessor's ideas as to how a bank should be run, and was at great pains to repudiate flatly many practices that Mr. Wiggin persisted in defending.

These differences were of sensational interest to the country in 1933, for in the minds of the general public, Mr. Aldrich meant the Rockefellers, and his placatory attitude was taken by the public to indicate a willingness on the part of the vast Rockefeller interests to cooperate with the still emerging New Deal. . . .

This revolution in the philosophy of the dominant Chase group was manifested first of all in the reversal of its long settled policy on the crucial question of bank affiliates. The Chase National Bank was well supplied with those useful adjuncts: whereas, as we have seen, the National City Bank had only one affiliate—the National City Company—the Chase National Bank, like the planet Jupiter, had at least five satellites. Chief among these was the Chase Securities Corporation. . . .

The Chase Securities Corporation was organized in 1917, following the example set by the National City and other banks. . . .

Altogether, the Chase Securities Corporation floated over six billion dollars of new security issues. This, while not as staggering an amount as the 20 billions of the National City Company, was sufficiently impressive;

especially in view of the fact that the Chase Securities Corporation did not "yield to the times"—as Mr. Wiggin put it—and commence to make public offerings, until 1928.

The total profits made by the Chase Securities Corporation, from 1917 to 1933, were over $41,000,000, more than $12,000,000 of which were made during the years of depression following 1929. But the activities of the Chase Securities Corporation were by no means confined to offering new securities. Just as in the case of the National City, its affiliates gradually led the Chase Bank not only into the field of investment banking proper, but into market pools, manipulations, and other kinds of dubious transactions. Yet Mr. Wiggin, as late as January 1933, saw no reason, so far as his own personal judgment was concerned, for requiring banks to stick to the business of banking, and forbidding them to engage, under a transparent corporate *alias*, in the business of stock gambling. . . .

Mr. Wiggin was not accustomed to condemnation, he was accustomed to praise. And to reward! His pride in the record of the bank may have been his supreme satisfaction, but it did not exclude more tangible satisfactions as well. As head of the Chase National Bank, for example, he received a salary of $175,000 in 1928, an equal amount in 1929, $218,750 in 1930, and $250,000 in 1931. As the reader will note, the deeper the depression, the higher Mr. Wiggin's salary. In 1932, Mr. Wiggin took a "cut" in salary, and received a mere $220,300. During these same depression years Mr. Wiggin, in his report to stockholders, was confidently denouncing the theory that high wages make prosperity, and declaring firmly that American business "may reasonably ask labor to accept a moderate reduction in wages, designed to reduce costs and to increase both employment and the buying power of labor." Needless to say, Mr. Wiggin saw no inconsistency between his views on wages in general and his own remuneration.

The above figures, moreover, represent only Mr. Wiggin's *regular* salary, as head of the Chase National Bank. He, and certain other leading officers, also received large additional sums as "bonus," awarded on the same generous principle that had inspired Mr. Mitchell and his brother officers to set up the famous National City Company "management fund." From this source, Mr. Wiggin received $100,000 in 1928, $100,000 in 1929, and, even in 1930, $75,000. Still further, while he received no regular salary from the Chase Securities Corporation, the bank's affiliate, he did receive from it large bonuses, which in some years ran as high as $75,000. . . .

These bonuses, to be sure, do not compare with the truly magnificent sums voted to themselves by Mr. Mitchell and his associates, out of the National City "management funds," and amounting . . . in Mr. Mitchell's case, to more than a million a year. As Mr. Wiggin sardonically remarked: "Our figures were small. It was a small bank."

Pity for Mr. Wiggin on this score, however, would be premature. To begin with, we must remember that being executive head of the largest bank in the country was only a part-time job for Mr. Wiggin and that in connection with his 59 variegated directorships, he was a member of numerous "finance committees," "executive committees," and the like. Quite frequently, he drew down handsome sums for his service in such capacities. . . .

Many of these corporations from which Mr. Wiggin received these helpful additions to his regular earnings, received large loans from the Chase National Bank, dominated by the same Mr. Wiggin. Mr. Wiggin, naturally, was quite positive that decisions on making those loans were in no way influenced by these circumstances, and it may indeed have been so. Yet it is obvious that these interlocking and possibly conflicting interests did not promote a healthy state of affairs.

But all this was only the beginning of Mr. Wiggin's lucrative activities. All his salaries and bonuses put together, would not have been great enough to begin to pay even the Federal taxes on his total income. Thus, in 1928, his salary as head of the bank was $175,000 and his bonus $100,000, a total of $275,000; but he, or certain private corporations which he and members of his family completely owned and controlled, actually had an income of over $6,800,000, and paid Federal incomes taxes of approximately $962,000! That is to say, his income for the year was over 25 times as great as the combined salary and bonus he received from the bank. . . .

To assist him in his private operations, Mr. Wiggin formed no less than six corporations, all of them owned and controlled by himself or members of his immediate family. Three of these were Canadian corporations, organized in the hope that they might prove useful in reducing income taxes. . . . [The other three had names formed from those of family members.]

There was very little sentiment, though, in the subsequent careers of these corporations. They were active and useful sources of profit, not incorporated heraldic monuments. When the Chase Securities Corporation, the bank's affiliate, was involved in what promised to be some especially profitable a bit of financing, for example, it was considered more tactful and proper to "cut in" the personal-sounding "Shermar Corporation," rather than crudely mention Mr. Wiggin by his everyday, noncorporated name. But chiefly, these corporations of Mr. Wiggin were used as the instruments through which he speculated, on a huge scale and with a minimum of risk, in the stock of the institution of which he himself was the chief fiduciary, that is, in the stock of the Chase National Bank itself.

Mr. Wiggin's private operations in Chase Bank stock for his own benefit, moreover, were intimately intertwined and synchronized with extensive and intricate manipulations of the same stock undertaken by the bank's own affiliates. The full story of these involved relationships is an incredible one. The National City Company, too, had traded on a stupendous scale in the stock of its own bank, but the lengths of which speculation and manipulation in Chase Bank stock were carried on for the benefit of "insiders," far transcended anything that was done in the National City.

Between September 1927, and July 1931, the Chase Securities Corporation, either directly, or through the Metpotan Corporation, which it owned, participated in and largely financed eight pools in the bank's stock. These pools were briskly conducted. One was no sooner wound up, than another was started. Sometimes several pools were in operation simultaneously. Mr. Wiggin, like other eminent financiers, did not like the term "pool," and preferred to call these operations by the more non-committal term, "trading accounts.". . .

However elegantly designated, the essential nature of the transactions could not be obscured. Altogether, they resulted in the purchase or sale of millions of shares of Chase Bank stock, involving $430,772,795 in purchases and $429,949,210 in sales, a total of over $860,700,000.

Mr. Wiggin could not be brought to admit that there was the slightest impropriety in the bank's encouragement of and participation in these gigantic pools in its own stock. In his opinion, they were "perfectly justified." Other participants in these pools, he conceded . . . were probably participating for the purpose of making money: but the Chase Securities Corporation itself, and the Metpotan, its subsidiary, were not similarly motivated. While not indifferent to possible profit, they were primarily interested, according to Mr. Wiggin, in "stabilizing the market," in increasing the number of stockholders, in "providing purchasing power," and in exercising a "steadying effect" upon the price of Chase Bank stock.

Unfortunately, despite their best efforts, they could not prevent the stock of the Chase National Bank from rising from 575, on September 21, 1927, the day the first of these eight pools was started, to the equivalent of 1415 (the stock had been split 5 for 1, and the high for the new stock was 283), in 1929, shortly before the bubble burst, at which price it was sold in large amounts to the public. By 1933, the new, split-up stock had declined to 17¾ (the equivalent of 89 for the old stock). It is evident that as a means of "steadying the market" in Chase Bank stock, these pools were a woeful failure.

It is quite true, however, that the amount of profits ultimately realized was by no means great. The Metpotan Corporation, the chief instrument through which the bank participated in these transactions, could show only the relatively negligible profit of $159,000 for the whole five years (1928–1932) trading in Chase Bank stock. . . .

A very different picture is presented when one turns to the private operations of Mr. Wiggin and his family corporations in the same stock and during the same period. It at once appears that Mr. Wiggin, in his private capacity, was marvelously more successful at this business of trading in Chase National Bank stock, than he was as head of the Bank. The contrast is astonishing. *Whereas Metpotan, as we have been, in pool transactions aggregating over $860,000,000, made only a miserable $159,000 profit for the whole period of 1928–1932, Mr. Wiggin and his corporations, during substantially the same period, from trades in the same stock, actually realized a cash profit of over $10,425,000—65 times as much!*

A part, but only a small part, of these millions came to Mr. Wiggin because the Chase Securities Corporation of Metpotan, obligingly "cut in" Mr. Wiggin's Shermar Corporation on some of the eight pools in the bank's stock already described. But the vast bulk of the money came from a different source, from transactions in which neither the Bank nor any of its affiliates shared a penny of profit.

Furthermore, a large part of this $10,425,000 which Mr. Wiggin made by trading in Chase National Bank stock, $4,008,538 to be exact, was reaped in the amazingly short period between September 19, 1929, and December 11, 1929, and in the very midst of the great Wall Street crash. To make four million dollars at any time is considered a brilliant achievement; to make that much money, in less than three months, and during the greatest collapse in the history of the stock market, would seem to call for a mysterious genius. But, like other mysteries, the answer, once found, was quite simple. Mr. Wiggin made all that money by selling Chase National Bank stock short. . . .

Mr. Wiggin not only sold short before the crash, he kept on selling short right through the crash, right through the fateful days of October and November 1929, when so many members of his own Wall Street community were frantically facing destruction, and while he himself was a leading member of the famous "bankers' consortium," organized to stabilize the market so far as possible. He did not stop until December 2, 1929, by which time he had sold 42,506 shares. Soon after, on December 11, 1929, he safely covered his short position, and realized that amazing profit of over $4 million.

Charles E. Mitchell

FERDINAND PECORA

Here, provided by Mr. Pecora himself, is a rather restrained description of the Charles E. Mitchell referred to in the Wiggin piece, and some highlights of Mitchell's testimony as the hearing's first witness. Sometimes known as "Sunshine Charlie," Mitchell and his National City organization came to epitomize what was "wrong on Wall Street" before the Crash and why a Securities Exchange Commission was a necessity after it. Basically a supersalesman, Mitchell was also a self-made man, a visionary, and possessed of a great capacity for focused hard work. To the end, however, he could not admit that many of his most successful personal moves involved a massive misuse of his bank and of his power in it.

The first to take the stand was Charles E. Mitchell himself, Chairman of the Board of the National City Bank. He was an impressive figure, forceful, self-confident, and persuasive. He was then about fifty-six years old, a self-made man in the American tradition, raised to the financial heights by his innate capacity and will, and a dominant and attractive personality. He had first become connected with the National City organization in 1916, and had risen rapidly to its leadership. While he insisted that he was by no means all-powerful, he admitted that "my associates considered that anything could not have been done if I had opposed it."

Under his sway the watchword was expansion to the limit. The National City Bank's branches in Greater New York rose to seventy-five; it also had branches scattered around the world in various countries. Its capital stock was increased to $110,000,000 par value. Its affiliate, the National City Company [an investment dealer], grew by itself into a vast organization. . . .

In 1929, the affiliate had, on its own account, no less than 1,900 employees and 69 branch offices in at least 58 cities, in addition to 26 branches of the Bank which acted as adjuncts to its sales force. It had 11,300 miles of private wire between its various offices, "up and down the coast . . . across the continent, with loops to Minneapolis and St. Paul, and so forth." The Company did business with hundreds of small investment dealers throughout the country, and used these too as channels for the distribution of its products. Many of these dealers were themselves banks with investment departments, out-of-town correspondents of the National City Bank. It had branches in London, Amsterdam, Geneva, Berlin, and a large number of correspondents in other countries. It was interested deeply in sugar, copper, and oil. It arranged mergers and dissolutions. It did an astonishing amount and variety of business.

Mr. Mitchell assumed, throughout his testimony, the loftiest moral tone, no matter how questionable the transactions were with respect to which he was interrogated. Yes, he was only human, "filled with error," and had made many mistakes; but so had everyone else. The bank, under his direction, had pursued some policies he now viewed as unsound—but hindsight was wiser than foresight. The public, it is true, had perhaps not in all cases been treated with maximum frankness—but the National City was itself spontaneously remedying all this, and "blazing a trail" to more adequate safeguards for the investor.

Mr. Pecora: The National City Company is the biggest investment house in the country, isn't it? Do you know of any bigger? . . .

Mr. Pecora: Yes; but isn't the National City Company the largest investment company selling securities to the public?

Mr. Mitchell: I should think probably; but I would not want to make any boast about that, Mr. Pecora.

Mr. Pecora: It would not have been unbecoming for the National City Company to have taken the lead in bringing about a change in custom with regard to putting out fuller information to the public?

Mr. Mitchell: We are doing it every day. We are issuing to the public today more complete information regarding the condition of the companies that we finance than we ever have in our history, and we are trying to go a very long way. We are trying to blaze a trail with respect to that.

Mr. Pecora: When did you commence to blaze that trail?

Mr. Mitchell: I should say a year and a half ago. We have learned much. We have all made mistakes, and a man that cannot profit by it certainly is not very worthy. We are trying to blaze the way for investment finance into a higher ground than it has been.

• • •

Yes, there had been a great gambling mania in 1927–1929, but the National City had nothing to reproach itself for in this respect: it had "tried to prevent overspeculation." Actions which others might find highly improper seemed to Mr. Mitchell to present "nothing criticizable." At all times, he was merely doing his "duty as a banker."

Mr. Mitchell's conception of his "duty as a banker," however, was a far different thing from the standards of that profession as they existed in previous times. To a large extent, of course, it was not a question of Mr. Mitchell's or any other individual's standards, but rather of a revolutionary change in the character of American banking itself. . . .

The National City alone, under Mr. Mitchell's pioneering direction, came to sell not less than $1,000,000,000 of securities per year, and sometimes $2,000,000,000—aggregating the enormous total of at least $20,000,000,000 in securities which the National City manufactured, or in the manufacture of which it participated, for the ten years preceding the Senate investigation. And the National City not only "manufactured" (the phrase is Mr. Mitchell's) these huge quantities of securities, "suitable for public distribution"—it likewise sold these securities like so many pounds of coffee to the public. (This analogy likewise is Mr. Mitchell's.) Under his leadership, the National City grew to be not merely a bank in the old-fashioned sense, but essentially a factory for the manufacture of stocks and bonds, a wholesaler and retailer for their sale, and a stock speculator and gambler participating in some of the most notorious pools of the "wild bull market" of 1929.

But how was this possible? For surely, the layman will protest, the law does not permit a bank to engage in such activities. A bank, especially a national bank, is, or is supposed to be, sacrosanct, its power strictly limited by Act of Congress, and its activities carefully and regularly examined by skilled examiners.

The layman is right. But he has reckoned without the ingenuity of the legal technicians and the complaisance of governmental authorities toward powerful financial and business groups during the lamented pre-New Deal era. With their superior advantages, a method was worked out whereby a bank could assume a veritable dual personality. In one aspect—the aspect which it presented to the bank examiner and as to which it was subject to governmental control—it observed strictly all the proprieties of a properly managed bank. In the other aspect, it knew no regulation and no limitations: it could, and did, engage in the most diverse, risky and unbanklike operations.

The technical instrument which enabled the bank to carry on in this Dr. Jekyll-Mr. Hyde fashion was known as the "banking affiliate." How the scheme was worked out may best be explained by telling the story of the organization of the National City *Company*—as distinguished from the National City *Bank*. The Bank was founded in 1812; the Company, only in 1911. At the time of the inception of the Company, its capital stock was fixed, for the time being, at $10,000,000. The certificate of incorporation, obtained from the State of New York, permitted the new Company to be almost *anything but a bank*, a railroad or an educational institution. But the beneficial title in the stock of this new, nonbanking corporation was owned by the very same persons who were the stockholders of the National City Bank, and they held their interests in the old and the new corporations in identical proportions.

And where did the $10,000,000 capital of the new corporation come from? It came from the proceeds of a special forty per cent dividend declared upon the stock of the Bank itself. Not a penny of new money was contributed by anyone. All the shareholders of the Bank, the recipients of this extraordinary dividend, agreed by mutual consent that the proceeds should go, not into their own pockets, but to the uses of the new Company. Now, who was to direct the destinies of this new Company? Not its real stockholders directly (who were identical with the stockholders of the Bank); instead, a "trust agreement" was set up, that is, an arrangement whereby the legal title and the voting control of the stock were vested in three individuals, who held the stock in trust for the real, ultimate beneficiaries—viz., the stockholders of the Bank.

And who were these three all-powerful "trustees" of the new Company? Originally, James Stillman, Sr., then the Chairman of the National City Bank; Frank A. Vanderlip, then President of the Bank, and Stephen S. Palmer, a director of the Bank. What is more, if one of the three trustees resigned or died, the other two could pick his successor, *but only from the ranks of officers or directors of the Bank*. If a trustee ceased to be an officer or director of the Bank, he ceased automatically to be a trustee of the Company, "it being intended that only officers or directors of the Bank shall act as trustees."

Each stockholder of the Bank was thus simultaneously the owner of a proportionate beneficial interest in the Company, through the trustees who had legal title to the Company's entire capital stock. Nor could a stockholder sell his interest in the Bank, without at the same time selling his interest in the Company, for it was provided that the two were inseparable. The very certificates of stock ownership in the Bank and of beneficial interest in the Company were printed on the reverse sides of the same sheet of paper, physically as well as legally indivisible. In brief, the two corporations—the Bank and the Company—were in all but name, one institution. . . .

Mr. Mitchell reigned undisputed. He had become President of the Company in 1916; in 1921, he became President of the Bank as well; in 1929, he became Chairman of the Board of the Bank, the Company, and the Trust Company.

The National City Bank and Company, at its zenith, was a gigantic monument to Mr. Mitchell's supersalesmanship, his limitless energy, and driving genius. But its sensational expansion was not attained without bringing with it equally sensational abuses. . . . At the root of most of the mischief there was always present, in some form or other, the influence of the banking affiliate—a ready facility for financial misadventure.

Charles E. Mitchell

EDMUND WILSON

"Charlie Mitchell has been arrested at the orders of the President of the United States and while we have got him, let us take a look at him." These words and the other language and expression in the next story convey something of the revulsion and near hate that Mr. Mitchell's appearance before the Senate Investigating Committee produced in the popular mind. As reported here in a 1933 excerpt from *The New Republic*, Mr. Mitchell's faults were not treated as circumspectly as they had been by the committee's Mr. Pecora. Here, he is made a figure of ridicule and denigration, ". . . a man of low order, caught in suspicious circumstances and hard put to it to talk himself out."

A young college man, according to a legend of the boom, went to work at the National City Bank. One day Charles E. Mitchell, then its president, came through on a trip of inspection. "Mr. Mitchell," said the young man in a low voice, "may I speak to you a moment?" The great banker and bond salesman scowled: "What is it?" The young man politely pressed him to step aside out of earshot of those present. Still scowling, Mitchell complied. Said the young man in a discreet whisper: "Your trousers are unbuttoned, sir." "You're fired!" flashed the great financier.

In those days, the trousers of Charles E. Mitchell could no more be unbuttoned than Louis the Fourteenth's grammar could be at fault. He was the banker of bankers, the salesman of salesmen, the genius of the New Economic Era. He was the man who had taken the National City Company, that subsidiary of the National City Bank which had been established, according to the practice of the New Economic Era, as a legally distinct but actually identical institution to set up shop for the disposal of the securities which the bank was forbidden to sell, and had transformed it in six years' time from a room with a stenographer, a boy and a clerk into an organization with a staff of 1,400 and branch offices all over the country, which sold a billion and a half dollars' worth of securities a year, the largest corporation in the country. At its summit, like an emperor, sat Mitchell, dynamic, optimistic and insolent, sending out salesmen in all directions as he preached to them, bullied them, bribed them; had them clerking in security shops on the street level of every provincial city where they sold bonds like groceries in A. and P. stores; had them knocking at

Edmund Wilson, *The New Republic*, June 28, 1933, pp. 176–178. Reprinted with the permission of The New Republic.

the doors of rural houses like men with Fuller brushes or vacuum cleaners; had them vying with each other in bond-selling contests; had them intimidated, intoxicated, always afraid of being fired if they failed to sell more and more bonds—"You cannot stand still in this business!—you fellows are not *Self-Starters!*"—till they resorted to faking orders merely to inflate the figures and invested their own salaries in these securities about which they knew as little as the people they were selling them to.

The days of the highly respectable banker who advised widows and young people, were over. The public had the salesmen always at their heels: the salesmen had always behind them the megaphone voice, the indomitable jaw, the nagging telegrams, of Mitchell. He sold the American public over fifteen billion dollars' worth of securities in ten years. He sold them the stock of automobile companies which almost immediately turned to water; he sold them the bonds of South American republics on the verge of insolvency and revolution; he sold them the stock of his own bank, which after October, 1929, dropped in three weeks from $572 to $220 and which was recently worth $20. In the minds of the public, of his minions, of himself, Mitchell had reached the apotheosis of the Caesars. In his days of greatness, it was boasted, he always traveled by special train. One of his salesmen, who was afterwards ruined by his investments in the Mitchell securities, described his master's brain as "spinning like a great wheel in a Power House" and spoke almost with trembling of the terror he inspired. . . . Mitchell blazed like the great central source of the energy and heat of the boom: his colleagues called him "Sunshine Charley."

Today that sunshine has faded. Charley Mitchell looks cheap in court. Through long sessions of the muggy June weather while the reporters go to sleep at their table and the judge invites the jury to take their coats off, among the pallid creatures of the courtroom whose skins have never known any other light than that of the soapy globes of the courtroom chandeliers, whose fat legs have never known any exercise other than stalking the courtroom floor, Mitchell sits behind the wooden railing that separates the spectators from the trial, broad-shouldered but short-legged, his grizzled hair growing down his neck and forehead, his long nose with its blunt end no longer driving salesmen out to their prey but bent humbly down toward the table. Against the neutral complexions and the tasteless clothes of the courtroom, he is conspicuous for his ruddy face and for the high stiff white collar, the blue serge suit, the white handkerchief sticking out of the breast pocket of the big downtown days of the boom. At first glimpse, when you only see his back, he seems dignified, distinguished; then you see that he looks sheepish. Behind him ledgers, suitcases, crammed briefcases are all that is left of the boom—those immense profits, those mighty transactions, the florid boasts of the bankers, the round-eyed hopes of the public, now merely a tableful of papers to be produced in court.

Sitting quiet, looking often toward the clock, he listens to the witnesses called to testify as to whether or not his sale to his wife of 18,300 shares of National City Bank stock, his sale of 8,500 shares of Anaconda Copper stock and his failure to report $666,666.67 from the management fund of the National City Bank, were devices to evade the income tax. Max Steuer, Mitchell's lawyer, has called him a "big fish victim of mob hysteria"; and the idea of big fish haunts you as you watch the officials of J. P. Morgan and of the National City Bank trying not to get their bosses in trouble. The boom produced its own human type with its own physical and psychological characteristics, its own more overblown and softer-headed species of the American business man. . . .

He tells deliberately a very halting story. The sales were real sales, his wife really wanted to buy the stock, he had the very best legal advice to guarantee their legality, etc. When he pledged his personal resources to help the National City Company buy National City Bank stock during the first stockmarket crash, he had not hoped to get anything out of it, he had merely been trying to save the bank. Yet Mrs. Mitchell . . . had not had enough income to pay even the interest on the loan from Morgan necessary to carry the stock she was supposed to have bought, but had not paid for; no transfer stamps had been attached to the letter recording the sale; and afterwards Mitchell had bought the stock back from his wife at the same price. He had bought the other stock back in the same way; and the $666,666.67 which has been asserted by the defense to have been a loan had, according to the prosecution, been written off the books of the bank as if it had been a bonus.

On the stand Mitchell's prestige evaporates. The perfect type of the big executive of the cigarette and success-course advertisements undergoes a degradation. Confronting the lawyers with his blue suit, his robust torso and grizzled crest, with his scowling brows of power and his forceful nose joined by coarse lines to his wide and common mouth, he throws out his hands in stock gestures of frankness and exposition, making things clear weakly; tries to put over points with a finger that no longer carries conviction; breaks down in the middle of sentences, frowning helplessly, his mouth hanging open. . . .

It is wrong to take out on individuals one's resentment against the abuses of institutions. Charley Mitchell, the investment superman, could never of course have been created without the mania of the public to believe in him. It was the climate and soil of the boom which made the ambitious boy who worked his way through Amherst by giving courses in public speaking, the smart clerk at Western Electric who used to pay out part of his weekly $10 to take business courses at a night-school—it was the climate and soil of the boom which nurtured this being and his fellows. . . .

Charley Mitchell has been arrested at the orders of the President of the United States and while we have got him, let us take a look at him. The head of the biggest financial institution in the country, whose arrogance was lately so great that it was reputed to constitute *lése majesté* to tell him his pants were unbuttoned and who, proceeding in the same spirit, did not even think it necessary to go through the formalities of covering up his frauds against the government, is a man with a full-fleshed common face and a fierce unconvincing eye—a man of a low order, caught in suspicious circumstances and hard put to it to talk himself out.

GREAT
FINANCIAL HOUSES

Alexander Baring

JOHN ORBELL

Alexander Baring was Francis Baring's second and most able son. Posted to the United States in 1795 at age 21, he soon proved his competence by enlarging and enhancing the firm's U.S. presence and by contributing importantly to America's successful acquisition of the Louisiana Territory from France. Later, after his return to Britain, he helped negotiate the Webster-Ashburton treaty governing border disputes between the United States and Canada. This historical glimpse is from a history compiled by the firm's archivist.

Alexander Baring moved with great ease amongst the elite of the business community of the United States, and the confidence he exuded, backed by the standing of his father's house, is reflected in the accounts he captured. These included the account of the Bank of the United States which acted as agent for the United States government in paying interest on its funded debt in London and Amsterdam, and in handling exchange matters. For Barings this was safe and lucrative business. Of greater importance were commissions undertaken for the United States government which began in 1795 and were renewed in 1798 when the house handled the government's purchase of weapons in Europe, and continued in the following year when it acquired the government's shareholding in the Bank of the United States for £267,516 enabling the liquidation of a debt to the Bank. In 1803 Barings was rewarded by being appointed to the highly prestigious office of financial agents in London for the United States but, its greatest triumph in American affairs was to come later that year.

In 1802 it became known that Spain had ceded the one million square miles of the Territory of Louisiana to France. A combination of United States fears for French aggrandizement in North America, coupled with the growing needs of the French government for funds for military campaigns in Europe, culminated in negotiations for the sale of Louisiana to the United States. Alexander Baring accompanied United States officials, Monroe and Livingston, to Paris where he acted as their financial adviser and, in bargaining with the French, was largely instrumental in scaling down their demands from 100 million to 60 million francs. The deal was mostly financed through the issue of $11.25 million United States government bonds to the French government which sold them to Barings and Hopes

John Orbell, Baring Brothers & Company, Limited, undated. Reprinted by permission of the author and with the compliments of ING Bank N.V.

who placed them in the London and Amsterdam markets. The addition of the Territory of Louisiana approximately doubled the area of the United States, with 15 states created out of it in whole or in part.

The scale of this business was immense. "It is of the utmost magnitude and importance, might stagger us in normal times," wrote a partner of Hopes, and Sir Francis complained he scarcely had "the nerves" for it. But the business was not without its problems, most of which turned on the ambiguity of the house's position in financing an enemy of the British Crown. The negotiations had been conducted in the wake of the Treaty of Amiens (1802), which had brought a temporary peace with France, when the British government thought "it would have been wise for this country to pay a million sterling for the transfer of Louisiana from France to America." With the resumption of hostilities in late-1803, attitudes changed and the Prime Minister, Henry Addington, advised Sir Francis that "in view to the projected invasion of this Kingdom, . . . I have . . . to desire that you would decline being party to any remittances to France on account of the debt due from the United States of America in consequence of the cession of Louisiana." Whilst the house immediately acquiesced to this demand, throughout 1804 it was making substantial sales of Louisiana stock in the London market in conjunction with Hopes. One estimate puts these at about $6 million although the means through which this was achieved are unclear.

Alexander Brown

FRANK R. KENT

The firm that Alexander Brown founded in Baltimore circa 1800 was parent to four firms; three continued 200 years. Brown himself was said to have had knowledge, judgment, character, courage, vision, and a zest for the mercantile trading game. He appears also to have been possessed of a certain instinct for doing things correctly. More than one of his correspondents spoke of this instinct as being "uncanny."

Alexander Brown . . . loved his work. [An exceptional trove of] letters to his sons and his customers covering the period from 1800 to 1834 breathe an unmistakable zest, a genuine love for the romance of business, a pride

---

Excerpted from Frank R. Kent, *The Story of Alexander Brown & Sons* (publisher unknown) 1925, pp. 22–23, 25–29, 47–50, and 111–113.

and joy in the vindication of his judgment and in the justification for the risks he ran. . . .

It is doubtful whether any other similar records exist in the United States. Certainly there are none covering so long and unbroken a period or disclosing quite the same sort of history. The fact that through 125 years they have been kept in a nearly perfect state of preservation is almost as remarkable as the records themselves.

There are nearly 100 volumes and, because of the story they tell, they are practically priceless. That all other business men of the time kept similar records is hard to believe. They entailed endless patience, labor, care. In those days, before the cable, the telegraph and telephone, business instruction in letters had to be of the most minute and detailed kind. Apparently every letter written by the firm of Alex. Brown & Sons, from the day of its foundation until the letter press came into use, was copied by hand in these "letter books."

From them is gleaned the history of the firm and the facts about the character and career of the great man who was its founder.

For he was a great man. No one can possibly go through these musty old books, now about to fall to pieces, and not grasp that fact. Through these thousands of letters, painstakingly written with his own hand, and almost all cold, formal, and rigidly restricted to business, touching politics and war only as they affected business—through them all there somehow breathes a spirit of genuine, unmistakable bigness. In the coldest and most condensed notes of acknowledgement you sense his character: upright, strong, dominant, determined, daring. It is curious in going through these books and reading these letters of long ago, signed "Alexander Brown," how extremely easy it is to pick out the ones that were written by Alexander Brown and those written by the sons. It is simply not possible to mistake them. There was a note of command, of decision, of authority in every line. . . .

They—these letters—reveal him, too, as more than merely a great businessman of his time. They show him as the leading figure of his community, a public spirited and philanthropic citizen, a clean thinking, constructive and patriotic man, whose mental range and vision were wide and clear. A big man, but by no means a perfect man, for these business letters also reveal that this first Alexander Brown could, when aroused by some moral transgression, display intolerance and an unforgiving spirit. . . .

From his business letters you get the impression of an eagle-eyed and keen-brained man who, through his agents, kept himself informed of conditions in every quarter of the globe, buying and selling as a result of ripened judgment, much experience and wide knowledge. His correspondents were located at the pivotal points, the pivotal cities at home and capitals abroad. They wrote him of political as well as financial conditions. He wrote back, analyzing the facts as presented to him, checking them up one against the other, forming his judgments and directing his agents to buy, sell, borrow or "stand pat," as the situation seemed to demand. . . .

Handicapped by the slowness in communication, the way in which that directing brain could marshal the resources of all those widely separated branches, hook them up together and successfully drive them, with each son playing his allotted part, pulling exactly the load given him, was a remarkable and thrilling thing even as it is partially disclosed by the cold and restrained letters of instructions written by the head of the firm. One cargo was balanced against another; one agent supplemented another; one brother pulled where the other left off—all working separately and yet all together, but none knowing the full scope of the deal except the father and head of the firm in Baltimore—and he never overlooked a vital factor: insurance, exchange, commissions, warehouse receipts, embargoes, politics. Slight scope for originality or initiative was allowed his sons and partners by Mr. Brown. Their job was to carry out his orders. He did the heavy thinking for them and the rebuke came swiftly and mercilessly when they failed or departed from the letter of instructions. In all the years in which he exchanged thousands of letters with his sons there appear amazingly few words of affection or evidences of sentiment. Yet they loved him devotedly and were so broken up by his death that, for a while, the decision as to whether or not to continue the firm as a going concern trembled in the balance.

• • •

In order to facilitate his operations it became necessary to establish agencies of the firm in Charleston, Savannah, New Orleans and Mobile. In each of these places Mr. Brown found a solid, reputable, reliable man. With each of them he made terms sufficiently liberal to insure absolute loyalty. To each of them, after a sufficient trial, he gave his complete confidence and friendship. It was a deliberate policy with him, laid down specifically in letters to his sons, that it paid to form business alliances only with the highest type and most trustworthy of men, and that, in dealing with such men, the utmost generosity and trust were required.

To his rigid adherence to these convictions is unquestionably due no little of his great success as a trader. It was not only cotton but tobacco, too, that he began to export, through these agents, on a large scale. As a natural consequence of these extensive importing and exporting activities there developed an international banking business as an indispensable adjunct. For this, the Brown firm was in an exceptionally good position, for, while other American merchants did not have connections abroad sufficiently close to make them eager to take the risk of buying commercial bills on Great Britain, Alex. Brown & Sons, through its branch in Liverpool and its family associations in England, had a complete knowledge of the standing and credit of most English merchants, which enabled them to purchase these bills freely, covering their transactions by selling their own drafts on Liverpool.

Thus it was that in those early days the Alexander Brown house acquired control of a considerable share of the sterling exchange business of this country. Alexander Brown's name on bills gave them currency in the markets of the world. That is an exact statement and that situation existed within 15 years after Mr. Brown landed in Baltimore. It was a remarkable tribute to his genius and judgment as a business man. Not only was the name of Alexander Brown on bills sufficient to give them credit practically anywhere but, conversely, Americans who wished to import goods, if their reputation abroad was not sufficiently well established to make direct purchases, applied to Alexander Brown for credits on his Liverpool house. No other firm in America was in quite the strategic position to do a general exchange and credit business and it was not long before this branch of the business became a very important part of the firm's activities, although while Alexander Brown lived, it was never allowed to become the dominant end.

• • •

The change from a strictly mercantile house to merchant banking, though rapid, was almost imperceptible. Alexander Brown became a banker and a financier largely for the reasons given in the foregoing chapters and because he grew so wealthy as a result of successful trading that this aspect of the business became of primary importance. To keep his money employed and his profits turning over, he had to offer credit to others. . . .

The banking end was a necessary adjunct of his business. He knew that end and neither neglected it nor minimized its importance, but it was in the shipping end, in the moving of cargoes from port to port, the buying of goods here at a low price, because of depression in the market or an over abundance of the crop, and selling them at a high figure in some other port of the world where there was a shortage and a demand that Alexander Brown excelled.

• • •

It is not possible to exaggerate the value the first Alexander Brown placed on his reputation and that of his firm. He kept it fresh in the minds of his sons through his letters when they were away from him, and by precept and preaching when they were at home. He never missed an opportunity to impress upon them the importance of keeping free from questionable transactions and shady people. "Do no business," he wrote time and time again to William in Liverpool, John in Philadelphia, and James in New York, "with those you cannot trust." "Better to lose the business than have an uneasy mind."

It was also a matter of pride with Alexander Brown that he and his firm should be identified with every progressive development and civic movement in Baltimore, the city in which he was located. It was this feeling that made him, in 1825, one of the incorporators of the Maryland Institute of Art; that made him throw his weight behind the erection of a municipal water works; that caused him to head the list of Baltimore subscribers for the relief of the sufferers from the great fire in Savannah; that prompted him to take a prominent part in the ceremonies of the laying of the cornerstone of the Washington Monument in 1815, and, in the same year, the laying of the cornerstone of the monument commemorating the Battle of North Point.

• • •

It was doubtless this spirit also that prompted him to do a perfectly characteristic thing. At great expense to his firm he fought for a principle when the immediate stake was but a few dollars. He employed the leading lawyers of his day and carried the case to the Supreme Court of the United States where Chief Justice Marshall rendered a decision laying down certain fundamental principles of Constitutional Law that had made the case one of the half dozen most important decisions rendered by the Court since its foundation. The case is known as *Brown vs. Maryland* and is recorded in 12 Wheaton p. 420.

The facts were, that the Maryland Legislature passed a law requiring all importers and wholesalers of imported goods to take out a license and pay a fee of $50 thereupon. For failure to take out such a license there was to be imposed a fine of $100 and forfeiture of the amount of the tax.

Here was but a small amount of money at stake, but a great constitutional principle was involved, as to whether or not the United States government had the exclusive power to regulate commerce. If the State of Maryland possessed the power to impose a license tax on imports, so did every other state, and if such power existed why should the states confine themselves to nominal taxes on imports alone?

Alex. Brown & Sons refused to take out a license. Alexander, George, John and James were indicted in the City Court of Baltimore for doing business without a license and judgment was rendered against them in the Maryland Courts. They took their case to the Supreme Court of the United States. William Wirt and Jonathan Meredith represented the Browns; Roger Brooke Taney and Reverdy Johnson the State of Maryland. It was an array of great lawyers arguing before one of the greatest judges of all history.

On March 12, 1827, Chief Justice Marshall delivered the opinion of the Court in favor of the Browns, laying down certain principles of power reserved to the national government. We now see clearly that this solid foundation and unit control were absolutely necessary as a base for the great international commerce of the United States.

The Court found that the Act under which the Browns were indicted was repugnant to that Article of the Constitution which declares:

"that no State shall lay any impost or taxes on imports or exports."

and in response to the argument that the duty was a very light one and was not of the character held repugnant by the constitutional provisions, the Court said:

> It is obvious that the same power which imposes a light duty, can impose a very heavy one, one which amounts to a prohibition. Questions of power do not depend on the degree to which it may be exercised. If it may be exercised at all, it must be exercised at the will of those in whose hands it is placed. If the tax may be levied in this form by a state, it may be levied to an extent which will defeat the revenue by impost, so far as it is drawn from importations into the particular state.

The Court also held the Act repugnant to the clause in the Constitution which empowers "Congress to regulate commerce with foreign nations, etcetera."

Johann Heinrich Schröder

RICHARD ROBERTS

Johann Heinrich Schröder's long life spanned the years from 1784 to 1883, a period of immense change and development in Europe. He and his firms participated fully in the evolution, extending and expanding considerably his family's original merchanting business. On becoming firmly establishing in England, he anglicized the name of his London firm to J. Henry Schroder Co., which his successors made into an international leader in investment management and merchant banking. This historical precis provides detail and perspective on the development process.

Johann Heinrich Schröder was born on 12 December 1784 and died 98 years later on 28 June 1883. At his birth, the Industrial Revolution was in its infancy but by the time of his death, factory production, railways, steamships and the electric telegraph were commonplace in the industrial nations. The creation of the modern industrial economy was accompanied

Excerpted from Richard Roberts, *Schroders: Merchants & Bankers*, MacMillan Press Ltd., 1992, pp. 26–42.

by an enormous increase in international trade, in the development of which Johann Heinrich's firms were involved. During the course of his lifetime he was a partner in four merchant firms conducting international trade. Initially, he joined J.F. Schröder & Co., the firm of an elder brother with whom he was in business for a decade and a half in London. Upon the dissolution of their partnership at the end of 1817 he formed his own firms in London and Hamburg and subsequently another in Liverpool—the three leading European seaports of the era. The business built by Johann Heinrich was an international trading organization with a growing emphasis on trade finance in London, the world's foremost financial centre.

The shipment of commodities, particularly sugar, coffee, cotton, indigo, tallow and grain, from producer countries to consumer markets was the activity with which Johann Heinrich's firms were principally involved. As merchants, they conducted business both as principals and as agents. Operating as principals, merchant firms purchased, shipped and sold goods on their "own account," assuming all risks and receiving all profits, or on "joint account" with other firms, sharing the risks and rewards. . . . Merchants also acted as agents for merchants in other cities. Acting as agents, they organized the shipment, insurance and sale of cargoes for a commission. This was less risky and required less capital, but the rewards were commensurately more modest than successful own account or joint account transactions. The firms of Johann Heinrich acted both as principals and as agents for one another and for the other Schröder family firms.

In the first half of the nineteenth century much of the trade in the import of commodities to Europe was conducted on a "consignment" basis. . . . Merchants in market centres, notably London, Liverpool and Hamburg, received cargoes of produce dispatched by planters or merchants in the places of origin. The goods were sold and the proceeds remitted to the shipper or held as a balance on his behalf, depending on the arrangements between the parties, the consignment merchant taking a percentage commission for his services. Although in principle the role of the consignment merchant was that of an agent, in fact he often assumed part of the risks of the transactions because it became common practice for an advance to be made to the shipper of up to two-thirds or three-quarters of the likely value of the consignment. . . . Advances to shippers were furnished in the form of bills of exchange; that is, an order signed by the consignment merchant promising payment on presentation of the bill at a future date, by which time he would have sold the goods received on consignment and be in a position to pay. If the shipper required cash prior to the maturity of the bill he could sell it to a local bank or some other party who in due course would present it for payment by the consignment merchant.

Exporters, whether operating on a consignment basis or by outright sale of goods, preferred payment in bills endorsed by a well-known firm of impeccable reputation. This gave rise to the specialist activity which in time came to be called "merchant banking," the practice of certain high-standing merchant firms guaranteeing payment of bills of exchange issued by firms of lesser standing and receiving a commission for providing this service. . . . Upon presentation of the bill, the merchant firm would acknowledge responsibility for payment by writing "accepted" across the face. Such bills became known as "acceptances" and the firms which provided this service as "accepting houses," or alternatively "merchant banks." Typically, payment was due 90 days after acceptance and in the meantime the bills were traded in the money market. The increasing specialization of certain London merchants upon acceptance business in the early nineteenth century led to the provision of credit facilities for clients on a regular rather than *ad hoc* basis by means of the granting of a "letter of credit," which was an authorization to a client to issue bills of exchange up to an agreed limit, an arrangement known was a line of credit. Firms granting letters of credit, such as Schröders, engaged a network of merchants and bankers in other cities to act as correspondents or agents, who agreed to make payment upon the presentation of bills issued under the firm's letters of credit. . . .

Johann Heinrich's London firm, J. Henry Schröder & Co., was an active participant in the development of the sterling bill of exchange as the foremost instrument for the finance of international trade. "Merchants & Bankers" was the term by which J. Henry Schröder & Co. styled itself well into the twentieth century.

• • •

The dissolution of the partnership between the Schröder brothers in London at the end of 1817 enabled Johann Heinrich to reorganize his business activities. It was the prelude to the creation of a unique network of firms in London, Hamburg and Liverpool which made Schröders different from the other merchant banking firms established in the City. At the beginning of 1818 Johann Heinrich founded his own firm in London, under the English name J. Henry Schröder & Co., and in 1819 he established a second firm, J.H. Schröder & Co., in Hamburg. The concurrent conduct of two firms in London and Hamburg was a bold business strategy in the era of the horse-drawn carriage and the sailing ship. Success required the support of trustworthy partners. For partners Johann Heinrich initially turned to his family, choosing merchants related by marriage in both London and Hamburg. . . .

He was very hard-working, ambitious and highly self-disciplined, traits which go a long way in explaining his outstanding success as a businessman. Family folklore was full of tales of his impeccable punctuality and of his intolerance of lapses in time-keeping by others; he even, it is said, called off an engagement to a girl who was unpunctual because he foresaw that it would be a source of friction between them. He had rigorous standards and could turn stern if disappointed. . . . He had strongly-held religious convictions and a highly developed sense of duty towards his family and the community, though unlike his father and other relations he did not become involved in the civic life of Hamburg.

From 1818, Hamburg was Johann Heinrich's home. On 26 January 1819, aged 34, he married Henriette von Schwartz, the 20-year-old daughter of Heinrich von Schwartz, a Hamburg merchant and the Prussian consul-general in Hamburg. In 1824, aged 40, he became a citizen of the city-state. . . .

Johann Heinrich returned to London in the summer of 1819, six months after his wedding in Hamburg. In July 1819, he became a member of the Russia Company and in the 1820s and 1830s J. Henry Schröder & Co. was one of the thirty or so firms in London known as "Russia merchants." . . . The firm was prominent in the shipment of indigo and raw sugar to St. Petersburg, particularly to H. E. Schröder & Co. . . . J. Henry Schröder & Co.'s other important business was the shipment of sugar to Hamburg, probably to J. H. Schröder & Co., on an "extensive" scale. . . .

In July 1839, Johann Heinrich established a third firm, J. H. Schröder & Co. in Liverpool, of which initially he was the sole proprietor. . . . The capital of the new firm was £50,000, a fairly typical sum for modest-sized merchant banks of the day, such as George Peabody & Co. or Frühling & Goschen. . . . However, Johann Heinrich informed the Bank of England's Liverpool branch that he was prepared to commit a further £150,000 to the undertaking should it be required, indicating substantial wealth. . . .

The basic business of J.H. Schröder & Co. of Liverpool was the receipt of consignments of cotton from the southern United States. At the time of its formation the cotton trade was reviving following a drastic downturn during the commercial crisis of 1836–37, which had bankrupted several of the leading transatlantic consignment merchants and weakened others. . . .

J. Henry Schröder & Co. celebrated its thirtieth anniversary in 1848. By this time it was a soundly established and well-reputed firm of moderate size, making profits of perhaps £500,000 in 1990 money. . . . The distinctive features of its business were its specialization in certain colonial and Baltic produce and its strong ties with Hamburg; all but one of the sixteen clerks who were employed . . . had German surnames. . . .

In 1849, Johann Heinrich reorganized the partnerships of both his London and Hamburg firms, moves which suggest his withdrawal from active participation in the business. . . .

Johann Heinrich was approaching his 65th birthday in 1849, so age was probably an important factor in his decision to retire. Perhaps also prompting him to seek a quieter life were the commercial crisis of 1847–48, the revolutions in many European countries in 1848, and the brief occupation of Hamburg by the Prussians in 1849, all of which must have been disruptive to the business of his firms. Maybe the persuasive inducement was the lure of his country estate at Schwansee in Mecklenburg, about 60 miles northeast of Hamburg, which he purchased in 1846. Charitable works absorbed him in retirement of which the most notable was the erection of a home for the elderly, the Schröder Stiftung, to which in 1850 he made an endowment of 1.5 million Bancomarks, £110,000 in sterling of the day— around £4.5 million in 1990 money. In 1868, in recognition of his benefactions the King of Prussia made him a Prussian Freiherr, Baron Johann Heinrich von Schröder, a very unusual honor for a Hamburg merchant.

Beside business, Johann Heinrich's greatest interest was his family. There were nine surviving children, three sons and six daughters. The eldest and youngest sons, Johann Heinrich and Wilhelm, were given charge of their father's London and Liverpool firms, while the middle son, Carl, inherited the family estate at Schwansee and pursued the life of a country landowner. All three were generally known by the English forms of their names . . . which was a common practice amongst Hamburg's Anglophile merchant families.

Nicholas Biddle

R. T. CONRAD

Nicholas Biddle, active in national affairs at a remarkably early age, served as president of the Second National Bank of the United States from 1823 to 1839 when it was the largest and most powerful business organization in the country. He was the nation's foremost banker in the first half of the nineteenth century, but had many other significant talents as well. Among his writings, he edited *Travels of Lewis and Clark*.

Nicholas Biddle, was born at Philadelphia, on the 8th day of January 1786. He began his education at the academy, whence he was introduced to the University of Pennsylvania, and passing through its successive probations, was about to take his degree in 1799, when his extreme youth, being then only 13 years of age, occasioned his being sent to Princeton, in New Jersey. He is described by those who knew him at this period, as a thoughtful and severe student and a youth of dauntless and indomitable spirit. A classmate and companion, since a distinguished citizen, says of Mr. Biddle, "I enjoyed an intimacy with him at that time, which gave me full opportunity of

Excerpted from R. T. Conrad, *The National Portrait Gallery of Distinguished Americans*, 1839, pp. 3–4, 7–8, and 10–13.

forming a judgment of his abilities, and I have a distinct recollection of having made up my mind that he was destined to be a great man."

Young Biddle remained at Princeton two years and a half, and graduated
in September 1801. . . . His standing and scholarship are shown by the fact
that, though the youngest person, it is understood, that ever graduated before or since that time in college, he and Mr. Edward Watts of Virginia, a
gentleman very much his senior, divided the first honor of the class, the
valedictory being assigned to Mr. Biddle.

On leaving college, he commenced the study of the law in Philadelphia. . . .

When three years of Mr. Biddle's term of study were about to expire,
General Armstrong was appointed minister of the United States to France,
and offered to take [Biddle] with him as secretary. He accordingly embarked in the year 1804, and spent the three succeeding years in Europe.
The period of his residence in France was one of extraordinary interest,
not merely from its embracing the career of Napoleon from his corona-
tion, but from the complicated relations between the United States and
France, and especially from the examination and payment in detail of the
claims of this country on France, which were paid out of the purchase
money for Louisiana. This duty devolved almost exclusively upon the
young secretary. The payments were made at the French bureau, and Mr.
Biddle, with untiring assiduity, attended to the disbursement. The officers
of the French government are mostly gentlemen of ripe years; Mr. Biddle,
then about 18, was even more juvenile in appearance than years, and the
advent among these grave dignitaries of this youthful depository of so important a trust was viewed with a wonder that was increased when they
found him performing his arduous duties with the ability, firmness, and
perseverance of a veteran statesman. . . .

But a measure of more general interest, and which occupied the attention of the union at large, drew upon the youthful statesman the eyes of
the whole nation. The charter of the Bank of the United States expired in
1811; and the question of its recharter was then agitated with as much violence as the same subject has, in later days, excited. Among the modes of
opposition practised by the enemies of the Bank, one was to procure instructions from the legislature to the members of Congress from Pennsylvania to vote against the recharter. A resolution of this character was
introduced, and it was in opposition to that resolution that Mr. Biddle
made his first speech. The speech produced a great sensation at the time,
and established the reputation of its author. It is remarkable not only for
its power and the soundness of its general principles, but from the strange
coincidence that he should begin his career by a prophetic warning of the
evil consequences of the destruction of the bank; that those evils should
have actually occurred; that the listeners to that warning, convinced by
melancholy experience of their error, should, when afterwards transferred

to Washington, have been the chief promoters of the charter of a new bank; and, finally, that this very youth should become the head of that bank, and in that capacity, vindicating his early positions, should acquire for himself and the institution a credit throughout the commercial world, of which the history of the country furnishes no parallel. It is no less remarkable that although the question was then wholly new, not having yet been discussed in Congress or elsewhere, the speech of Mr. Biddle embodies, in a condensed form, almost everything—the leading principles and general facts—which has been since developed in the multitudinous discussions that have succeeded. The speech itself elicited universal applause, and received, what is more valuable than any general praise, the most decided eulogium from the late Chief Justice Marshall. It was circulated generally, and eagerly read, and did much to extend and establish the reputation of its author in all sections of the union.

At the close of the session he declined a reelection, and retired from public life, dividing his time between his studies, which were always pursued with the most vigorous diligence, and agriculture, for which he has manifested, throughout life, a decided predilection. . . .

In the year 1819, he first became connected with the Bank of the United States, an incident which contributed to give a direction to his subsequent career, and secured to the country the aid of his extraordinary abilities in the important field of finance. The institution was at that time justly considered in great jeopardy. Its affairs had been investigated by a committee of Congress, and the report of that committee tended to inspire distrust and apprehension. To add to these difficulties, its president had resigned; and the position and prospects of the bank became so critical, that the most vigorous exertions were deemed necessary to revive the public confidence. For this purpose, President Monroe, without the knowledge of Mr. Biddle, nominated him as a director of the bank on the part of the United States. This mark of confidence was not only unexpected, but unwelcome to Mr. Biddle, for he had previously declined being a director on the part of the stockholders; but thus summoned, by the national executive, to what had become a serious and important trust, he did not feel himself at liberty to decline the task. He accordingly took his place in the bank at the same time that Mr. Langdon Cheves, who had been previously elected president, assumed the duties of his station. In conjunction with that gentleman he labored with great industry in arranging the affairs and establishing the character of the institution, and, having no special employment at the time, was enabled to turn into that channel the almost undivided energies of his mind. . . .

In the year 1821, he removed permanently to his farm in Bucks county. While residing there, the resignation of Mr. Cheves as president of the United States Bank occasioned a general convention at Philadelphia of all the stockholders of the bank throughout the United States. The selection of a successor was regarded as a matter of great delicacy and importance, not merely in relation to the interests of the institution itself, but from its influence upon the credit and commercial prosperity of the country at large. The subject was, therefore, anxiously canvassed as well in the public prints as among the stockholders. The station called for commanding abilities, a genius practical, fertile in resources, profoundly skilled in finance, and versed in all the comprehensive and diversified interests connected with trade. Public opinion pointed to Mr. Biddle as preeminently fitted for the arduous and momentous trust, and he was accordingly invited to accept the presidency. The result elicited general applause, and the government manifested its approbation of the choice by appointing Mr. Biddle a director on the part of the United States. He entered upon the duties of the office in January 1823. His previous service of three years in the bank had made him familiar with its concerns, and had given him some peculiar views of its administration, which he now proceeded gradually and cautiously to develop. The details of this subject belong to history, and cannot, of course, be given in the present brief and hurried notice; but the general purpose of the change of system may be made intelligible in a few words. By the charter of the bank, all its notes were made receivable in all payments to the government. It was objected that as these notes were payable in so many places, provision must be made to pay them in those places, so that a greater amount of specie must be kept in reserve than the amount of notes in circulation. Application was made to Congress to alter the charter so as to make the notes payable only where they were issued, and it was declared by the bank to Congress, that unless the change was made, the bank would be not only useless but injurious. With this view of the subject, there could, of course, be no general circulation of its notes, no regulation of the domestic exchanges—the whole amount of notes on the first of January 1823, being about three and a half millions of dollars, and the amount of domestic bills on hand less than two millions of dollars.

With these opinions Mr. Biddle did not at all concur. He thought that the universal receivability of the notes, so far from being injurious, was highly beneficial to the bank and to the country; and that there was no danger of issuing the notes, if the branches issuing them were careful to provide funds for their redemption at the points to which the well known course of trade would necessarily carry them. He considered this very provision beneficial in another point of view; he believed that it would enable the bank, by the policy just mentioned, to regulate the domestic exchanges and effect the great object of its creation. Having matured the project in his own mind, he proceeded to carry it out. Years of patient and anxious labor, directed by the most vigilant sagacity, were necessary to bring all the parts of this original and admirable system into full action. That consummation was, however, at last attained, when, as in 1835, there had been established nine new branches, making the whole consist of the bank at Philadelphia and *25 branches*; sustaining a wholesome circulation of 24 millions, based on 24 millions of current bills of exchange, with 15 or 16 millions of specie.

The change thus gradually and quietly effected, was regarded throughout the world as one of the miracles of genius. It brightened the aspect of the whole country, and inspired health and animation in all the various pursuits of trade and industry. The effect of Mr. Biddle's system is thus explained by the report of the Committee of Ways and Means of the House of Representatives: "It may be confidently asserted that no country in the world has a currency of greater uniformity than the United States, and that no country of any thing like the same geographical extent, has a currency at all comparable to that of the United States on the score of uniformity"; and again: "It has actually furnished a circulating medium more uniform than specie." The committee of finance of the Senate characterized with equal force the success of Mr. Biddle's administration. "This seems to present a state of currency approaching as near to perfection as could be desired"; and again; "It is not easy to imagine, it is scarcely necessary to desire, any currency better than this."

Stephen Girard

GUSTAVUS MYERS

Stephen Girard, self-described as the neglected "ugly duckling" of his family, was an exceptionally tight man of forbidding demeanor. He made a large fortune in shipping and trade with China, then expanded it through banking in Philadelphia. He was shrewd, venal and remorseless in pursuit of profit. Charity, it was said while he was alive, had no place in his heart. Yet, he left almost all his wealth to worthy causes, in addition to founding a college for orphans that bears his name.

Girard was born at Bordeaux, France, on May 21, 1750, and was the eldest of five children of Captain Pierre Girard, a mariner. When eight years old he became blind in one eye, a loss and deformity which had the effect of rendering him morose and sour. It was his lament in later life that while his brothers had been sent to college, he was the ugly duckling of the family

From *History of the Great American Fortunes* by Gustavus Myers, © 1907, 1910, & 1936. Reprinted by permission of Random House, Inc.

and came in for his father's neglect and a shrewish step-mother's waspishness. At about 14 years of age he relieved himself of these home troubles and ran away to sea. During the nine years that he sailed between Bordeaux and the West Indies, he rose from cabin boy to mate. Evading the French law which required that no man should be made master of a ship unless he had sailed two cruises in the royal navy and was 25 years old, Girard got the command of a trading vessel when about 22 years old. While in this service he clandestinely carried cargoes of his own, which he sold at considerable profit. In May 1776, while en route from New Orleans to a Canadian port, he became enshrouded in a fog off the Delaware Capes, signaled for aid, and when the fog had cleared away sufficiently for an American ship, near by, to come to his assistance, learned that war was on. He thereupon scurried for Philadelphia, where he sold vessel and cargo, of which latter only a part belonged to him, and with the proceeds opened up a cider and wine bottling and grocery business in a small store on Water street.

Girard made money fast; and in July 1777, married Mary Lum, a woman of his own class. She is usually described as a servant girl of great beauty and as one whose temper was of quite tempestuous violence. This unfortunate woman subsequently lost her reason; undoubtedly her husband's meannesses and his forbidding qualities contributed to the process. One of his most favorable biographers thus describes him: "In person he was short and stout, with a dull repulsive countenance, which his bushy eyebrows and solitary eye almost made hideous. He was cold and reserved in manner, and was disliked by his neighbors, the most of whom were afraid of him.". . .

During the British occupation of Philadelphia he was charged by the revolutionists with extreme double-dealing and duplicity in pretending to be a patriot, and taking the oath of allegiance to the colonies, while secretly trading with the British. None of his biographers deny this. While merchant after merchant was being bankrupted from disruption of trade, Girard was incessantly making money. By 1780 he was again in the shipping trade, his vessels plying between American ports and New Orleans and San Domingo; not the least of his profits, it was said, came from slave-trading.

• • •

Girard's greatest stroke came from the insurrection of the San Domingo Negroes against the French several years later. He had two vessels lying in the harbor of one of the island ports. At the first mutterings of danger, a number of planters took their valuables on board one of these ships and scurried back to get the remainder. The sequel, as commonly narrated, is represented thus: The planters failed to return, evidently falling victims to the fury of the insurrectionists. The vessels were taken to Philadelphia, and Girard persistently advertised for the owners of the valuables. As no owners ever appeared Girard sold the goods and put the proceeds, $50,000, into his own bank account. "This," says Houghton, "was a great assistance to him, and the next year he began the building of those splendid ships which enabled him to engage so actively in the Chinese and West India trades."

From this time on his profits were colossal. His ships circumnavigated the world many times and each voyage brought him a fortune. He practiced all of those arts of deception which were current among the trading class and which were accepted as shrewdness and were inseparably associated with legitimate business methods. In giving one of his captains instructions he wrote, as was his invariable policy, the most explicit directions to exercise secretiveness and cunning in his purchases of coffee at Batavia. Be cautious and prudent, was his admonition. Keep to yourself the intention of the voyage and the amount of specie that you have on board. To satisfy the curious, throw them off the scent by telling them that the ship will take in molasses, rice and sugar, if the price is very low, adding that the whole will depend upon the success in selling the small Liverpool cargo. If you do this, the cargo of coffee can be bought 10 percent cheaper than it would be if it is publicly known there is a quantity of Spanish dollars on board, besides a valuable cargo of British goods intended to be invested in coffee for Stephen Girard of Philadelphia.

By 1810 we see him ordering the Barings of London to invest in shares of the Bank of the United States half a million dollars which they held for him. When the charter expired, he was the principal creditor of that bank; and he bought, at a great bargain, the bank and the cashier's house for $120,000. On May 12, 1812, he opened the Girard Bank, with a capital of $1,200,000, which he increased the following year by $100,000 more. . . .

His wealth was now overshadowingly great, his power immense. He was a veritable dictator of the realms of finance; an assiduous, repellent little man, with his devil's eye, who rode roughshod over every obstacle in his path. His every movement bred fear; his verist word could bring ruin to anyone who dared cross his purposes. The war of 1812 brought disaster to many a merchant, but Girard harvested fortune from the depths of misfortune. "He was, it must be said," says Houghton, "hard and illiberal in his bargains, and remorseless in exacting the last cent due him." And after he opened the Girard Bank: "Finding that the salaries which had been paid by the government were higher than those paid elsewhere, he cut them down to the rate given by the other banks. The watchman had always received from the old bank the gift of an overcoat at Christmas, but Girard put a stop to this. He gave no gratuities to any of his employees, but confined them to the compensation for which they had bargained; yet he contrived to get out of them service more devoted than was received by other men who paid higher wages and made presents. Appeals to him for aid were unanswered. No poor man ever came full-handed from his presence. He turned a deaf ear to the entreaties of failing merchants to help them on

their feet again. He was neither generous nor charitable. When his faithful cashier died, after long years spent in his service, he manifested the
most hardened indifference to the bereavement of the family of that gentleman, and left them to struggle along as best they could.". . .

The reestablishment and enlarged sway of the [Bank of the United
States, in which Girard invested] bank were greatly due to his efforts and
influence; he became its largest stockholder and one of its directors. No
business institution in the first three decades of the nineteenth century
exercised such a sinister and overshadowing influence as this chartered
monopoly. The full tale of its indirect bribery of politicians and newspaper
editors, in order to perpetuate its great privileges and keep a hold upon
public opinion, has never been set forth. But sufficient facts were brought
out when, after years of partisan agitation, Congress was forced to investigate and found that not a few of its own members for years had been on the
payrolls of the bank.

In order to get its charter renewed from time to time and retain its extraordinary special privileges, the United States Bank systematically de-
bauched politics and such of the press as was venal; and when a critical time
came as it did in 1832–1834, when the mass of the people sided with President Jackson in his aim to overthrow the bank, it instructed the whole press
at its command to raise the cry of "the fearful consequences of revolution,
anarchy and despotism," which assuredly would ensue if Jackson were re-
elected. To give one instance of how for years it had manipulated the press:
The *Courier and Enquirer* was a powerful New York newspaper. Its owners,
Webb and Noah, suddenly deserted Jackson and began to denounce him.
The reason is, as revealed by a Congressional investigation, that they had
borrowed $50,000 from the United States Bank which lost no time in giv-
ing them the alternative of paying up or supporting the Bank.

Girard's share in the United States Bank brought him millions of dollars. With its control of deposits of government funds and by the provisions of its charter, this bank swayed the whole money marts of the United
States and could manipulate them at will. It could advance or depress
prices as it chose. Many times, Girard with his fellow directors was se-
verely denounced for the arbitrary power he wielded. But—and let the fact
be noted—the denunciation came largely from the owners of the state
banks who sought to supplant the United States Bank. The struggle was
really one between two sets of capitalistic interests.

• • •

In all his 81 years charity had no place in his heart. But after, on December 26, 1831, he lay stone dead and his will was opened, what a surprise
there was! His relatives all received bequests; his very apprentices each got
$500, and his old servants annuities. Hospitals, orphan societies and other
charitable associations all benefited. Five hundred thousand dollars went

to the City of Philadelphia for certain civic improvements; three hundred thousand dollars for the canals of Pennsylvania; a portion of his valuable estate in Louisiana to New Orleans for the improvement of that city. The remainder of the estate, about $6 million, was left to trustees for the creation and endowment of a College for Orphans, which was promptly named after him.

A chorus of astonishment and laudation went up. Was there ever such magnificence of public spirit? Did ever so lofty a soul live who was so misunderstood? Here and there a protesting voice was feebly heard that Girard's wealth came from the community and that it was only justice that it should revert to the community; that his methods had resulted in widows and orphans and that his money should be applied to the support of those orphans. These protests were frowned upon as the mouthings of cranks or the ravings of impotent envy. Applause was lavished upon Girard; his very clothes were preserved as immemorial mementoes.

Jacob Henry Schiff

CYRUS ADLER

Jacob Schiff emigrated to America from Germany in 1865, joined Kuhn, Loeb in 1875, and became its head only ten years later at age 38. Concentrating on railroad finance, he built a great firm and a great fortune. He was also an active philanthropist and deeply engaged in Jewish affairs. Here are two pieces that tell us a great deal about him: the first is a sensitive biographical sketch, while the second illustrates just how principled a man he was.

Jacob H. Schiff was known in all parts of the American continent, in every country of Europe, in Palestine, in Japan, in fact throughout the civilized world. Vaguely he was considered as the combination of a great financier and a great philanthropist, but in neither capacity had the extent of his deeds been brought home to any considerable proportion of the vast numbers to whom his name was familiar.

What manner of man was this who, of no ruling family or exalted official station, so impressed himself upon the imagination of people in many climes and in all conditions of life? To answer this question is well

Excerpted from *Jacob Henry Schiff: A Biographical Sketch*, The American Jewish Committee, 1921, pp. 3–12; and *Jacob H. Schiff: His Life and Letters*, Doubleday, 1929, pp. 249–254.

nigh impossible in a brief sketch. And yet the attempt should be made, for mankind is enriched by the story of great personalities, and future generations are stimulated to high deeds by the knowledge of the acts of those who have gone before.

Jacob H. Schiff was born at Frankfort-on-the-Main on January 10, 1847, and died in New York on September 25, 1920. He was descended of a family known to have been settled in Frankfort since 1370. The pedigree carefully worked out in the *Jewish Encyclopedia* presents the longest continuous record of any Jewish family now in existence. The earliest Schiff, named Jacob Kohen Zedek, was dayyan (ecclesiastical judge) of the Frankfort community in the fourteenth century. . . .

It is impossible and indeed inappropriate even to endeavor to give here an outline of the history of this distinguished family. The few facts mentioned are intended to indicate that for over six hundred years there can be traced an unbroken line of rabbis, scholars, men of affairs, and communal leaders, all of whose qualities went to make up the background of the very remarkable man who is the subject of this sketch and in whose single person nearly all the traits of this long line of ancestors were blended—some appearing in greater proportion than others, but all nevertheless present.

His immediate forbears were Moses Schiff and Clara Niederhofheim. The father, a man of high sense of duty, exact and stern, was rigorously devoted to religious observances, and demanded a similar devotion on the part of his children; the mother was a woman of sweet and conciliatory nature. The distinctive traits of both of these personalities were found in the son, for Mr. Schiff set before himself a life of exacting duty, whilst toward others he showed great kindliness and consideration.

His education, both secular and religious, was thorough for a layman. In the course of time, by wide reading and contact with men, he acquired a broad, general cultivation. He had a good knowledge of the Hebrew language, and could freely quote the Bible in the sacred tongue. He read some favorite commentaries, and kept himself abreast of the developments in biblical studies. His exactness in method and his knowledge of, and interest in, Jewish learning undoubtedly went back to the excellent if severe training of his boyhood days.

In 1865 he left Frankfort ostensibly for England, but he had already determined upon America as his future home. As the voyage across the Atlantic was in those days still a fearsome enterprise, he stopped in England long enough to write a series of letters to his mother which were left in the hands of a friend to be mailed at regular intervals, so that the mother should be spared the anxiety of his passage across the ocean until a letter would have been received from New York announcing his arrival there.

In New York he was employed for a time in the brokerage firm of Frank and Sons, and later became a partner in the firm of Budge, Schiff and Company. After the death of his father, in 1873, he went to Germany, intending to live with his mother, but the spirit of America had entered his soul, and his mother, to whom he was deeply attached, herself suggested that he should return to the United States.

On January 1, 1875, he became a member of the banking firm of Kuhn, Loeb and Company, and before many years the older members of the firm, recognizing his financial genius, were glad to accord him the headship of the house. . . .

. . .

It became one of the two most influential private international banking houses on the Western Hemisphere. It was a characteristic of Mr. Schiff that as a banker his activities were all creative, looking to the development of the resources and the extension of the commerce of the United States. Hence, he was particularly concerned in the financing of railway enterprises, recognizing that the prosperity of a great country depended, in large measure, upon the extent and efficiency of its transportation agencies.

He believed it important for America to bring the Atlantic and Pacific closer together, thus aiding in uniting the citizenship of the United States economically and politically. In 1897 he reorganized the Union Pacific Railroad which was described at the period as being "battered, bankrupt and decrepit"—an achievement of the first rank and constructive in the best sense.

Mr. Schiff had faith in his intuition of men, and being swift to recognize genius, gave his support to Edward H. Harriman. According to financial authorities the Harriman-Schiff railway combination became the most powerful, the most aggressive, and the most successful that America had ever known.

In like manner he was one of the first supporters and associates of James J. Hill, who, by the building of the Great Northern Railway, virtually became the founder of a vast empire in the Northwest. Mr. Schiff was for many years a director of the Great Northern, retiring only after a conflict of interest developed between it and the Union Pacific Railway. The operations of Kuhn, Loeb and Company as bankers for railways began with their association with the Chicago and Northwestern some 50 years back. One of their most important connections was with the Pennsylvania Railroad system which came especially to the notice of the general public under the presidency of A. J. Cassatt, who dreamed the dream of a tunnel under the Hudson and of a Railway Station in the City of New York commensurate with the importance of the great city. Kuhn, Loeb and Company succeeded in floating for the Pennsylvania Railroad Company large loans in this country and abroad. Two checks drawn to the order of the Company on February 17, 1915, for the amount of $49,098,000, and on June 1, 1915, for $62,075,000, which hang in the modest frames in the offices of Kuhn, Loeb and Company, attest the magnitude of their loans.

Other railroads whose financial operations his firm aided were the Baltimore and Ohio, the Chesapeake and Ohio, the Delaware and Hudson, the Illinois Central and Southern Pacific. Of many of these railroads Mr. Schiff became a director, but his participation in large financial enterprises was by no means limited to them. He also financed a number of important industrial undertakings, such as the Westinghouse Electric Company, the United States Rubber Company, Armour and Company, the American Telephone and Telegraph Company, and the Western Union Telegraph Company. He served as a director of the Western Union Telegraph Company, of the Equitable Life Assurance Society, of the National City Bank, of the Central Trust Company, of the American Railway Express Company, and of the Fifth Avenue Trust Company.

His advice was sought in these and many other enterprises because of his wide knowledge of affairs in America and Europe and of the sound conclusions he was able to draw from this knowledge. His confidence in the great transcontinental railways was heightened by his repeated journeys to the West and the South, so that he appreciated from personal observation the richness of our great national domain. He was alive to the fact that agriculture was the backbone of commerce, and once, when asked what the stock market indicated with regard to business possibilities of the season, said that he did not follow the stock market but rather the crop reports.

As to the correctness of his judgement, B. C. Forbes, a well-known financial writer, has declared, in speaking of him, that "Kuhn, Loeb and Company have issued more good investments and fewer bad ones than any other banking concern in America."

The Japanese loan of 1904–1905, which Mr. Schiff financed, attracted world-wide attention, and had important consequences. . . .

Beside the Japanese loan, he financed loans for other foreign governments such as Sweden, Argentine, Cuba, Mexico, and China. . . .

Mr. Schiff on numerous occasions refused to participate in Russian loans, and used his great influence to prevent the entry of Russia into the money markets of America, solely because of the ill-treatment of the Jews by the Russian government. On various occasions, when Russia was pressed for funds, offers were made by agents of the Russian government to relax the restrictions upon the Jews in a particular province in exchange for a loan of $50 million. Mr. Schiff invariably rejected such advances, declining to buy better treatment for a section of his coreligionists which he held should be accorded them as a matter of right.

• • •

As for the business operations of Kuhn, Loeb & Co. during the war period, the most interesting question before 1917 was doubtless that which arose in connection with the problem of financing for the belligerent governments. Schiff maintained relations with individuals in Germany until the entrance of the United States into the war, but from the very outbreak of the war in 1914, his firm did no financing directly or indirectly for the German government or its allies.

On the other hand, they placed considerable loans in 1916 for the French cities of Paris, Bordeaux, Lyons, and Marseilles, which were issued primarily for humanitarian purposes. Naturally, his German friends inquired whether his firm would do for Frankfort or Hamburg what they had done for Paris or Bordeaux, and he replied that they would, if satisfactory assurances could be obtained that the proceeds would not be used for war purposes. But just then there broke out a new submarine controversy between the United States and Germany, which determined him not to consider even such loans to German cities.

He was sympathetically disposed towards the Anglo-French Loan, but he could not bring himself to aid [Czarist] Russia, one of the Allies, while it remained under the form of government it had at that time. His own formal statement on the subject was issued on October 1, 1915:

> With differing sympathies on the part of individual members of our firm, we decided at the outbreak of the war to refrain from financing public loans for any of the governments of the belligerent nations. Concerning the present Anglo-French Dollar Loan, we have felt that as American bankers we should assist in what we believe will result in promoting the interest of the country's commerce and industries, but it not having been found practicable to give any actual assurances that the Government of Russia—against whose inhumanity the members of our firm have ever raised their voices—is not to derive benefit from the funds that are to be raised through the Anglo-French Loan, I have felt constrained to advise my firm to refrain from becoming participants in the loan.

This dramatic statement was made under the following circumstances. When the Anglo-French Commission came to New York late in the summer of 1915, to negotiate the conclusion of the first of the great loans in America, its members were advised by the leaders of the banking group to which they addressed themselves that it would not be possible to raise a loan of more than $250,000,000, and that, moreover, the loan would have to be secured by marketable collateral.

The Commission was greatly surprised and disappointed. Lord Reading, the leading member, took occasion to ask various opinions on the subject, and among others that of Otto Kahn and Mortimer Schiff. They told him that they were convinced that a loan of $500,000,000 could be raised, and that no collateral need be given, and advised him to insist on both these things and to take the attitude that he would rather go home empty-handed

than to yield on either point. He thereupon asked whether Kuhn, Loeb &
Co. would be prepared to back that opinion by joining in the business.

They replied that, as far as they personally were concerned, he knew
that they individually were favorably disposed, but that they were unable
to commit the firm of Kuhn, Loeb & Co., as they had to submit the matter to their colleagues, particularly the senior of the firm, Jacob Schiff.
They added that he was aware that Mr. Schiff's position had been to stand
aloof, mainly because he could not get himself to do anything which would
give aid and comfort to Russia, the nation which for many years had dis-
criminated against, oppressed, and persecuted the Jews. Lord Reading answered that he was well aware of Mr. Schiff's position, and while greatly
regretting it and disagreeing with his reasoning, he could not but honor
him for his motives.

They reported this conversation to Schiff and their other associates.
Schiff was greatly distressed at being confronted with the proposition. On
the one hand, he realized fully the vast advantage it would be to Kuhn,
Loeb & Co. to join in the leadership of this and subsequent Anglo-French
business. On the other hand, he could not bring himself—he who year after
year had rejected overtures to do business with the Russian government—
to share in a transaction the financial results of which would inevitably be
utilized in part for the benefit of Russia, allied as she was with England and
France, and would thus aid, and in a sense help to perpetuate, the existing
Russian régime. He ended by saying: "Let us all consider the matter for 24
hours and reach a conclusion at a partners' conference tomorrow."

They met the next day. He was very grave and evidently much disturbed.
He opened the discussion with words to the following effect: "I have
thought about this situation all night. Before asking your opinions, I want
to tell you that my mind is made up, unalterably. I realize fully what is at
stake for the firm of Kuhn, Loeb & Co. in the decision we are going to
make. But come what may, I cannot run counter to my conscience, I cannot
sacrifice my proudest convictions for the sake of whatever business advantage, I cannot stultify myself by aiding those who, in bitter enmity, have
tortured my people and will continue to do so, whatever fine professions
they may make in their hour of need. I ought not to be asked to do so. It is
not fair to put me in this dilemma. I will tell you what is the limit to which
I can honorably consent. I am willing that Kuhn, Loeb & Co. should join in
the loan and the leadership of the transaction, provided that we are assured
in writing by the commission, on behalf of the British and French governments, that not one cent of the proceeds of the loan will be given to Russia.
I know your objections and counter-arguments and criticisms. They do not
and cannot affect my conclusion. This is a matter between me and my conscience, and no one but I myself can solve it for me. You are younger men.
Some of you do not feel as I do on what I consider the morally controlling
element of the question. I cannot have many more years to live. The future

of the firm is yours. Realizing my duty by the firm and by you, I have gone to the limit of what I can sanction."

Feeling as they all did toward Schiff, there was, of course, no room for discussion. Most eager though some of them were to join in the leadership of this vastly important affair, and realizing as they did that there was hardly a possibility of Schiff's condition being complied with, they acquiesced in his conclusion. Mortimer Schiff and Otto Kahn went to see Lord Reading to tell him so. As they had anticipated, though his attitude was very sympathetic and he did full justice to the motives actuating Schiff, he said that no government could accept such conditions of discrimination against one of its allies in the war, and, even if it did, it could not in fact fulfill them.

The episode is characteristic of Schiff's strength of conviction and his adherence to his principles, regardless of all other considerations. He knew full well not only that his firm would suffer in business, but that his motives would be misunderstood and, furthermore, that this misunderstanding would affect the younger members of his firm, who were more exposed to public and private criticism than was a man of his years. He realized the distress which it caused them, as it did him; yet he could not yield.

Mr. Morgan, Mr. Carnegie, and the Great Steel Industry Consolidation

FREDERICK LEWIS ALLEN

J. Pierpont Morgan and the Wall Street House he headed so dominated American finance for so long that his image still towers over the horizon nearly a century after his death. He had remarkable eyes, a commanding presence, and a reputation for making abrupt, final judgments. The respect accorded his views was such that, by simply making them known he once saved the country from the consequences of a great financial panic. Here we see him at his best, thinking hugely, concluding with finality, implementing with vigor and assurance, and completing the transaction on terms virtually guaranteed to return Morgan a handsome profit. This success was, perhaps, the greatest of his banking career.

It was in the late summer of 1897 that Pierpont Morgan got his first real glimpse of the possibilities of combination in the great steel industry.

His life that year had been full of variety. Early in January he had given a million dollars to the Lying-in-Hospital for a new building. Then he had taken a short subzero winter holiday at his friend W. West Durant's camp in the Adirondacks, enjoying the place so much that he bought it the following year. In March he had promised to build a new rectory for the Church of the Holy Innocents at Highland Falls, of which he was senior warden (as he was of St. George's in New York). On March 24, he had departed from Wall Street and No. 219 Madison Avenue for his annual trip abroad, sailing this time on the *Teutonic* with his daughter Louisa. While in England, he had supervised the affairs of his London banking house, had prepared the way among British investors for the refunding of the New York Central mortgage debt and had also found time to make heavy purchases of objects of art, for himself and for the Metropolitan Museum, in which he was now taking an expanding interest. And returning from Europe in June, he had divided his summer attention between financial affairs and his plans for the annual regatta of the New York Yacht Club, of which he had recently been elected commodore.

They were big plans, for the new commodore liked to do things in a spacious way. The yachts were to assemble at Glen Cove, Long Island, proceed to New London and then Newport and then Vineyard Haven, and then go on the longest jaunt in their history—a race round Cape Cod and all the way to Mt. Desert, Maine. Morgan offered gold and silver cups for the winners. And at the beginning of August he filled his 204-foot black *Corsair* to capacity with guests and set out upon the festivities of regatta week. . . .

It was not long after this regatta that he was waited upon in New York by Judge Elbert H. Gary, a Middle Westerner who had himself been vacationing that summer, in a somewhat less spectacular way—taking his first trip to England and dutifully doing the cultural round there, from Bunyan's grave and Dickens' "Old Curiosity Shop" to the British Museum and the Tower of London. Gary—whom Morgan had met before—had now come to New York on behalf of John Warne Gates, a rising manufacturer of barbed wire who had already, with Gary's help, combined a number of steel and wire companies into one, and who now wanted to combine a great many more—to form an 80-million-dollar American Steel & Wire Company.

Charles Coster had already examined the data which Gary had brought with him, and had reported that the project was worth his chief's attention. Morgan talked with Gary, was favorably impressed, and gave his provisional OK to the ambitious project; and Gary and Gates thereupon went to work trying to line up the numerous manufacturers of wire for the great merger.

Morgan was dealing now with two quite different men. Gary, born and bred in an Illinois farm town, had become a leading Chicago lawyer, had been mayor of Wheaton, Illinois, had served two terms as a country judge, and had been president of the Chicago Bar Association; recently, as legal adviser for Gates, he had become an expert matchmaker among corporations. . . . But there was nothing about Gary's friend Gates that remotely resembled a bishop. Gates was a plunger, a gambler, a large, genial all-night poker player, once described by his secretary as a "great boy with an extraordinary money sense annexed." He had made his start in business as a barbed-wire salesman. . . . Now he had become a big shot in the wire industry and was ready to become a bigger one. They called him "Bet-a-Million" Gates; he was said to have spent a rainy afternoon on a way train betting with a companion on which of the raindrops coursing down the windowpane would reach the bottom first—at a thousand dollars a race.

All that fall and early winter the negotiations over the proposed wire combine went on, but in February Morgan would go no further. What he said was that he was disturbed by the financial showing of one of the companies that was to be included in it. But there may have been other reasons. The American battleship *Maine* had just been sunk in Havana Harbor, and there was a threat of war in Spain; perhaps that fact contributed to Morgan's uncertainty. Or the main factor may have been distaste for Gates and the "Waldorf crowd" of speculative plungers who surrounded him. At any rate, Morgan would not say yes—whereupon Gates and Gary went ahead without him. The result was the formation, first, of a small combination, and then, a few months later, of a larger one called the American Steel & Wire Company, put together without aid from 23 Wall Street.

But Morgan had had his initiation into the steel industry. And he had found Gary both able and reliable. And so, in the summer of 1898—while the brief Spanish War was being won by the United States with one hand tied behind its back—he willingly embarked with Gary upon another combination scheme: a scheme for tying together the Illinois Steel Company, and an ore company, and several other concerns, to form what was to be known as the Federal Steel Company. And when, by September, the job was done, he called Gary to his office and said, with his customary brevity:

"Judge Gary, you have put this thing together in very good shape. We are all very well pleased. Now you must be president."

Gary was amazed. He had had no inkling of any such plan. He said he couldn't think of it.

"Why not?" said Morgan.

"Why, Mr. Morgan, I have a law practice worth $75,000 a year and I cannot leave it."

"We'll take care of that," said Morgan. "We must make it worth your while."

"But I must think it over," said Gary desperately.

"No, we want to know right now."

"But who are the directors to be?"

"You can select the directors, name the executive committee, choose your officers, and fix your salary."

Gary begged for a week to think the matter over. Morgan gave him twenty-four hours. Gary accepted.

And so, the following month, the Chicago lawyer came East at the behest of the New York banker to become the head of what had become the second biggest steel concern in the country. He was not a steelmaster, knew little about steel manufacturing. He was there because the banker trusted him.

• • •

So contagious did the idea of combining steel companies become during the next two years that it was as if a giant magnet had moved over the surface of the industry, pulling together into compact groups the innumerable separate particles of which it had previously consisted. Morgan himself helped to bring together two more groups—the National Tube Company and the American Bridge Company. And as for the Moore brothers, they worked with such diligence as to produce the National Steel Company, the American Tin Plate Company, the American Sheet Steel Company, and the American Steel Hoop Company. Each of these constituted a merger of a number of hitherto competing businesses; and each, as it acquired a partial monopoly of the operations in its special field of steel manufacture, lifted its prices sharply. The profits accordingly rolled in. During its very first year Gary's Federal Steel Company was handsomely in the black and paid dividends on its preferred and common stock, despite its heavy capitalization; early in 1900 American Steel & Wire paid a seven per cent dividend.

Inevitably, now, a new notion popped into many minds. *Why not combine the combinations?* Why not make them into a mammoth supercorporation, the biggest and most powerful thing of its kind in the world? Since the Spanish War, America had suddenly become conscious of being at last a world power; could not such a colossus of American steel capture the market not only of its own continent but of other continents, too?

But there was one thing which stood squarely in the way of such a dream. The biggest, most efficient, and most fabulously successful unit in the industry was the Carnegie Steel Company, the control of which was held tightly in the hands of that twinkling little genius, white-bearded Andrew Carnegie. And while the new combinations which had been put together by Gary and Gates and Morgan and the Moores concentrated almost without exception upon making finished articles—wire, pipe, rails, girders, steel plate, etc.—Carnegie dominated the making of the crude steel from which they fashioned their wares. Obviously any supercombination must include Carnegie's company, or its life would be precarious indeed. Carnegie, who was in his middle sixties, was known to be looking forward to retirement. Perhaps he would sell. The trouble was that his company had become so incredibly prosperous, as the business boom of the late nineties continued, that men gasped at the size of the sum of money which would be required to buy out the principal stockholder. It would run into hundreds of millions.

Two of Carnegie's colleagues, Henry Clay Frick and Henry Phipps, toyed with various plans for buying Carnegie out. They engaged in a flirtation with the Moore brothers in the early months of 1899, and actually induced Carnegie to give them an option on the purchase of his company on behalf of some unidentified clients. (They did not dare tell Carnegie that the Moores were in on the deal, for if he had known it he would never have consented; he disliked everything that these speculator-promoters represented.) The scheme failed because too many other people distrusted the capacity of the Moores to manage such an undertaking; they could not get substantial financial backing. Morgan was among those who were approached, and would have none of any such deal. He too would not go into partnership with the Moores. Later, in the spring of 1900, Carnegie's chief aide, the brilliant Charles M. Schwab, went to Gary to propose that Federal Steel should buy Carnegie out, and Gary consulted Morgan. "I would not think of it," said Morgan; "I don't believe I could raise the money." He was well aware that so many New Jersey holding companies had been launched during the past two or three years—not only in steel but in other industries—with lavish issues of stock, that the stock market was suffering from what he called "undigested securities." Thus the matter rested. A supercombination seemed impossible.

• • •

Whereupon, in the summer of 1900, there began a ferocious struggle within the steel industry. The various new combinations which made finished steel products were conscious of the need for "integrating" their businesses—for producing their own crude steel and even acquiring if necessary their own sources of iron ore, so as not to be dependent for their very existence upon the whims of Andrew Carnegie. They were so prosperous that they could save or raise money for the installation of blast furnaces or the leasing of ore fields. And so they began to make themselves ready to go into the manufacture of crude steel, in the hope of thus achieving independence. On behalf of American Steel & Wire, John W. Gates sent word to the Carnegie Company that he was canceling his contract for crude steel; in the future he would make his own. The Moore brothers sent identical notices on behalf of Steel Hoop and Sheet Steel. And word came that National Tube and American Bridge expected likewise to stop ordering from Carnegie.

Carnegie was idling that summer at Skibo Castle in Scotland, but there was nothing idle about his reaction to these rebuffs. He had noted for several weeks that the orders from some of these concerns had been dwindling, and had written to his colleagues in Pittsburgh that if the Steel Hoop people stopped ordering crude steel, the Carnegie Company should reply by going promptly into the manufacture of steel hoops. Now, when the full scope of the impending crisis became clear, he decided on a full declaration of war. The Carnegie Company would go into making finished products of all sorts. . . .

Schwab, who was Carnegie's right-hand man, went over to Scotland to visit him, bringing plans for a great new steel works. . . . "Go on and build the plant," ordered Carnegie, the fire of battle in his eyes.

The prospect that this decision opened up was staggering. All the steel combinations that had been effected during the past three years were in deadly peril. For Carnegie could produce steel more cheaply than anyone else on earth. He had immense resources. And he didn't mind stopping dividends entirely in order to pour the earnings of his company into new construction. . . .

Morgan was uneasy; and not on the score of Carnegie's steel operations alone. For Carnegie had declared war on the Pennsylvania Railroad too. The Pennsylvania had raised Carnegie's freight rates, and now in answer to this move the little warrior was negotiating with George Gould for the building of a new railroad link to connect the Western Maryland with Pittsburgh, thus destroying the Pennsylvania's monopoly of freight traffic between Pittsburgh and the seaboard. . . . "Carnegie," he was heard to say, "is going to demoralize railroads just as he has demoralized steel." Morgan tried to get Schwab to come and see him for a talk. Schwab did not come. Carnegie drove ahead with his plans. Apparently there was no stopping him.

• • •

But on the evening of December 12, 1900, two New Yorkers, J. Edward Simmons and Charles Stewart Smith, gave a dinner to Schwab at the University Club; Morgan accepted an invitation to attend, and was seated next to Schwab; and after dinner Schwab, who had a fine voice and was something of an orator, made an extraordinary speech on the future of the American steel industry. He told how the demand for steel was growing, and how America could dominate the steel trade of the entire world, if only the industry could be fully integrated for complete efficiency. . . . Only a single corporation which could carry the manufacture of steel through every stage from the mining of the ore to the completion of the finished product could accomplish this, said Schwab. And so great would be the economies such a company could achieve, that it would not have to hoist prices to prosper, as had the recent combinations; it could even cut prices and still make millions.

Morgan was vastly impressed. The picture that Schwab had drawn was of an orderly and disciplined industry, at peace with itself; how much better than this crazy, wasteful warfare! And the idea was big, very big indeed. Morgan liked things big. "After the cheers had subsided"—I quote from Burton J. Hendrick's life of Carnegie—"he took Schwab by the arm and led him to a corner. For half an hour the two men engaged in intimate conversation. The banker had a hundred questions to ask, to which Schwab replied with terseness and rapidity." Then Morgan went home to No. 219, and Schwab took the night train for Pittsburgh. But in the days that followed it was clear that Morgan was thinking long and hard about Schwab's idea, and was wondering how it could be turned into a reality. He would have to negotiate with Andrew Carnegie. How could this best be done?

He sent for Bet-a-Million Gates, who even if unreliable surely knew his way round, and asked whether Gates thought there was a chance that Carnegie would sell. Gates thought he might. . . . Schwab was the man to work through. All right, said Morgan; can you arrange this? Gates thereupon called up Schwab on the long-distance telephone and suggested that he come on to New York for a talk with Morgan.

Schwab didn't like the idea of talking with Morgan without telling Carnegie in advance; but Gates persuaded him that there would be no disloyalty to Carnegie if he, Schwab, were to happen to go to Philadelphia on a certain day and Morgan just happened to be there—say at the Hotel Bellevue. The date was accordingly set, and Schwab went to Philadelphia—only to find, instead of Morgan, a message to the effect that Morgan was laid up with a cold, and wouldn't Schwab be so good as to go on to New York and talk with Morgan that evening at No. 219? Schwab politely agreed to do so, and took the train to New York.

Whereupon there began, that very night, a momentous conference in the high-ceilinged, mahogany-paneled library at No. 219 that lasted until daylight. Four men took part in it: Morgan; his handsome and substantial partner Robert Bacon; the knowledgeable, easygoing Gates; and the young, self-made, energetic Schwab. They discussed what companies ought to be included in a merger, what companies omitted. . . . Gradually the picture of a new giant steel company began to take shape. Morgan asked Schwab whether he thought Carnegie would consent to sell; Schwab said he couldn't be sure, for the Scotchman was changeable, unpredictable. But Morgan had made up his mind to try. When the night-long session came to an end, Morgan asked Schwab to convey a firm proposal of purchase to Carnegie and to ask his price.

Schwab was a little uneasy at the prospect of confronting his chief with such a proposal, and asked Mrs. Carnegie's advice as to how to proceed. She suggested that a game of golf might put her husband in the most approachable humor; and so Schwab challenged the older man for a match the following morning at the links of the St. Andrews Golf Club in Westchester County. The two men played round the wintry links, and adjourned for lunch afterward to Carnegie's stone cottage on the hilltop above the club. There Schwab broke the news of Morgan's offer.

Now it must have occurred to the reader—it has occurred to a great many people—that possibly Carnegie had all this time been playing an elaborate game with a view to inducing just such a result as the Morgan offer: that his announced invasion of the territory of the other steel companies, and his threat to do battle with the Pennsylvania Railroad, had been conceived to this very end, and that he had concocted the idea of the Simmons-Smith dinner, and of getting Morgan to attend, and of turning loose upon him some carefully contrived oratory of the sort at which Schwab excelled. Perhaps; but there is no evidence of anything quite so Machiavellian. . . . But presently he realized that the time had at last come. This was it—the inevitable and desirable end of his years as a steelmaster—the moment when he could satisfy his long-standing wish to stop making money and begin making a career of giving money away.

On a slip of paper he jotted down in pencil a few figures. He gave the slip to Schwab and asked him to present it to Morgan.

What Carnegie proposed was that for every $1,000 in bonds of the Carnegie Company there should be exchanged $1,000 in securities of the new corporation which was yet to be formed; that for every $1,000 in stock of the Carnegie Company there should be given $1,500 in securities of the new corporation; but that he would take his own personal payment wholly in bonds. . . . To Carnegie himself, who owned some 58 percent of Carnegie Company stock, this would mean a payment in bonds to the amount of no less than $225,639,000 (par value). For all the bonds and stocks of the Carnegie Company, it would mean a payment of bonds and stocks to the amount of $400,000,000—later increased by throwing in some extra common stock for Carnegie's partners, so that the total reached $492,556,766 (par value). A huge transaction.

Schwab took the slip of paper to Morgan. Morgan glanced at it and said, "I accept."

Not only was there no bargaining over terms, but it was not until weeks later, when Morgan was drawing contracts with the other concerns in the deal, that he suddenly woke up to the fact that he had no signed agreement from Carnegie at all—nothing but those penciled figures on a slip of paper. Suppose Carnegie should drop dead? Or utterly change his mind? Hurriedly Morgan sent for Stetson and for Carnegie's lawyer, and they prepared a suitable letter which Carnegie obligingly signed.

During this interval of time it occurred to Morgan that he and Carnegie had not met for a long time and that perhaps they should have a friendly chat. Being accustomed to meeting people on his own ground, he called up Carnegie and suggested that he come down to 23 Wall Street for a visit. Carnegie replied that since the distance from Wall Street to Fifty-first Street was no greater than the distance from Fifty-first Street to Wall Street, and since he, Carnegie, was the senior of the two, perhaps Mr. Morgan would care to call upon him. Morgan at once went, and the two men talked together in a closed room for just fifteen minutes; after which Morgan departed, saying as he shook his host's hand, "Mr. Carnegie, I want to congratulate you on being the richest man in the world!"

To this remark there is a postscript to be added. A year or two later the two men met on shipboard. Said Carnegie, "I made one mistake, Pierpont, when I sold out to you."

"What was that?" asked Morgan.

"I should have asked you a hundred million more than I did."

"Well," said Morgan, "you would have got it if you had."

J. Pierpont Morgan, Jr.

RON CHERNOW

Jack Morgan was J. Pierpont Morgan's son—and no doubt suffered from comparison with that legendary figure. He succeeded to the mantle as head of their firm, enjoyed his business role immensely and lived in a mansion grander than any of his father's. An Anglophile, he spent a great deal of time in England, where his principal residence came complete with a village and villagers. He bequeathed his family's London townhouse to the U.S. government for use as the residence of our Ambassador.

Jack Morgan moved through the twenties like a monarch. One journalist described him embarking from his limousine at 23 Wall: "I saw two other men inconspicuously draw themselves up in an attitude of attention, like soldiers in mufti, acting on their instincts or through force of habit. . . . The great doors with their huge panes of spotless glass and their polished brass swung open and shut.". . . He enjoyed his spot at the top of the Morgan empire. About to present Pope Pius XI with restored Coptic texts in 1922, he made this observation: "My special job is the most interesting I know of anywhere. More fun than being King, Pope, or Prime Minister anywhere—for no one can turn me out of it and I don't have to make any compromises with principles.". . .

Jack lived regally at his 250-acre island estate, Matinicock Point, off the North Shore. Visitors passed through enormous wrought-iron gates and down an endless drive shaded by linden trees; in season bloomed several thousand tulips and daffodils under the direction of Jessie Morgan. The estate required several dozen full-time gardeners. There were also cows, horses, greenhouses, boxwood and rose gardens, cottages for the staff, and a dock down at the Sound.

Amid open lawns and high trees, the red-brick mansion was grander than any of Pierpont's residences. It was designed by Grant La Farge with an imposing columned entrance. Inside, three famous ladies—Rubens's Anne of Austria, Gainsborough's Lady Gideon, and Sir Thomas Lawrence's countess of Derby—stared down from the walls of a house specially fireproofed for them. The majestic stairway of the forty-five-room house was lined with beautiful floral arrangements.

Jack liked quiet, domestic pleasures. Delicate and sedentary, a born dabbler, he enjoyed detective novels and crossword puzzles. His literary hero was Rudyard Kipling. He disapproved of contact sports, and when his two sons, Junius and Harry, went to Groton, he protested the introduction of football, calling it immoral, dangerous, and brutal. . . . He loved taking drives in his chauffeured cars and had four of them—two Rolls-Royces, a Lincoln, and a Buick roadster.

He was fanatical about his privacy and hostile to the press. . . .

Only once did Jack submit willingly to press photographs. One day, as a motorboat was taking him out to the *Corsair* [the large yacht inherited from his father] the photographers were in their usual hot pursuit, when Jack's Panama hat blew into the Sound. A photographer fished it from the water and gave it to Jack's boatswain, saying, "Your boss hasn't treated me with much courtesy, but I am glad to do him a favor.". . . Like Pierpont, Jack was sentimental and could be disarmed by a gallant gesture. When he heard the story, he ordered the photographer up on deck and posed for twenty minutes of pictures.

Both Jack and Jessie loved England, which they visited each spring and summer. When the London *Times* tagged him an English squire, Jack was thrilled. . . . He had a London townhouse at 12 Grosvenor Square and bequeathed Princes Gate, the old family townhouse, to the U.S. government as a residence for the American ambassador. Just as George Peabody had hosted annual Fourth of July dinners, Jack hoped future ambassadors would "live like gentlemen and have their Fourth of July receptions in adequate surroundings.". . . Later on, Princes Gate would be the wartime residence of Ambassador Joe Kennedy, who finally slipped into the House of Morgan through a back door. It was the house opposite Hyde Park fondly remembered by the Kennedy sons.

Jack's major British residence was Wall Hall, his three-hundred-acre estate north of London with artificial lakes and gardens. He ruled the village like a whimsical Prospero. He didn't simply live in the village, he owned it. . . .

To an extraordinary degree, he was a creature of custom and comfort. So that he could drive without removing his plug hat, he had an English firm design a car with a special high top. He corresponded with a haberdasher about socks that didn't slide smoothly enough over his heel. Perhaps fearing his own emotions—or else in homage to his Yankee-trading ancestors—he always wanted things around him to proceed tidily. He was obsessed with punctuality. At Wall Hall, he had so many clocks that someone came in weekly just to rewind them. For gifts, he often gave his partners rare gold watches.

The year had its unchanging rhythms for Jack. The high spot was August 12—the Glorious Twelfth that launched the Scottish grouse-hunting season. "Nearly everybody I know has started for shooting in Scotland," he once wrote a partner in early August. . . . Who else in America could make such a statement? . . .

After his father's death, Jack hadn't been able to pursue collecting and was preoccupied with settling the estate. Now, in another parallel to Pierpont's life, Jack widened his collecting as he moved into his midfifties. Once again, Belle Greene went on buying trips to Europe, and Jack regarded her with affection and slightly fearful awe. When four rare manuscripts owned by the earl of Leicester came on the market, Greene was afraid to commit so much money on her own. She asked Jack to negotiate. He went to Europe and after a sleepless night bought them for an estimated $500,000. Jack told the seller: "My librarian told me she wouldn't dare spend so much of my money. But just the same, I wouldn't dare face her if I went home without the manuscripts.". . .

Jack hadn't yet erected the sort of monument to Pierpont that Pierpont had to Junius. In 1924, he incorporated the Pierpont Morgan Library in his father's memory, with Belle Greene as the first director; he provided a $1.5-million endowment. Perhaps recalling the brouhaha over the art collection's breakup, he summoned reporters for a wistful interview. Seated in the West Room, where Pierpont had worked and Junius stared down from above the mantel, Jack said, "This is the room where my father literally lived. I think it is probably the most peaceful room in New York. You never hear a thing here except occasionally a bad automobile horn.". . .

As he took reporters around the library, he snatched up interesting items and talked about them. Taking up a Dickens manuscript, he said, "Scrooge and all the rest of them are there. Isn't that nice?" In his remarks may be heard the plaintive note of a man seeking public love—love that he felt he deserved but was always denied. At the end of his tour, he asked, "Now what do you think of it? Have I done a good thing in making this gift?". . .

Jack suffered two emotional blows from which he never recovered. In 1924, he lost his mother, who was still living in the original Madison Avenue mansion; it was torn down only after her death. She had survived into her eighties, by then a stone-deaf old woman. Jack, as a boy, had gravitated toward his mother's warmth and gentleness. His own close marriage to Jessie probably recapitulated the earlier relationship.

Like Fanny, Jessie Morgan became somewhat weak and sickly, but there were major differences. Jessie was a natural executive and extremely efficient in running four giant households, supervising butlers, footmen, and housekeepers. She had a shy, matronly look that hid steely discipline. . . .

Jessie served Jack, adored him, and advised him in every aspect of his life. She was the invisible safety net that stopped him from falling, and he relied on her judgment implicitly.

Then, in the summer of 1925, Jessie contracted a sleeping sickness—an inflammation of the brain—then prevalent in the United States. It was thought to derive from the influenza pandemic of 1917–18. Jessie fell into a coma and had to be fed through a tube. Antibiotics weren't yet available, and eminent physicians could only counsel patience. They told Jack the disease was running its course and that Jessie would eventually wake up. A trusting person, Jack waited and prayed. Afraid of submitting to melancholy, he put on a brave front and reported to 23 Wall every day, taking comfort from Jessie's smallest stirrings and from the fact that, as she slept, she was well nourished and gaining weight. . . .

By mid-summer, Jessie had slowly improved, and Jack was buoyed by reports that her condition was better than at any time since the onset of the illness. Doctors assured Jack he could go to work, without fear. On August 14, 1925, he went to the office only to receive a late-morning call to return home at once. By the time he arrived, Jessie was dead. Her heart had stopped from what doctors thought was an embolism. They were stunned by the sudden reversal.

Still recovering from his mother's death, Jack was distraught, inconsolable. He mourned deeply and reverently, much as Pierpont had mourned the sainted Mimi. In a moving outburst of grief and affection, he told Lamont, "Well, I have all these years to look back upon, everything to remember and nothing to forget.". . .

Solitary, clad in tweeds, and smoking his meerschaum pipe, Jack wandered about his formal gardens, a melancholy widower. His partners noticed his loneliness. Easily wounded, he had had a tendency toward melodrama and self-pity, both of which now became pronounced. Writing of his fourteen grandchildren in 1928, he told a friend, "It makes a great difference to me in my life, which is necessarily very lonely.". . . Sometimes he asked his chauffeur of twenty-five years, Charles Robertson, to drive him down to the Morgan Memorial Park. He would sit beside the chauffeur and stare silently at the water. For all his money, he now thought himself the loneliest of men.

Lehman Brothers

JOSEPH WECHSBERG

Lehman Brothers' early history in many ways exemplified the adventuresome spirit by which a number of firms eventually established themselves in Wall Street. Their transition from Würzburg to Montgomery to Manhattan took only 22 years.

In 1844, Henry Lehman, the 21-year-old, enterprising son of a Würzburg cattle merchant, arrived in America. Like many other immigrants he began his career as an itinerant peddler. He was honest and hard-working, and the people trusted him. A year later he settled in Montgomery, Alabama, and hung out a small sign, H. LEHMAN, outside his little shop on Commerce Street. By 1850 he had been joined by his younger brothers, Emanuel and Mayer, and the three brothers formed a partnership called Lehman Brothers. The Montgomery directory listed them as "grocers." Actually the store supplied clothes, utensils, food, and a great many other articles needed by the local cotton farmers.

Business was excellent in booming Montgomery where the war cry was "Cotton is king!" Many customers paid in raw cotton instead of cash. The Lehman brothers were resourceful traders. They first made a profit when they acquired the cotton and then resold it again at a profit. A shrewd sense of profit-making is characteristic of the beginnings of all merchant-banking dynasties. These men prospered because they were just a little smarter than the next fellow. Gradually Lehmans' retail trade became less important as it devoted more energy to the cotton-brokerage business.

Henry Lehman was known as something of a hypochondriac. He was always haunted by the fear that he was going to die of yellow fever. . . . When the dreaded disease broke out in Montgomery in 1855, Henry hurriedly left town and went to New Orleans where Lehman Brothers was going to have a branch office. A few weeks after he arrived there he caught yellow fever and died, at the age of 33.

In 1858 Emanuel Lehman opened an office in New York where the big opportunities were. But Emanuel was, above all, a Southern patriot, and when the Civil War broke out, he hurried back to Montgomery, the Cradle of the Confederacy.

Excerpted from Joseph Wechsberg, from Ron Chernow's *The House of Morgan*, Touchstone Books, year unknown, pp. 262–269.

The Lehmans served the South well. Emanuel fought in the Confederate Army. Later he helped to sell Confederate bonds in London, and then
he went on to the Continent, trying to sell cotton. It was a great chance
for an ingenious merchant who was not afraid of running the blockade. He
could buy cotton in the South cheaply and sell it in Germany at 10 times
the price. It may not have been very patriotic; it may even have involved
him in some smuggling. . . .

In 1866 Emanuel Lehman went to New York to operate a cotton-
brokerage business at 176 Fulton Street. Two years later Mayer followed
him there and they moved to Pearl Street where they stayed 10 years,
when they moved again to larger quarters, at 40 Exchange Place. . . .

Lehman Brothers prospered during the economic and industrial expansion in the United States in the second half of the nineteenth century. They
kept their original firm in Montgomery until 1912. The New Orleans
branch lasted until 1936. But they concentrated their energies in Manhattan. Emanuel remained the firm's conservative "inside" man, while the
more aggressive Mayer saw the outside contacts. For many years the two
brothers alone managed the affairs of the firm. They were among the
founders of the New York Cotton Exchange, became members of the Coffee
Exchange and of the first New York Petroleum Exchange. In 1887 the firm
acquired a seat at the New York Stock Exchange.

Toward the end of the century, Lehman Brothers, still primarily a commodity house, began to engage in enterprises which led to investment
banking. It acted as "private bankers" to industry, and was appointed Fiscal
Agent of the State of Alabama. It sold the state's bonds (not an easy job in
view of the South's bad credit rating) and serviced Alabama's debts, interest payments and other obligations. Becoming interested in the industrialization of the South, it backed cotton mills in Alabama and Louisiana.

After Mayer Lehman's death in 1897 and Emanuel's retirement shortly
afterwards, a second generation of Lehmans—Philip, Sigmund, Arthur,
Meyer H. and Herbert—took over and directed the firm's activities toward investment banking. . . .

At the beginning of the twentieth century, partnership in Lehman
Brothers was limited by a family law to blood relatives bearing the name of
Lehman.

Tokushichi Nomura II

ALBERT J. ALLETZHAUSER

Tokushichi Nomura II built his father's small money-changing entity into what became the world's largest and most profitable securities business. Here, we learn of his first high-stakes adventure in the Japanese stock market, read about how he capitalized on his early perception of the value that securities research might have, and follow the course of a series of breathtaking stockmarket bets made by a man possessed not only of strong convictions, but of iron nerves as well.

According to family legend, Tokushichi Nomura I, the father of the founder of Nomura Securities, was the misbegotten son of a samurai and his serving girl. He was born in 1850, toward the end of the Tokugawa era (1603–1867), the romantic age of feudal lords and samurai, in a Japan closed to the outside world. The era took its name from the Shogun Ieyasu Tokugawa, who by the year 1603 had united the battle-torn Japanese fiefdoms into a nation, moving the capital to Edo, the eastern city today called Tokyo. Although the ultimate source of political legitimacy was still the Emperor, in practice he was no more than a puppet of the Tokugawa shogunate and never left his palace in the ancient capital of Kyoto. Life was much harsher than the poems and woodblock prints suggest; the Shogun ruled the general populace with an iron hand.

Toshitsura Doi, Nomura's father, was thirteenth in an exalted line of samurai who served the Shogun. He was the keeper of the monumental Osaka Castle and one of the nation's richest men. He disavowed any blood relation to young Tokushichi and banned him from using his noble name. Tokushichi took his mother's name, Nomura, a fairly common Japanese surname, and a wealthy landowner was paid to rear him. At the age of ten he was apprenticed to a moneychanger named Yahei Osakaya.

Apprenticeship was the normal form of school for male Osaka children in the nineteenth century. Tokushichi's tasks in the Osakaya household included sweeping the street in front of his master's money-shop and sprinkling it with water from the communal well to keep the dust down. Any Japanese shopkeeper, then as now, who failed to maintain tidiness in his small area by watering it during the day was considered lazy by his neighbours and his shop destined to failure.

Excerpted from *The House of Nomura* by Albert J. Alletzhauser, HarperCollins, 1990–1991, pp. 25–26 & 40–49.

Later, Osakaya gave him the arduous work of wheeling copper coins around in a cart. These heavy coins were in constant use for daily transactions, and it was Tokushichi's duty to haul them around to customers who wanted to exchange them for silver or to break a silver coin into smaller change.

In the mid-nineteenth century Osaka was Japan's main entrepot centre, an intensely practical and entrepreneurial city. Not until the twentieth century would Tokyo become Japan's commercial centre. . . .

Known as the "kitchen of Japan," Osaka derived its status as a hub of economic activity, and much of its character, from its central role in rice trading. Rice was then the key to the Japanese economy, the staple against which wealth was measured and though which power was maintained. The Dojima rice market, located on a small island at the delta of three main rivers in northern Osaka, supported more than 1,300 registered rice dealers. Established in 1688, it provided a clearing mechanism for surplus rice that enabled rice-growers to sell their crop ahead of a harvest if they felt an exceptionally good year would drag down prices. Or, if a poor harvest was anticipated, they could buy rice and sell it later at an inflated price.

The feudal lords saw an additional use for the rice exchange. When money become tight, as often happened during the costly annual pilgrimage to the Tokugawa shogunate in Tokyo, they could sell rice tickets, receipts for rice stored in warehouses or for crops not yet harvested. These tickets became a form of currency in which rice dealers were only too happy to trade and this secondary market at Dojima became the world's first futures market.

• • •

In 1902, after his three obligatory years in uniform, Nomura found himself back at his father's moneychanging shop as general manager. The next three years were spent building up the family business, studying the stockmarket and persuading clients to buy and sell shares. This was his real love. He had no interest in buying and selling copper, silver and gold, a task he left to his brother Jitsusaburo. In Nomura's eyes, moneychanging had a limited role for the future. Banks were beginning to handle most money transactions and, with the introduction of the yen, Japan now had a proper currency. The future of money-making lay in the stockmarket.

Japan declared war on Russia in February 1904, following the continuing dispute over spheres of influence in Korea and Manchuria. Tokushichi decided it was the perfect time to expand Nomura Shoten from a middle-sized moneychanging house that only dabbled in stocks to a fully fledged stockbroking firm. He had seen the stockmarket gallop ahead during the Sino-Japanese War eight years earlier. At that time he had been too young to take advantage of the bull market, but now he was determined to become rich. He understood that modern war fuelled industrial expansion.

There was one obstacle—his father. Although Nomura was general manager of Nomura Shoten, and his father, often drunk, was seldom in the shop, he had to uphold the tradition of filial piety and somehow persuade his father to accept the new direction for the family business. Nomura pleaded with him to see the wisdom of committing capital to the stockmarket at such a time.

His father, however, stubbornly refused Nomura access to the family funds, partly because stock dealers were detested in Osaka and partly because his son had been so unsuccessful in his previous market forays. It tortured the younger Tokushichi to think of the money he could be making in the market if only his father would allow it. He became obsessed with the thought of the money sitting idly in the company safe. Not until June 1904, when his mother died, was Nomura able to wear down his father's resistance.

"How much do you need to start a stock business?" asked his father. "Half the family fortune," Nomura replied. *Twenty thousand yen*, more money than the average Osaka man made in his entire working life. Tokushichi was stunned by the amount of money his son wanted as capital—speculative capital—but he suddenly relented: he intended anyway to retire one day and turn everything over to his eldest son.

Nomura quickly changed the name of Nomura Shoten to Nomura Tokushichi Shoten and later that year he married Kikuko Yamada, the daughter of a well-to-do merchant, a match arranged by his father. For Nomura it was a timely marriage, since Kiku's job was to wash, cook and care for the house, chores that had been neglected since his mother's death in the summer. Her presence was fortuitous in helping to soften his father's outrage when he suddenly hired thirteen employees in anticipation of a stockmarket boom. Later Kiku produced two sons, Yoshitaro and Tokio.

Nomura's intuition proved correct. Japanese business prospered and in 1905 Japan dealt Russia crushing defeats at Tsushima and Port Arthur, marking the nation's graduation into the world of military and industrial might. The Tokyo and Osaka stockmarkets rallied sharply.

In 1905 Nomura made his first major stockmarket investment. Fukushima Boseki was a textile company rumoured to be headed for bankruptcy. But Nomura knew otherwise. Unlike most other stock traders of the early twentieth century, he took the trouble to visit the management of companies whose shares were quoted on the stock exchange. The spinning company had been set up by his brother-in-law, Yutaro Yasuhiro, to whom he had been apprenticed. The company was located just up the street from his own shop. Nomura would occasionally stop by for tea and to discuss business with Yasuhiro. To him it was clear that the rumours were being generated by stock traders who had taken short positions, selling shares in the company they did not have, and were trying to stir up a selling panic so that they could buy shares to cover their positions.

One day, after a particularly sharp sell-off in Fukushima Boseki shares, Nomura pestered the management into showing him their order-books. What he found was that instead of being on the verge of collapse, the firm was thriving as a result of wartime demand for uniforms, socks and tents. The order-books were bulging, the spinning looms were running at full capacity and profits had never been better.

The next day, when Nomura returned to the floor of the Osaka Stock Exchange, he started quietly buying up Fukushima shares. Other traders noticed his buying and questioned him, but he casually told them he had earlier sold short, and was now buying back to cover his short positions. He began buying shares at twenty yen and within days the price hit twenty-five. He kept on buying until the price reached thirty. Nervously, some of the traders who had sold shares they did not own began to panic and scrambled to buy them back. To their alarm they found Nomura had bought up most of the available shares and they were unable to buy back their stock without forcing the price still higher. Quick-witted dealers turned the short sellers' predicament into a "short squeeze," a buying panic that fed on itself.

Nomura sat back as the price rose each day, hitting thirty-five, then forty, forty-five, fifty. By the end of 1905 the price of Fukushima Boseki had rocketed fourfold to 100 yen and Nomura had earned on paper the 20,000 yen he had borrowed from his father earlier. He sold a few shares in the market on the way up, but was so thrilled with his first stockmarket killing that he kept most of his shares as a long-term investment. He refused to part with his holding even later when he became rich and famous. Nomura group companies have adhered to the wish of their founding father, so that in the 1990s, over eight decades after Tokushichi Nomura II purchased his first investment, they retain a 15 per cent stake in that same textile company, now known as Shikibo. And, as if to symbolize the Nomura group's bond with Shikibo, a distant relative of Tokushichi Nomura II reigns as president.

Nomura was crudely acting out intuitive market precepts which soon amassed him a considerable fortune. He played the crowds, mastering their psychology and getting the better of them. When emotion overtook reason in the stockmarket, he was there to buy from the distressed and sell to the eager, exploiting the mass mentality that led people to make impulsive and often irrational decisions.

Nomura decided that the best way to invest and beat the crowd was to hire someone to poke around individual companies, talk to management, check order-books and, if possible, calculate stock-price movements related to cycles in the Japanese and world economies. He hired an investigative journalist named Kisaku Hashimoto to run Nomura Tokushichi Shoten's newly formed research department. Hashimoto was a star reporter for the *Osaka-Mainichi Shimbun* who had many contacts who could pass him inside information on corporate Japan. He was the ideal man to be the nation's first research analyst. Moreover, he was a college graduate and at the time no college graduate would normally have considered joining a stock-dealing firm. In hiring Hashimoto, Nomura also improved the reputation of Nomura Shoten, differentiating the firm from the crude dealers on the floor of the Osaka Stock Exchange.

Tokushichi was harsh in his criticism of his own profession: "The biggest obstacle to our success is low-life personalities in the stock business." Bringing Hashimoto on board in 1907 began two precedents that set the company apart from other Japanese firms. First, Nomura was subsequently able to persuade even the smartest college graduates to join stock-broking; and second, to entice these graduates and to encourage them to stay, Nomura paid his employees salaries far in excess of those paid in any other securities firm. Tokushichi compellingly relates in his autobiography how his "blood boiled" at Japan's characterization of stock dealers as virtual outcasts. But it was not until 1987 that the status of stockbrokers—and of Nomura Securities in particular—came anywhere near that of bankers.

Hashimoto spent a lot of time visiting companies, following up rumours, formulating new ideas and writing the Nomura weekly stock comment. If one or two Kitahama dealers bought a certain spinning-company share in a conspiratorial manner because of an enormous purported contract with the government, Hashimoto would pry his way into the company and extract the truth. Some of his most valuable moles were in the nation's largest trading company, Mitsui Bussan, and by discerning which companies made the most frequent use of Mitsui as their agent to sell their manufactured products, he was able to keep track of order flows. Trading companies were—and still are—firms that acted as intermediaries in matching buyers and sellers of every imaginable product. Friends in Nippon Yusen, the large shipping company, informed Hashimoto which firms were chartering the most space in its fleet, giving Nomura Shoten a rough picture of who was exporting overseas. Tokushichi Nomura in turn used this information to buy and sell stock on the Osaka stockmarket.

In 1906 the Osaka stockmarket was in the midst of an unprecedented boom. Nomura had optimistically added ten telephones to his three existing lines, employing a woman with a seductive manner to operate the switchboard and receive customers, thinking she would encourage his male clients to place orders. Tokushichi's small sales force went knocking from door to door (as it still does), pressing clients and potential customers to buy stock in the market.

Nomura himself handled the riskier work of buying and selling stock and stock futures for the house account. For every stock he bought—and physically appropriated to stash away in his company safe as a longer-term investment—he also bought the stock's considerably more speculative futures contract. He bought shipping stocks in firms such as Japan Postal Service Shipping, the government freight operator, which in 1906 leapt from eighty to 190. At the same time, his investment in Fukushima Boseki, which had already earned him his initial start-up capital of 20,000 yen, kept hitting new highs. Fukushima Boseki reached 150 in May, inched up to 160 by June and to 175 by July. Then it really began to roar: 222 in August, 324 in October and 421 by the end of 1906.

The great 1906 bull market—one of the greatest in the history of Japan—spread like wildfire. Stocks would suddenly burst into life, setting new highs and doubling or tripling in a matter of weeks. A buying panic would ensue on the Osaka Stock Exchange floor, as dealers pushed and shoved one another to buy the latest fast-moving stock, only to find that interest had subsided, having leapt to yet another stock.

Nomura had been buying stock since 1905 and was sitting on vast profits in both his long-term portfolio and his stock-futures portfolio. To be rich in Japan in the early twentieth century meant having a net worth of at least 100,000 yen (about $50,000 then, $1.5 million in current real terms) and Tokushichi Nomura was worth ten times that amount. In December 1906 his brother Jitsusaburo, always inclined to caution, advised Nomura to sell his shares. After all, why allow excessive greed to risk the million yen he had made? Nomura saw the wisdom of his brother's advice, but his thirst for market excitement, his *need* always to be at risk in the stockmarket, exerted a stronger pull. Not content with banking his profits, he calculated he would make twice as much by betting the market would fall.

Nomura had no doubt that the 1906 bubble would burst. He and Hashimoto did some research and found close similarities with the conditions before the stockmarket plunge following the Sino-Japanese War. They began to examine the daily data on the market closely as Nomura's scouts tracked the selling and buying patterns of major Osaka dealers. Then, on 10 December, they detected a subtle change, noting that a few big dealers had begun selling. That day Nomura took action and began selling out his long-term portfolio, eliminating one third of his holdings by the end of the week. At the same time, he started selling share futures short, betting that the market would fall and he would be able to buy back at a cheaper price. Prices continued to rise, however, as the big Tokyo dealers unexpectedly began buying Osaka shares. Jitsusaburo urged him not to take additional risks by selling short. "Only sell your long-term holdings," he told Nomura, but his elder brother was unmoved. His mind was set—he wanted to add another bag of gold to the swelling family coffers.

Nomura's selling had little impact on the market. Prices rose daily and Jitsusaburo pleaded desperately with Tokushichi to cover his short positions. Then, on 26 December, five medium-sized stock dealers paid a visit to Nomura's offices to ask him to persuade his childhood friend Einosuke Iwamoto, now one of Kitahama's most successful stock dealers, to start selling in the hope of triggering a big sell-off. They needed help, but Nomura refused his fellow dealers on the grounds that he would be taking advantage of his special relationship with his friend. The dealers left Nomura and decided to solicit Iwamoto's support themselves. Surprisingly, he agreed to help them and the next day led the selling charge on the floor of the Osaka Stock Exchange. But their efforts were useless. The buying spree continued.

Each day Tokushichi, who had sold out his entire long-term holdings to finance his futures positions, waited for the market to show signs of weakness and each day the market moved against him. He was now losing considerable sums of money. The bull market of 1906 carried on into 1907. Tokushichi, distressed with the abnormal rise of the market, went so far as to place a large advertisement in a local Osaka newspaper warning investors of danger ahead.

Although the market was still moving against him, Nomura stepped up the pace of his short selling. Inevitably, margin calls from the market traders who dealt for him began to arrive. Japanese investors at that time needed little cash to make vast speculations on the market. If they made money, everything was fine and the profits were added to their trading accounts. But if the market did not go their way, they needed to remit funds on a daily basis.

The money Nomura had placed on consignment was rapidly being whittled down, so that by early January the fretful brokers began to press him even more brusquely. Years later, Nomura recounted how he had hidden under his desk to avoid creditors. He eventually resorted to hiring a rickshaw for the day and furtively wheeling around the streets of Osaka—in the middle of winter—stopping in obscure back-street cafes where he was sure not to run into irate creditors or fair-weather friends from Kitahama. Tension mounted at Nomura Shoten as salesmen, clerks and secretaries realized their jobs were in danger unless the market began falling soon. But day after day it continued to rise.

By late January 1907 Tokushichi was desperate. He decided to seek the aid of a banker named Washio Shibayama who was manager of the Konoike Bank, one of the three leading banks in Osaka at that time. Shibayama faced a delicate situation. A Nomura Shoten bankruptcy could take down the bank, but Nomura Shoten was one of his most important customers. Like his counterparts at other banks, Shibayama had virtually unlimited powers of discretion when lending to customers, playing a supportive role in nurturing Japan's early industrialization. Little documentation was needed to lend money. Instead, bankers relied on friendship, instinct and judgment—often in that order.

Nomura played with Shibayama's emotions in his bid to ensure No-mura Shoten's survival.

"How much do you need?" Shibayama asked.

"One million yen," came the reply.

Shibayama stuttered, "That is one third of our bank's entire paid-up capital and I am only the manager of a single branch."

Shibayama listened carefully as Tokushichi explained in detail why he believed the stockmarket would collapse. In a crowning flourish he handed Shibayama a list of all his personal assets and pledged them to the bank. "I am betting my life that I am correct," said Nomura, in the ultimate Japa-nese pledge of honour. "If someone considers a matter thoroughly and does nothing, the outcome is the same as if he had considered nothing at all. I have never been wrong."

Then, in a final act of bravado, Nomura secretly offered Shibayama a high-ranking job with Nomura Shoten—conditional, of course, upon the loan. In case he should be fired by Konoike's president, Shibayama thought it prudent to accept the offer, and advanced Nomura the money.

Tokushichi now had a reprieve and could meet his consignment pay-ments. But the next two days proved nerveracking. The market surged still higher on a renewed wave of buying. In Osaka the index was up fifty-eight points, or nearly 8 percent, on 16 January and jumped another fifty-one points the following day. Another peak, 774 on the index, was scaled two days later. Somehow Tokushichi and the other dealers, including Iwamoto, kept their nerve. This could not go on forever.

Then, on a snowy 19 January, it happened: the market began to crack. Jitsusaburo was first with the news. He ran in the snow from the stock ex-change to Nomura's office, only to find Tokushichi, on the brink of a vast fortune, dozing.

"Wake up!" he shouted. "The selling has begun."

Nomura groaned and rolled over to go back to sleep.

"Wake up!" his brother shouted again. "Prices are falling." This time Tokushichi heard his brother. He jumped off his futon and began hugging Jitsusaburo. "I knew it. I saw it would happen. We are saved."

• • •

Within days, the great bull market of 1906 became the great bear market of 1907, one of the most dramatic declines in the history of the Japanese stockmarket, comparable to the collapse of the St. Petersburg exchange in 1917 and of the Shanghai stockmarket in 1949. In the twelve days from the peak of 19 January 1907 to the end of the month, the market shed one third of its value. By the end of 1907 the selling bloodbath had reduced the market's value by 88 percent. The final reading on the index at the end of the year was a mere 92, down from 774.

Nomura made three million yen—the equivalent to $60 million in current real terms. He became a legend. Traders, fond of labels, nicknamed him "the great general of the stockmarket." Aged twenty-eight, he was worth over five million yen, including the million he had made in the bull market and another million he had made speculating in property.

. . .

In 1928, when Tokushichi had reached the age of fifty, he was awarded the highest personal accolade of his life. Emperor Hirohito elevated him to the House of Peers, the noble legislative arm of the imperial family, whose members were selected by Japan's conservative aristocracy or appointed by the Emperor. . . .

At first the highbrow members sneered at the son of an Osaka money-changer, but eventually the quality of the speeches Tokushichi gave on financial matters won him favour.

Jonathan Binns Were

Jonathan Binns Were came to what was then Port Phillip, Australia, as a colonial seeking opportunity in 1839, aged 30. He became an integral part of its growth and development and remained a community leader for over forty years until his death in 1885. Though twice brought to the verge of bankruptcy, he died in comparative affluence. He was buried in the churchyard of St. Andrews, Brighton, land he had given to the church early in his prosperous career. His firm, J.B. Were, continues to prosper.

[Jonathan Binns Were] was born at Wellington, Somerset, on 25th April, 1809. After finishing school he received a business training for 10 years in the house of Collins and Co., merchants and bankers, of Plymouth, who were largely interested in trade with the colonies. In 1833 he married Sophia Mullett Dunsford, a member of the Society of Friends, a woman of great charm and ability. In his thirtieth year Were resolved to settle in Australia. Possibly the action of his father and elder brother in breaking the entail of the Were properties had some influence on his decision, but he had doubtless also been attracted by the trade of his employees with New South Wales, and what he had heard from their clients of the opportunities that awaited a man of enterprise and courage.

Excerpted from *The House of Were*. Used with permission.

At any rate, when the properties were sold and the proceeds were divided among father and sons, J. B. Were received £9000. How well he invested this money may be judged from the fact that the goods he purchased with it brought £70,000 in Australia. It is not clear whether he actually chartered the ship *William Metcalfe*, in which he sailed, but it is certain that the bulk of her cargo was his. His purchase included a house in sections, ready for erection on his arrival at Port Phillip, and a number of tents. At Oporto he added a consignment of port wine in gallon glass decanters, engraved with the name J.B. Were.

We went aboard the *William Metcalfe* in Plymouth Harbour in July 1839. With him went his wife, his infant son, Jonathan Henry, afterwards a partner in J.B. Were & Son, his four-year-old daughter, Sophia Louisa . . . his brother-in-law, Robert Stevenson Dunsford, and two servants. Under the command of Captain Phillipson, the *William Metcalfe* set sail on 26th July, 1839, bound for Port Phillip. After a voyage of 113 days she arrived on 15th November, 1839. . . . She was one of the largest vessels on the Australian run. In addition to a small group of independent settlers, she carried 230 assisted immigrants, the largest shipload up to that time. The *William Metcalfe*, with the *David Clarke* (229 immigrants), the *Palmyra* (43) and the *Westminister* (208), all of which arrived between October and December 1839, ushered in an era of assisted immigration which was to increase the population of Port Phillip from 5,000 to 20,400 in two years. . . .

The scene that greeted the early arrivals in Port Phillip has been vividly pictured by a number of pioneers who left records of their impressions. . . . When they reached the settlement proper, with its straggling houses and huts running up the slopes of market and Queen Streets to Collins Street, only just beginning to look continuous, they must have realized they had come to a primitive new world. The stream of arrivals was so great that accommodation was available for only a fraction of the new settlers. The rest set up tents on the south side of the Yarra, where there was an ever-growing encampment.

Were had laid his plans with meticulous care. While most newcomers were seeking in vain for tradesmen to build them houses he unpacked his imported house and erected it on a site on the south-western corner of Collins and Spring Streets. . . . Were purchased the land at £3/10/-an acre. It was on the outskirts of the settlement. The home was named "Harmony Lodge."

• • •

Were was [industrious, capitalized on several opportunities and was soon] prosperous. But there were troublous times ahead, and he with others was brought almost to the verge of ruin during the period known as the "Hungry Forties." With increasing population, due partly to vigorous immigration, an era of speculation set in, particularly in land. At the first sales in 1837 land had brought moderate prices; but after 1839, when the second sales were held, a land boom developed. Values rose to unjustifiable heights, which might have been sustained but for the depression that over-took the main industry of the settlement—the production of wool. Be-tween 1837 and 1843 the price of wool underwent a steady recession, bringing disaster to all sections of the community. This was Victoria's first lesson in the effects of overseas affairs on Australian conditions, for the setback to the wool industry was the result largely of the depression in the textile industry in England. Victoria could not sell her wool abroad at profitable prices, and the effect was to reduce the value of sheep purchased at 23/- to 30/- per head to as little . . . as 2/- per head, with the pastoral properties thrown in.

• • •

The business of J.B. Were & Co. was already widely diversified, and the changed conditions [that came with the dawn of] the "gold era" gave it still greater scope. In particular, it laid the way open to more extensive exchange dealings and to important operations in the field of bullion broking. In Oc-tober 1831 an advertisement appeared in the Melbourne papers announcing that J.B. Were & Co. were cash purchasers of gold dust, wool and tallow, or would make liberal cash advances on such commodities consigned to their agents, Messrs. Frederick Huth & Co., London. . . .

In the early stages of the gold boom Were does not appear to have taken any direct interest in gold-mining, apart from his dealings as gold buyer and broker. . . .

Were reached out for a substantial share of the bullion broking busi-ness. Some advances were made against gold, the balance being payable less a discount of 10 percent on realisation in London, but diggers preferred to make the best terms possible at the moment and sold outright. . . .

The middle of 1853 was a period of transition from the old order to the new. Like practically every other business man, Were found the years of adaption to the requirements of the growing community a time of per-sistent difficulty and anxiety. For eight years from 1853 he was engaged almost continuously in unravelling the tangle into which his personal and business affairs had fallen. Until 1st September, 1853, the firm con-tinued under the style of J.B. Were & Co. On that date Robert Kent, a Melbourne merchant, was taken into partnership, and the firm was known as J.B. Were, Kent & Co. . . .

From the end of 1853 there was a growing list of insolvencies. The only people who appeared to benefit were the lawyers, who reaped a rich har-vest from the litigation arising from the failures which followed the burst-ing of the early gold boom. Several of the 80 barristers and 260 attorneys practising in Melbourne were, indeed, able to make incomes ranging from £7000 to £14,000 a year. While Were's troubles were partly attributable to business difficulties, they were due in part also to personal misfortune. In 1834, when he went to England, his affairs had already taken a turn for the worse, but he was still a man of considerable means. In his absence, however, a large proportion of his firm's funds was invested in a shipment of gold which, through some oversight, was uninsured. The ship was lost with all hands off the coast of New Guinea, and Were and his partners lost a fortune.

It may have been a desire to leave his troubles behind for a time that prompted his departure [for] England on 25th March, 1854. With his wife and family he embarked on the P. & O. steamer, *Chusan*, bound for England, via Singapore and Ceylon. His stay in England was prolonged and Victoria was not to see him again until early 1856. While he was in England his twin sons, Arthur Bonville Were and Charles Brooking Were were born at Westbourne Terrace, Hyde Park, London.

• • •

Were arrived back in Melbourne early in 1856. In his absence his business affairs had fallen into chaos, and his troubles were accentuated by the fact that many individuals and firms who owed him money were also in grave difficulties. In a statement which Were made to the Court in 1857, he said that the business first began to be unsuccessful during his absence in England from 1854 to 1856. Up to March 1857 he believed himself to be solvent. . . .

Despite his preoccupation with his own business and personal troubles, Were still found time to devote to public affairs. The Bill providing a constitution for the Colony of Victoria . . . received the Royal Assent on 16th July, 1855, and the Constitution came into force on the 23rd, November. [Were was elected a member of the Legislative Assembly by an overwhelming majority.]. . .

Were's political career was brief, and there is little to show that he took more than cursory interest in Parliamentary happenings. This was probably due to the fact that he was engrossed in unravelling the tangle into which his personal and business affairs had fallen. Early in 1857 Were resigned from Parliament. He never again sought to enter politics.

• • •

Late in 1856 the firm of J.B. Were, Kent & Co. was dissolved. From that time until 1st October, 1861, Were traded under the name of J.B. Were and Company, or J.B. Were. He retained his shipping agencies, and continued merchandising activities, but he was devoting more and more attention to stocks and shares, to which, ultimately, his activities were solely confined, thus laying the basis for the present firm of J.B. Were & Son.

This was a natural development for a man who had proved capable of continuously adapting himself to changing circumstances in a new and rapidly developing country, particularly one who had maintained a position of leadership in all departments of trade and finance.

• • •

A group of brokers, headed by J.B. Were, came together in October 1859, and established . . . Melbourne's first regular Stock Exchange. Of this institution, which devoted its attention wholly to stocks and shares and held regular calls daily, J.B. Were was the first chairman, and, at the outset, acted also as a secretary.

• • •

Up till the middle of 1885, though then in his seventy-seventh year, he had continued to play his part in public life and maintain his leadership in the troubled waters of the Stock Exchange. In June of that year, however, he became ill and [in December] passed away at his home.

Were was a true pioneer. Forty-six years before he had given up a life of comfort in the Homeland to cast his lot in a tiny settlement with a population of 5000 and only the rudiments of civilisation. He had seen the settlement grow into a flourishing Colony of nearly a million people; he had watched the spread of settlement out into previously uninhabited areas; he had lived through the epoch-making gold boom; and he had taken a leading part in shaping the destiny of the growing Colony. During the course of his career, his activities had covered the whole range of trade, finance and industry, and though twice brought to the verge of bankruptcy through coming to the rescue of business friends, had, with characteristic determination, rebuilt his fortunes to die in comparative affluence. In the meantime, he had taken a part in every notable public movement.

Some Unusual Investors

Sir Thomas Gresham

REV. FRANCIS WRANGHAM

Thomas Gresham, who founded the Royal Exchange as a matter of personal pride, was the propounder of Gresham's Law. He restored the credit of the British crown and was a financial advisor to Queen Elizabeth. He also became a very wealthy man.

The revolutions in the commercial affairs of Europe characterize the age of Elizabeth almost as strikingly as those of religion, with which they were at this time intimately connected; and, perhaps, there is not to be found in the annals of any other nation a combination of events so effectively concurring, at almost the same instant, to fix the renown of the Sovereign, and to insure the prosperity of the state. . . .

Thomas Gresham was the descendent of an ancient family, which . . . had already produced several eminent men in the earlier periods of British history. Nor was Sir Richard Gresham, the father of this gentleman, undistinguished. From his success in the business of a mercer [i.e., a dealer in expensive fabrics], he had been enabled to purchase considerable estates, became sheriff of London in 1531, and received the honour of knighthood from Henry VIII., who made him his principal agent for the negotiation of his fiscal concerns at Antwerp, during his wars with France. He, subsequently, discharged the office of Lord-Mayor. But what rendered him still more memorable as a citizen, was his having obtained leave for private merchants to become bankers, and to negociate bills of exchange without a special licence. This privilege being first exercised by merchants residing in Lombard-street, it was there that he proposed to build an Exchange: but it was reserved for his son Thomas to realise the project. . . .

Sir Richard left two sons, of whom John, the eldest (an eminent mercer in the reign of Edward VI.) accompanied the Protector Somerset in his expedition to Scotland, and was knighted by him upon the field after his victory at Musselburgh in 1547. The younger, the subject of this memoir, was born at London in 1519, and was bound apprentice to a mercer when he was extremely young: but he certainly did not long continue with him, as we find him subsequently a student at Caius College under its celebrated founder Dr. Caius, who in commendation of his proficiency stiled him *Doctissimus*

Excerpted from Rev. Francis Wrangham, *The British Plutarch*, 1816, pp. 535–545.

Mercator, 'the very learned merchant.' The profits of trade however were at that time so great, and such large estates had been acquired by it in his own family, that he also engaged in it, and was made free of the Mercer's Company in 1543. He married about this time, it is supposed, the daughter of William Fernley of Suffolk, relict of William Reade, Esq. of Middlesex.

Sir William Dansell had succeeded Sir Richard Gresham, as the King's agent at Antwerp; but by his bad management, instead of supplying his Majesty with money, he involved him so deeply in debt, that the merchants of that city refused to make any further advances. This greatly embarrassing the royal affairs at home, a letter of recall was dispatched to Dansell, which he refused to obey. Mr. Gresham was now summoned by the Council, and requested to advise by what means his Majesty could best be enabled to discharge the debt (amounting to 260,000£) or put it in such a train of liquidation, that his loans might proceed as usual. His suggestions upon this point must have been highly satisfactory; as without any solicitation on his part he was appointed agent, and removed with his family to Antwerp in 1551. Here, he . . . transmitted a plan to England for discharging the debts in question at Antwerp in two years. His proposal was, that the Council should remit with the utmost privacy about 1300£ a week, of which he would make such a discretional use in the market, as should prevent the artificial fall of the exchange. . . . He further proposed, that his Majesty should take the commerce of the lead-mines into his own hands, and forbid the exportation of that metal, except on the sovereign's account, for five years. This measure had the desired effect; and the price of lead rose considerably in the Flemish markets. By these two mercantile stratagems he turned the balance in favour of England, and the royal debts were punctually discharged within the term proposed. The credit likewise of the English crown, which was previously questioned by the Flemish merchants, rose to such a height, that Mr. Gresham could borrow whatever sums he thought proper on equitable terms.

The demise of Edward retarded, for a time, the honours earned by these eminent exertions. Upon the accession of Queen Mary, he was recalled: but he had been rendered independent by the munificence of his grateful employer, who beside lands to the yearly value of 300£, about three weeks before he died settled a pension of 100l£ upon him and his heirs forever; making use of these words, with other honorable expressions in the patent, "You shall know, that you have served a king.". . .

When Elizabeth succeeded to the crown, he was one of the first taken into favour. Soon after her accession, she employed him to furnish the royal arsenals with arms, and the year following conferred upon him the honour of knighthood, and appointed him her agent in foreign parts. Being now in the highest esteem with his fellow-citizens, and in great credit at court, he resolved to fix his residence in the city, and to live there in a manner suitable to his rank and fortune. For this purpose he built a large and sumptuous house on the west side of Bishopsgate Street.

The merchants of London still continuing to meet in Lombard Street in the open air, exposed to the inclemencies of the weather, Sir Thomas resolved to revive his father's plan of erecting for them, on the plan of the Bourse at Antwerp, a commodious Exchange. This he generously offered to do at his own expense, if the corporation would assign over to him a proper spot of ground, sufficiently spacious for the purpose. The city most gratefully accepted his proposal. . . .

The edifice was completed, and the shops opened, in 1569; and in January, 1570, the Queen attended by her nobility came from Somerset House to Sir Thomas' residence in Bishopsgate Street to dinner, on her return through Cornhill entered the new building, and having viewed every part thereof, caused it to be proclaimed by a trumpet and a herald the 'Royal Exchange. . . .'

To remedy the scarcity of silver-coin, which obstructed inland trade, Gresham, knowing that one Reggio (an Italian merchant) had lodged 30 thousand Flemish ducatoons in the Tower for security, and that he had likewise a considerable quantity of the same pieces in the hands of private friends in London, advised the Queen to make a purchase of them, and to coin them into English shillings and sixpences, by which she would at once gain three or four thousand pounds, and retain all this fine silver in her realm. . . . To effect this, Elizabeth borrowed the amount from the London merchants for two years, at moderate interest. At the same time, Sir Thomas sent five sacks of new Spanish ryals, his own property, to the Mint; and this example encouraging others, when the new coinage was issued, silver currency became so plentiful, that the greatest part of the royal debts in Flanders were paid with it: the residue being soon afterward remitted in bills of exchange on Hamburgh, to her Majesty's honour, and the further advancement of the commercial credit of the realm.

These wise regulations, of course, abolished the office of queen's agent for money-matters in foreign parts: but Elizabeth, to show her high regard for Sir Thomas Gresham, and that he might not lose the dignity of a public character in the city, put him into a commission with the Archbishop of Canterbury. . . . This honour he held, as occasion required, from 1572 to 1578.

He had now acquired very considerable landed property in some of the distant counties; but his activity of mind would not permit him to be absent long together from the bustle of the mercantile world. He loved to visit his favourite Exchange, and to associate with merchants: upon which account, instead of retiring to any of his new purchases, he built a magnificent seat at Osterley Park, near Brentford in Middlesex. . . . Here he indulged himself with short intervals of relaxation, but his mind was always so full of plans for the promotion of useful industry, that even here he made business part of his amusement: for within his park he erected paper, oil, and corn-mills, thus liberally finding constant employment for various descriptions of workmen, who were at all times devoted to his service. . . .

John M. Keynes

ROY HARROD

John Maynard Keynes—one of the most brilliant phenomena in the modern world of economics—was also a splendidly original and successful investor. Needing financial independence in order to afford his expensive tastes, Keynes turned to finance, and in particular to speculation in currencies, to create the affluence he needed. This sketch presents an engaging account of the early segments of Keynes' quest.

Although he entered with zest into his teaching work, and enjoyed it thoroughly, Keynes had never felt attracted by the prospect of the life of an ordinary college tutor. Something had always beckoned him to a wider field of action. Could he not find a way of combining his work for King's College, which he loved, with other work in London, which might be more remunerative and would keep him in touch with the center of affairs?

Money was certainly a problem. He had no inheritance and, so far, had had no business connections. But he felt that his experience in the Treasury could be turned to good account; one who had managed the external finances of the nation during the war with acknowledged success would surely have some market value in the world of finance. He must look around. By temperament he was courageous and always ready to take risks. In June 1919, he decided to reduce his university and college commitments, in the hope that something would turn up.

During August and September he was immersed in writing his famous book (*The Economic Consequences of the Peace*), but not so immersed that his mind could not dwell on other matters also. Early in August he began a new career, which he was not to relinquish for many years, that of a speculator. Depositing a modest cover with O.T. Falk's firm, he began buying and selling foreign currencies forward in large quantities. His operations included

Excerpted from Roy Harrod, *Fortune*, December 1950, pp. 113–114, 174–176. Reprinted by permission of Time, Inc.

the rupee, the dollar, the French franc, the mark, the lira, and the Dutch florin. Broadly, he tended to be a bull of dollars and a bear of the European currencies. His trading was active and continuous, large amounts being bought and sold every few days, but it was always based on his judgment as an economist, and not on rumors of the market place. He soon found that he was making substantial profits.

In September, through the intervention of Mr. Falk, he was invited to join the Board of the National Mutual Life Insurance Co., of which he became Chairman in 1921, a position he retained until 1938. His financial career was beginning.

Macmillan was doing his book. He was anxious that the first edition should be a large one and consist of at least 5,000 copies. He had confidence that it would interest the public. After discussion it was agreed that he should take the risk himself and pay for the publication, giving Macmillan a royalty of 10 percent. By paying for the publication he gave himself the prospect of much bigger profits, should the sales prove large. In the long run this arrangement with Macmillan was highly advantageous for him, since his other books were published on the same basis.

The Economic Consequences appeared in England at the end of 1919, and a month later in the United States. Its impact on the public mind was immediate and its reception tremendous. Long reviews appeared in all the papers, in the United States sometimes with banner headlines. For a month it was the main topic of conversation.

In the Easter vacation, 1920, he went to Rome with Duncan Grant and Vanessa Bell. These settled down to painting, while Keynes spent much of his time in a social round. He was feted by Italian liberals as a great man. He found at the British Embassy an old King's man, Mr. Haslam, and they had much to talk of. This revival of an acquaintanceship had further consequences, for on Mr. Haslam's return to England a couple of years later he proposed to the Provincial Insurance Co. that Keynes and Mr. Falk should be invited to act as economic advisers. In 1923 Keynes joined the Board and became president of their Finance Committee, where he guided the investment policy of the company. He remained a member of the board throughout his life, and this was one of his City connections that he valued most.

Good news came to Rome of his financial speculations. Since leaving England he had made a profit on francs of about £22,000 to set against losses on dollars of about £8,000. He was "indulging in an orgy of shopping of all kinds of objects which in spite of the difficulty of getting them to England are amazingly cheap. I should think we have bought about a ton so far, including quantities of furniture." When tired of gaieties, he went with the others to the Sabine hills and thereafter proceeded to the Berensons'. Thus the ways of peace were revived, and his personal prospects seemed fair.

Soon after his return to England they became overcast. His speculations were based on his judgment of economic trends, but they were carried out in day-to-day operations with a very narrow margin of cover. This technique was not really suited to the basis on which his risks were taken. At least he would require the most consummate skill if he was to match the one to the other. In the later days of May the dollar showed an obstinate refusal to appreciate, and the mark showed an obstinate refusal to depreciate. It was contrary to reason, but such was the case. The mark underwent a surprising and substantial revival. . . .

The movement of the mark at this time may merely have been a reaction from its earlier collapse; the other continental currencies also showed an upward tendency. All these movements were short-lived, and when another three months had elapsed the previous trends had been resumed.

Keynes could not wait for three months. As the later days of May ebbed away, it became clear that he was ruined. Between the beginning of April and the end of May he had lost £13,125. A small syndicate, for part of the resources of which he was morally responsible, also lost £8,498. Previous gains were wiped out, and his small cover. Sales had to be effected. His firm asked him to pay in £7,000 to keep the account open. It gave him favorable treatment, which helped to carry him through.

It is clear that, in the last resort, such a call was not beyond the means of his parents. Dr. Keynes (his father) had capital and would be ready to help. Keynes himself argued in retrospect that at the worst point his own assets were just enough to meet his liabilities, on the assumption that he sold all his pictures, books, and other possessions; there may have been a little wishful thinking here. However, the position was clearly not irretrievable. It would indeed have been a disaster if the man who had so recently set world opinion agog by claiming to know better than the mighty of the land had himself become involved in bankruptcy. One can imagine the banner headlines. He was never really near such complete disaster.

In this event the call of his firm was met in part by a loan of £5,000 from a famous financier, with whom he had no close personal relations but who knew, through a third party, of his work at Paris and admired it greatly. This was repaid in December. For the rest he had another resource. There was *The Economic Consequences of the Peace*. He had already had large sales in England, and in the course of business Macmillan had advanced him £1,000. That had already gone. The publisher would not ordinarily settle Keynes's account till after July 1. He wrote to request an advance settlement in respect of what was due. He promptly received a check for £1,500. Did he finger it lovingly? This was the reward for his masterpiece, a work of passion and anguish of spirit. He had torn himself away from the hateful coils of Paris in order to drain all his resources of knowledge and skill and art into persuading the world to be more wise and generous. It was the great work of his life so far; perhaps he would not achieve such another. There was the £1,500 lying on his desk. It was a just reward. But it was no longer his. It would be paid into his bank and at once paid out again, to swell the balances of those sagacious persons who thought that the mark had a rosy future and the dollar a poor one.

His parents, whom he took into his confidence about the setback, did not offer reproaches but advised caution in the coming year. We may be confident that he had learned his lesson. The intellectual apparatus would be brought to bear to make quite sure that this would not recur. To expect caution was perhaps asking too much—this was beyond his range; prudence he might conceivably achieve. Within a few weeks he was deeply in again, working on the same general lines. He was temperamentally daring and confident of his own reasoning. It would have been against his nature not to back it with all he had. Besides, this was his fight for freedom. He had no inheritance that he could enlarge by more orthodox financial methods. In the previous year there had been some hint that he might be offered a place on the board of one of the great British banks; his book had made that quite out of the question now. He was determined not to relapse into salaried drudgery. He must be financially independent. He felt that he had that in him which would justify such independence. He had many things to tell the nation. And he wanted a sufficiency. He must be able to take stalls at the Russian ballet whenever he wished—and entertain the dancers, if that struck his fancy. He must be able to buy his friends' pictures—and pay them handsomely. These other dealers in money merely squandered their earnings on banal conventional luxuries. He must use his brains to put some of their money into his pocket, where it would fructify, not only financially but in supporting the arts and people who really mattered, and in giving his own powers scope.

So he went deeply in. By the end of 1924 he reckoned that the value of his assets, after deducting his large overdrafts and not counting pictures and books, was £57,797. By the beginning of 1937 it was £506,450. He died in 1946 leaving about £450,000, if we include the value of pictures and books.

It is proper to mention that from time to time rumors have circulated among those who did not know Keynes well that he made his fortune by using inside information when in the Treasury. Such rumors were especially apt to occur among those who disagreed with his opinions on political economy. They may be scotched by the facts.

He had no foot in the Treasury (or any other official position) between June 1919, and July 1940. His speculative account opened on August 14, 1919, and his fortune reached its peak in 1937.

We may add that to those who knew him at all well the charge appears quite fantastic. He was punctiliously honorable in all financial matters. Not only would it have been entirely inconsistent with his character to have taken advantage of official information, but he had a certain idiosyncrasy, well known to those who worked closely with him, which made it extremely distasteful to him to use ordinary "inside" business information acquired in a straightforward manner. This was partly based on intellectual grounds. He believed that the safest way to earn was to consider a proposition in the light of the general economic situation and his own judgment as to how that would develop, and to back his judgment. He believed that inside information more often than not led investors astray. It was a favorite dictum of his in the thirties that "the dealers on Wall Street could make huge fortunes if only they had no inside information!"

There was also a moral side to this idiosyncrasy. There seemed to him to be something wrong in taking advantage of special knowledge, even when that knowledge had been gained in a thoroughly proper way in the ordinary course of business. It was not quite playing the game. The game was to pit one's intelligence against others who had the same public information at their disposal, so that the reward, when it came, would be subject to the inevitable risks, the prize of superior judgment.

In the management of his own capital the aim in early days was to get a quick enlargement of capital, and the method one of extreme boldness, decisions being taken on an economic appraisal of the general situation. At the bursary of King's College he had to look at matters very differently. Extremely long-term considerations were all-important. He soon acquired a dominating influence over investment policy there, becoming First Bursar in 1924.

In the case of the National Mutual and the Provincial insurance companies, he had a different problem again. As with the college, caution was necessary—he was prepared to cultivate this virtue when dealing with money not his own. But in the case of the insurance companies much greater stress had to be laid on liquidity. His success in increasing the revenues of King's was spectacular, and the insurance companies also prospered. It is fair to add that his own capital and that of the institutions whose investments he managed felt the full brunt of the slump of 1929–1931. In all cases there were large advances thereafter beyond the pre-slump positions.

Keynes gave zealous and unremitting attention to these investment problems. He had the difficult intellectual task of keeping distinct his three strands of thought, that relating to his own affairs, that relating to the college, and that relating to the insurance companies. To most men this would seem well-nigh impossible, and there were moments when even Keynes complained that he had set himself too hard a task. Yet we may be sure that basically this very difficulty kept his interest alive in it. It afforded the kind of intellectual conundrum that he thoroughly enjoyed. His work was performed in bed in the morning. Financial intelligence came to him from the various brokers and he assimilated the information provided by the newspapers. He pondered upon the implications of what he learned, and made his decisions. He reckoned that the whole business took him about half an hour each morning.

George Ross Goobey

ALASTAIR ROSS GOOBEY

George Ross Goobey was a large man, obviously an athlete even in his 80s, with an engaging, forceful personality to match. He was also a great storyteller who has combined a rare ability to think deeply about central issues and form independent judgments with a gift for persuading others to accept his decisions. In 1948, for example, he persuaded his trustees to buy equities before the great postwar bull market commenced and to sell Daltons (or "consols," the perpetual, nonredeemable Treasury bond) before they lost three-quarters of their value. Later, his advice took them for the first time into the property market. His son, himself a money manager, wrote this sketch.

Born in 1911 into a nonconformist shopkeeping family in London's East End, Ross Goobey's opportunity came with entrance to Christ's Hospital, the famous Bluecoat charity school in Sussex. An able mathematician but unable to go to university through family circumstances, Ross Goobey joined the British Equitable, a proprietary life office, as an actuarial student in 1928. The years of exams on paltry pay were a struggle, especially since a distinguished sporting career and the War intervened; and it was not until 1941 that he actually qualified as an actuary, having worked for, among others, Legal and General and the Royal Exchange Assurance, which took over British Equitable. . . .

In 1948 he was appointed investment manager of Imperial Tobacco Pension Fund, based in Bristol and then valued at £12 million. Like so many pension funds of the time, the fund, although based on final salaries, was almost exclusively invested in gilt-edged stock [i.e., in Britain, government bonds] which at the end of the 1940s was giving a running yield of less than the current yield on the equity market. The premise on which this yield gap was based was that inflation, after the wartime boost, was going to settle to the nil to negative trend it had followed between 1921 and 1938. At the beginning of 1948 undated gilts yielded 3.0 percent, and an average portfolio of UK equities, based on the de Zoete and Bevan Equity Fund, yielded 4.3 percent. The prevalent wisdom of the time was that equities should have a higher initial yield than gilts because they were more 'risky' than gilt-edged stocks, which were after all guaranteed by the government. What Ross Goobey had realised from a reading of two papers given at the Institute of

Excerpted from Alastair Ross Goobey, *The Money Moguls*, Woodhead-Faulkner, date unknown, pp. 72–74.

Actuaries by H. E. Raynes of Legal and General, in 1927 and again in 1937, was the undoubted fact that, even in periods of deflation, dividends of companies had risen in real terms, and in periods of inflation, modest though that inflation might be, dividends on company shares had risen in real terms, and of course in absolute terms: the consequence had been that the higher initial yield on the portfolio of equities had been but the starting point of their advantage over gilts.

He presented the facts to the investment committee of Imperial, a conservative body of men headed by R. J. ("Rab") Sinclair, later Lord Sinclair of Cleeve, and P. J. Grigg, the former minister in Churchill's Wartime Government. Ross Goobey carefully briefed and convinced Grigg, the critical committee member who was also a director of the Prudential Assurance. Despite the misgivings of some of the committee members, the recommendation to switch the portfolio from gilts to equity stocks was approved. One of the stumbling blocks was the reluctance of some members to take the loss of £1 million on book cost that the gilt portfolio . . . would have to suffer.

The consequence of this astonishing change in policy from the accepted wisdom of the time was very positive for the fund, and for Ross Goobey's reputation. He has become known as the Father of the Equity, although he would say that there were others at the time who may have had similar views, but not such foresighted trustees. The portfolio which Ross Goobey built up in the next ten years would give a modern portfolio manager the vapours; he bought shares in almost every company quoted at the time. As he says now, the market was a lot less sophisticated, and research into equity shares almost unknown; indeed, it was not until the 1960s that brokers ceased calling their modest research efforts the statistical department. The yield on the fund, the only basis on which performance was measured in those days, rose dramatically over the next 15 years, moving into double figures on cost—this in a period of lowish inflation. In the 1960s, Ross Goobey was also among the leaders of the move to take pension funds into the direct property market. . . .

The interesting point about Ross Goobey's career is that, despite being perhaps the best-known man in his field, he remained an employee of Imperial until he retired. At one point he was offered a full-time directorship of M. Samuel, the merchant bank which merged with Philip Hill, Higginson, Erlanger to become Hill Samuel; he was sorely tempted by the money involved but felt some loyalty to Imperial, which responded by allowing him to become a non-executive director of M. Samuel and, in due course, by promoting him on to the main board of Imperial Tobacco.

Georges F. Doriot

GENE BYLINSKY

Georges Doriot, who taught a course at Harvard Business School simply called "Manufacturing" from 1926 to 1966, presided over the growth of American Research & Development Corp. (the first public venture capital company). He inspired many to conceive of business as an adventure of commitment and charmed all with his Gallic, Lutheran, humorist style.

General Doriot, as he is widely known (he won the rank of brigadier general as a U.S. Army reserve officer in World War II), puts much more than money into new companies and expects to get much more than money out. He has no use for easily attained wealth. He's much more concerned with guiding scientist-dreamers and keeping up their enthusiasm and hopes just when those hopes need nurturing. He is, in short, not a man looking for a fast return on his money, but a nursemaid of dreams.

But as the driving force of ARD [American Research & Development Corp.], Doriot has demonstrated how a highly personal, patient upbringing of new companies can pay off in terms of money too. Infant enterprises in which ARD has invested have pioneered in the manufacture of atom smashers and novel machines to desalt brackish water, have been among the first to make small transistorized computers, and have led in the design of pallets for air freight. While they were making their contributions to technological innovation, many of them have performed well—some spectacularly—in the stock market. And there are more promising entrants coming along to keep ARD's net-asset value climbing.

In the beginning, ARD's performance was anything but spectacular. In 1947, its first full year of operation, the company realized a net capital gain of $87; it lost $241,228 in 1950, made $138,414 the year following, lost $1,436 in 1954. But since 1955, ARD has consistently reported gains, and it made a record $2,555,134 last year. Its net asset value, just under $3,400,000 at the end of its first year, zoomed to $93 million at the end of 1966 and continued to $160 million by the end of this year's first quarter. In one way or another and at one time or another, ARD has involved itself in the affairs of 97 companies. Today it has an interest in 45. In only six of

Excerpted from Gene Bylinsky, *Fortune*, August 1967, pp. 103–107 & 130–136. Reprinted by permission of Time Inc.

these does it list its investments below their original cost—a showing that most venture capitalists would envy.

It is typical of Doriot's approach, however, that he does not let himself be overwhelmed by good fortune. "Success is a very dangerous period," he is fond of remarking. "It goes to our heads." And in any case, sensational performance in the stock market is not his measure of success. Many other venture capitalists think in terms of getting a desired rate of return from their investments within a specified time. Not Doriot. He often refers to his companies as "children" (he is married but childless himself). "When you have a child, you don't ask what return you can expect," he says. "Of course you have hopes—you hope the children will become President of the United States. But that is not very probable. I want them to do outstandingly well in their field. And if they do, the rewards will come. But if a man is good and loyal and does not achieve a so-called good rate of return, I will stay with him. Some people don't become geniuses until *after* they are 24, you know. If I were a speculator, the question of return would apply. But I don't consider a speculator—in my definition of the word— constructive. I am building men and companies."

"Your sophisticated stockholders make five points and sell out," he scoffs. "But we have our hearts in our companies, we are really doctors of childhood diseases here. When bankers or brokers tell me I should sell an ailing company, I ask them, 'Would you sell a child running a temperature of 104?' "

• • •

In applying this operating philosophy, Doriot constantly surprises people. He impatiently dismisses the idea, which even preoccupies some of his scientist-dreamers, that a new company should show profits from the start. Sometimes a beaming young industrialist will rush in to trumpet proudly the news of early success—only to be knocked back on his heels by the soft, French-accented warning, "That may do you a lot of harm."

Something of an ascetic himself, Doriot worries that his "boys," the young scientists and engineers, will succumb to the temptations of early success. He fears that their efforts will slacken and that "they'll start buying 20-cylinder Cadillacs, 50-room mansions, go skiing in summer, and swimming in winter."

These fears, in most cases, have proved spectacularly unjustified. . . . ARD's original investment of $70,000 in Digital Equipment had rocketed by early summer to a market value of about $125 million, an 1,800-fold increase.

Naturally, not all ARD-financed companies have done that well; a few have been painful disappointments. Some years ago ARD poured $1,600,000 into the stock of a tape-recorder manufacturer called Magnecord, Inc. . . . By the time ARD got out it had lost more than a million dollars. The Magnecord situation, says Doriot, "was poorly handled." It was also a case of Doriot's becoming too enamored with a company, a failing to which he admits.

• • •

If Doriot's approach is unusual, so is the base from which he operates. When ARD was started by a group of pioneering Bostonians in 1946, very few investors were prepared to put their capital into venture situations. . . .

Doriot, although no scientist (he did study mathematics, physics, and chemistry in college, however), was recruited at first as chairman of the board of advisers. He had originally been the ARD board's choice for president, but be couldn't assume that job right away because he was still in the Army. . . .

At the Pentagon, Doriot had served first as director of military planning for the Quartermaster General, and later as deputy director of research and development for the War Department General Staff. He gained a reputation for spurring on researchers and production men to accomplish things they didn't think they could do. "When one little unit was in trouble, he'd spend three weeks on it and it would blossom," recalls a wartime colleague. He was an innovator, too. Under his supervision the Army developed, among other things, new dehydrated foods and uniforms with new thermal properties and abrasion resistance.

• • •

Stimulating people, inspiring them to delve into the future, often startling them with his seemingly unorthodox beliefs and techniques—these had long been Doriot trademarks. He was born in Paris almost 68 years ago, the son of a pioneering automotive engineer. His parents, both Lutherans, were strict disciplinarians. . . . Doriot recalls that his father would spank him when he wasn't first in his class. "I am still scared, and have been ever since I was eight years old, of classrooms and professors."

Nevertheless, Doriot became a professor himself. After coming to the United States in 1921, he graduated from the Harvard Graduate School of Business Administration, became an instructor there, and advanced to the post of assistant dean. Along the way he acquired a number of directorships in companies, and even served as president of McKeesport Tin Plate Corp. and chairman of National Can Corp. for a short time before leaving for the Pentagon. He managed to combine these business activities with teaching, and remained on the faculty at Harvard until last year. He taught so memorably and controversially that many old-time students who have forgotten other professors' names still remember Doriot vividly.

The course he taught was ostensibly about how to run a company. But in fact it consisted of a series of lectures expounding Doriot views on life, business, and even on picking a wife. He hammered into his students' heads three main themes: self-improvement, attention to detail in daily work, and an active concern with the future. . . .

Doriot himself maintains a work pace that would tire a man 40 years younger. He is up at seven and soon is walking briskly from his home on Beacon Hill across the Public Garden to the stately John Hancock Building, where ARD has its offices on the twenty-third floor. During the day he talks with investment bankers, university professors, patent lawyers, hopeful would-be industrialists, and coaches his staff on dealing with people and problems in the affiliate companies. He usually eats lunch in a cafeteria in his building. At night, he takes papers home to read, and occasionally paints with a palette knife when he can't sleep or doesn't feel like working. He ordinarily goes to sleep at eleven, but regularly wakes up at two "to worry," and starts scribbling notes on a blue pad in the dark.

● ● ●

The decisions Doriot is called upon to make require plenty of contemplation. First, and foremost, he has to decide where to put ARD's money. There is never a shortage of ideas, but in the Doriot scheme men rank first and ideas second.

But Doriot looks for specific attributes in people: a combination of courage and caution, endurance, imagination, and above all resourcefulness. "A man comes in here and says he invented the pencil," says Doriot. "Okay. What I want to know is whether he can improve the pencil. If the pencil goes out of fashion, can he have another idea?"

Judging ideas goes hand in hand with judging men. Doriot and his aides keep abreast of the latest technological developments, and they meet hopeful industrialists with an open mind. "We're good listeners," says Doriot. And when in doubt themselves, they can always call on first-rate scientists for advice.

It is easier, Doriot believes, to find a field of interest than to locate the proper vehicle to exploit it. Since such a vehicle must be manned by "grade-A" men, only a few hopeful industrialists wind up in the ARD starting line. Of the uncounted thousands of proposals received, it has investigated about 4,700 and invested in less than 100.

● ● ●

When it decides to back a brand-new company, ARD may buy voting control, but this does not mean it will run the company. "ARD directors on my board don't try to enforce a party line," says the president of one small firm. If a company is an already functioning enterprise, ARD usually invests in less than 50 percent of its stock. A favorite way of financing is to give a fledgling firm a loan, repayable in installments usually with options or warrants to purchase stock.

Sometimes ARD's terms for buying into a company sound pretty harsh. The founders of Digital Equipment, for instance, sold 78 percent of their company for $70,000. But like many other men whom ARD helped get started, they put up only a few hundred dollars of their own money, and they wound up millionaires.

• • •

The preliminaries of setting up a new company are the easiest part of the job, as far as Doriot is concerned. An avalanche of problems is unleashed when the company finally starts operating. . . . "Many of our companies have been close to sudden death at least once. In a small company human failures and weaknesses often are magnified in inverse proportion to the size of a company." . . .

At this stage, Doriot's role is to "watch, push, worry, and spread hope."

• • •

Ordinarily, ARD shies away from changing the top management of a company it backs. . . . On the other hand, ARD often considers it a good idea to put in experienced business and financial managers. In a company run by scientists and engineers, this usually meets with strong resistance. . . . As a last resort, ARD has tried to force management changes, especially in companies where it had voting control. . . .

ARD has a small staff that not only watches over investments but actively lends a hand when a company needs assistance. . . . They would never actually try to run a company, but they often serve as on-the-spot expert consultants. . . .

What its fledglings most appreciate in ARD is its way of encouraging them even in the dark days when the balance sheet looks disappointing—of "picking us up off the floor after we had been dropped," as one president puts it. "This is a lonely job and there aren't many people I can talk to about the problems," says another. "I got plenty of psychic income from Doriot—and that was very important."

Benvenuto Cellini

BENVENUTO CELLINI

Investors have been misled, conned, and deceived in many ways for many years, but few have fallen prey to as devious a group of rascals as did the great sculptor Benvenuto Cellini—who recounts this tale of woe in a passage from his autobiography.

It pleased God, who rules all things for our good—I mean, for those who acknowledge and believe in Him; such men never fail to gain His protection—that about this time a certain rascal from Vicchio called Piermaria d'Anterigoli, and surnamed Lo Sbietta, introduced himself to me. He is a sheep-grazier; and being closely related to Messer Guido Guidi, the physician, who is now provost of Pescia, I lent ear to his proposals. The man offered to sell me a farm of his for the term of my natural life. I did not care to go and see it, since I wanted to complete the model of my colossal Neptune. There was also no reason why I should visit the property, because Sbietta only sold it to me for the income.[1] This he had noted down as so many bushels of grain, so much of wine, oil, standing corn, chestnuts, and other produce. I reckoned that, as the market then ran, these together were worth something considerably over 100 golden crowns in gold; and I paid him 650 crowns, which included duties to the state. Consequently, when he left a memorandum written in his own hand, to the effect that he would always keep up these products of the farm in the same values during my lifetime, I did not think it necessary to inspect it. Only I made inquiries, to the best of my ability, as to whether Sbietta and his brother Ser Filippo were well off enough to give me good security. Many persons, of divers sorts, who knew them, assured me that my security was excellent. We agreed to call in Ser Pierfrancesco Bertoldi, notary at the Mercantanzia; and at the very first I handed him Sbietta's memorandum, expecting that this would be recited in the deed. But the notary who drew it up was so occupied with detailing 22 boundaries described by Sbietta,[2] that, so far as I can judge, he neglected to include in the contract

---

Reprinted from *The Autobiography of Benvenuto Cellini* translated by John Addington Symonds (1927), Chapters 102, 103, and 104, pp. 463–68, by permission of Random House, New York.

[1] What Cellini means is that Sbietta was to work the farm, paying Cellini its annual value. It appears from some particulars which follow that the entrate were to be paid in kind.

[2] The word confini, which I have translated "boundaries," may mean limiting conditions.

what the vendor had proposed to furnish. While he was writing, I went on working; and since it took him several hours, I finished a good piece of my Neptune's head.

After the contract was signed and sealed, Sbietta began to pay me the most marked attentions, which I returned in like measure. He made me presents of kids, cheese, capons, fresh curds, and many sorts of fruit, until I began to be almost ashamed of so much kindness. In exchange for these courtesies, I always took him from the inn to lodge with me when he came into Florence, often inviting a relative or two who happened to attend him. On one of these occasions he told me with a touch of pleasantry that it was really shameful for me to have bought a farm, and, after the lapse of so many weeks not yet to have left my business for three days in the hands of my work-people, so as to have come to look at it. His wheedling words and ways induced me to set off, in a bad hour for my welfare, on a visit to him. Sbietta received me in his own house with such attentions and such honours as a duke might covet. His wife caressed me even more than he did; and these excellent relations continued between us until the plans which he and his brother Ser Filippo had in mind were fully matured.

• • •

Meanwhile I did not suspend my labours on the Neptune, which was now quite blocked out upon an excellent system, undiscovered and unknown before I used it. Consequently . . . I hoped to have it soon completed, and to display it on the piazza simply for my satisfaction.

It was a warm and pleasant season; and this, together with the attentions of those two rascals, disposed me to set out one Wednesday, which happened to be a double holiday, for my country-house at Trespiano.[3] Having spent some time over an excellent lunch, it was past twenty o'clock when I reached Vicchio. There, at the town-gate, I met Ser Filippo, who appeared to know already whither I was bound. He loaded me with attentions, and took me to Sbietta's house, when I found that fellow's strumpet of a wife, who also overwhelmed me with caresses. I gave the woman a straw hat of the very finest texture, the like of which she told me she had never seen. Still, up to this time, Sbietta had not put in his appearance.

Toward the end of the afternoon we all sat down to supper in excellent spirits. Later on, they gave me a well-appointed bedroom, where I went to rest in a bed of the most perfect cleanliness. Both of my servants, according to their rank, were equally well treated. On the morrow, when I rose, the same attentions were paid me. I went to see my farm, which pleased me much; and then I had some quantities of grain and other produce handed over. But when I returned to Vicchio, the priest Ser Filippo said to me:

---

[3]From Cellini's Ricordi it appears that he bought a farm at this village, northeast of Florence, on October 26, 1548. In 1556, he also purchased land there.

"Benvenuto, do not be uneasy; although you have found here not quite everything you had the right to look for, yet put your mind to rest; it will be amply made up in the future, for you have to deal with honest folk: You ought, by the way, to know that we have sent that labourer away, because he was a scoundrel." The labourer in question bore the name of Mariano Rosegli; and this man now kept frequently repeating in my ear: "Look well after yourself; in the end you will discover which of us here is the greatest villain." The country-fellow, when he spoke those words, smiled with an evil kind of sneer, and jerked his head as though to say: "Only go up there, and you will find out for yourself."

I was to some extent unfavorably influenced by these hints, yet far from forming a conception of what actually happened to me. So, when I returned from the farm, which is two miles distant from Vicchio, toward the Alpi,[4] I met the priest, who was waiting for me with his customary politeness. We then sat down together to breakfast; it was not so much a dinner as an excellent collation. Afterward I took a walk through Vicchio—the market had just opened—and noticed how all the inhabitants fixed their eyes upon me, as on something strange. This struck me particularly in the case of a worthy old man, who has been living for many years at Vicchio, and whose wife bakes bread for sale. He owns some good property at the distance of about a mile; however, he prefers this mode of life, and occupies a house which belongs to me in the town of Vicchio. This had been consigned to me together with the farm above mentioned, which bears the name of Della Fonte. The worthy old man spoke as follows: "I am living in your house, and when it falls due I shall pay you your rent; but if you want it earlier, I will act according to your wishes. You may reckon on never having any disputes with me." While we were thus talking I noticed that he looked me hard in the face, which compelled me to address him thus: "Prithee, tell me, friend Giovanni, why you have more than once stared at me in that way?" He replied: "I am quite willing to tell you, if, being the man of worth I take you for, you will promise not to say that I have told you." I gave the promise and he proceeded: "You must know then that that worthless priest, Ser Filippo, not many days since, went about boasting of his brother Sbietta's cleverness, and telling how he had sold his farm to an old man for his lifetime, and that the purchaser could hardly live the year out. You have got mixed up with a set of rogues; therefore take heed to living as long as you are able, and keep your eyes open, for you have need of it. I do not choose to say more."

• • •

During my promenade through the market, I met Giovan Battista Santini, and he and I were taken back to supper by the priest. . . . We supped at the early hour of twenty, because I made it known that I meant to return to

---

[4]The Alpi are high mountain pastures in the Apennines.

Trespiano. Accordingly they made all ready; the wife of Sbietta went bustling about in the company of one Cecchino Buti, their knave of all work. After the salads had been mixed and we were preparing to sit down to table, that evil priest, with a certain nasty sort of grin, exclaimed: "I must beg you to excuse me, for I cannot sup with you; the reason is that some business of importance has occurred which I must transact for my brother Sbietta. In his absence I am obliged to act for him." We all begged him to stay, but could not alter his determination; so he departed and we began our supper. After we had eaten the salads on some common platters, and they were preparing to serve the boiled meat, each guest received a porringer for himself. Santini, who was seated opposite me at table, exclaimed: "Do you notice that the crockery they give you is different from the rest? Did you ever see anything handsomer?" I answered that I had not noticed it. He also prayed me to invite Sbietta's wife to sit down with us; for she and that Cecchino Buti kept running hither and thither in the most extraordinary fuss and hurry. At last I induced the woman to join us; when she began to remonstrate: "You do not like my victuals, since you eat so little." I answered by praising the supper over and over again, and saying that I had never eaten better or with heartier appetite. Finally, I told her that I had eaten quite enough. I could not imagine why she urged me so persistently to eat. After supper was over, and it was past the hour of twenty-one, I became anxious to return to Trespiano, in order that I might recommence my work next morning in the Loggia. Accordingly I bade farewell to all the company, and having thanked our hostess, took my leave.

I had not gone three miles before I felt as though my stomach was on fire, and suffered such pain that it seemed a thousand years till I arrived at Trespiano. However, it pleased God that I reached it after nightfall with great toil, and immediately proceeded to my farm, where I went to bed. During the night I got no sleep, and was constantly disturbed by the motions of my bowels. When day broke, feeling an intense heat in the rectum, I looked eagerly to see what this might mean, and found the cloth covered with blood. Then in a moment I conceived that I had eaten something poisonous, and racked my brains to think what it could possibly have been. It came back to my memory how Sbietta's wife had set before me plates, and porringers, and saucers different from the others, and how that evil priest, Sbietta's brother, after giving himself such pains to do me honour, had yet refused to sup with us. Furthermore, I remembered what the priest had said about Sbietta's doing such a fine stroke of business by the sale of his farm to an old man for life, who could not be expected to survive a year. Giovanni Sardella had reported these words to me. All things considered, I made my mind up that they must have administered a dose of sublimate in the sauce, which was very well made and pleasant to the taste, inasmuch as sublimate produces all the symptoms I was suffering from. Now it is my custom to take but little sauce or seasoning with my meat, excepting salt; and yet I had eaten two moderate mouthfuls of that sauce because it was so tasteful. On further thinking, I recollected how often that wife of Sbietta had teased me in a hundred ways to partake more freely of the sauce. On these accounts I felt absolutely certain that they had given me sublimate in that very dish.

• • •

They attended me more than six full months, and I remained more than a whole year before I could enjoy my life and vigour.

Ulysses S. Grant

DANA THOMAS

> Ulysses S. Grant may have suspected that Wall Street played him for a patsy during and after his two terms as President of the United States—and he would have been right.
>
>   The final blow came when the brokerage house in which he was a figurehead partner went bankrupt, leaving him bewildered, penniless, and deeply in debt. He repaid those debts in a final heroic act, writing his Civil War memoirs while dying of throat cancer. The memoirs, published by Mark Twain in two volumes, were best sellers.

Ferdinand Ward, sizing up the General as an ideal front man, became friendly with Buck Grant, the General's son. Ward was introduced to the General through Buck, flattered the old man and suggested that he go into the brokerage business with him. The General was told that he need not do any work but simply lend the prestige of his name.

As soon as the brokerage firm of Grant & Ward was organized, Ward began using Grant's name as an "open sesame" to wangle influential connections. He went to New Yorkers who had substantial bank balances, offering them a chance to invest with him in ventures that would bring big profits but which, he hinted, were of a delicate nature. They had to be handled quietly because they involved Government contracts and quasi-political deals. Ward implied that Grant's influence in high Washington circles would bring home the bacon but that the General's role had to be

From pp. 48–52, 161–7, 232–9 from *The Plungers and the Peacocks (Revised Ed.)* by Dana Thomas. Copyright © 1989 by Dana Thomas. Reprinted by permission of HarperCollins Publishers, Inc. & William Morrow.

kept in strict confidence since he could very possibly be nominated for a third term in the White House and the disclosure of these dealings would provide ammunition for his political enemies.

The story about Government deals was a fabrication. Ward was doing nothing more than putting his investors' money into ventures open to anybody without any political influence. For a time he did a profitable business, repaying his clients handsomely. But then he went into several unfortunate speculations; he lost heavily in Southern mining shares and West Shore bonds. And, finding it impossible to continue to pay dividends legitimately, he began borrowing money at exorbitant interest rates, hoping to make a big enough killing in the market to wipe out his debts. When this failed, he resorted to a shopworn device, paying his earlier investors out of the capital of later arrivals. The technique worked for two years, during which the Grant family, assuming that everything was on the level, put its entire capital into the brokerage firm. On the books, between April 18, 1882, and May 1, 1884, Grant & Ward showed a fictitious profit of $2.6 million. Actually it was careening toward bankruptcy. Grant's savings continued to be poured down the drain. And, in addition to his father's money, Buck sank his own and his wife's cash into the brokerage house. Then, he borrowed $500,000 from his father-in-law, ex-Senator Chaffee, of Colorado, to put into the leaky ship.

By the spring of 1884, Ward was in serious trouble. He had borrowed large sums on collateral and had been rehypothecating his securities. To raise capital he had been discounting the firm's notes, paying up to 30 percent in interest. To add to his difficulties, the stock market went into a slump, eliminating any chance he had of getting his money back. A number of his clients who had been squeezed heavily in the market asked for the cash they had deposited with him.

Ward was on the board of directors of the Marine National Bank, whose president, James Fisk, had become involved with him, loaning him a major part of the bank's funds to try to shore him up. Now Fisk was at the end of his tether.

Ward came to the ex-President and put matters to him casually so as not to alarm him. He said that the Marine National Bank was in temporary trouble; it was short of a few hundred thousand dollars in its cash reserves. If Grant could borrow $150,000, Ward said he would try to raise an equal amount and the pressure on the bank would be relieved.

Grant accepted at face value Ward's assurance that this was merely a temporary crisis; suspecting no fraud, he decided to visit his old friend William Vanderbilt, the son of the Commodore, who had amassed the greatest fortune in America up to that time, in railroad operations. Ushered into Vanderbilt's office, the General wasted no time in coming to the point. He told Vanderbilt he urgently needed a loan and he offered him as security his war medals and other souvenirs of the battlefield.

Vanderbilt shrugged and said, "I don't care anything about the Marine National Bank. It can fail without disturbing me. And as for Grant & Ward—what I've heard about the firm would not justify me in lending a dime." He paused. "But for you, General Grant, I'll give $150,000 personally—on your word alone."

Vanderbilt's check was unable to halt the disaster. On Tuesday morning, May 6, the Marine National Bank suddenly closed its doors on stunned depositors. It had lent Grant & Ward over $4 million—most of it on uncollectible notes. The brokerage firm was bankrupt, with assets of $67,000 against liabilities of $16.7 million. Grant's own share in the business, which had been carried on the books at $2.6 million, had been whittled away to nothing. The failure of the firm touched off a sharp drop in the stock market. A chain reaction of bankruptcies hit financial houses that had been dealing with Grant & Ward or the Marine National Bank.

Grant was astonished. Not till the very last moment, when the brokerage house was on the verge of declaring bankruptcy, had the ex-President learned the true state of affairs. He hurried down to the offices to examine the books and see for himself the extent to which he had been hoodwinked. A mob of reporters gathered outside to cover his visit.

The General presented a tragic sight. He had fallen on the sidewalk in front of his home several months earlier and he was walking on crutches. Alexander Dana Noyes, a financial writer of the time, reported afterward in his reminiscences: "What followed is perhaps the most vivid picture in my own memories of Wall Street. The outer door slammed open. It admitted General Grant, followed by his Negro servant. Moving rapidly across the room on crutches . . . the General looked neither to the right nor the left. He made for the partners' private office, unaware that nobody was there. To me, it was a never-to-be forgotten picture . . . here, on this strange occasion, there was passing before us in a flash the stock figure with the grizzled beard and smoothed-down sandy hair which hundreds of magazine pictures had made as familiar as that of an everyday acquaintance. Probably all of us remembered at that moment the description by every war correspondent, of the inevitable cigar at which the General puffed reflectively on the eve of a battle; for as he moved across the room . . . (we noticed this at once) he held tightly clenched between his lips a cigar that had gone out. Nobody followed him or spoke to him, but everyone in the cynical, 'hard-boiled' group took off his hat as General Grant went by. I have always liked to think that this was not so much tribute of respect to a former Chief Magistrate as spontaneous recognition of the immense personal tragedy which was enacting itself before our eyes."

The Grants' savings were virtually wiped out. An old friend, the Mexican Ambassador, reading of the family's difficulties, paid a call and although Grant strenuously objected, left a check for $1,000. A stranger,

Charley Wood, sent a check for $1,000, requesting "that this amount be accepted as a loan on account of my share for services ending in April 1865."

Worried about Vanderbilt's $150,000 loan, Grant called on the financier and insisted on signing over all his assets, including the deed to his house on East 66th Street, his farm in Missouri, the trophies he had collected during the war. Vanderbilt refused, urging the General to forget the debt. But Grant insisted and a compromise was worked out. At Vanderbilt's suggestion, he agreed to turn over his war trophies to the Smithsonian Institution for the benefit of the nation.

It was an unhappy day when the moving van arrived to haul away the General's souvenirs. They had been lugged down to the parlor for a final look. Here were buttons snipped from the General's uniform—one for each battle he had taken part in. Here were the epaulettes he had worn during the siege of Richmond; his sword; a replica of the table in the farmhouse at Appomattox where he and Lee had signed the treaty ending hostilities. Here was the pen he had used to write his field orders; a medal awarded him by Congress after the Battle of Vicksburg. Here was a collection of Oriental money and a gift of ivory tusks from Siamese royalty. As piece by piece these objects were carried from the parlor and placed in the van to be carted away, tears filled the eyes of Mrs. Grant, and the General bowed his head.

His life was changed now. Gone was the carriage with the high-blooded horses, the retinue of servants and the other hallmarks of gracious living. The General brooded hour after hour over the tragedy he had inflicted on his family and the people who had invested with his firm. When ever anyone visited him, he would take him aside and speak bitterly of Ward's betrayal. He lived it over and over again like a recurrent hallucination.

Winston S. Churchill

WILLIAM MANCHESTER

Winston Churchill, often cited (including at least once by himself) as a Great Man, was *not* a Great Investor. He was a disaster, and would have been an even greater disaster had it not been for Bernard Baruch, as this story illustrates.

. . . . Men who have done something with their lives interest him—indeed, they are the only men who do. He is particularly impressed by military men; any winner of the Victoria Cross is embraced, and when he meets Sir Bernard Freyberg, the New Zealand war hero, Churchill insists that the embarrassed Freyberg strip so that his host can count his 33 battle scars. Similarly, men who have amassed fortunes while he has struggled year after year with creditors, hold enormous appeal for him. . . .

It . . . explains, in part, Winston's fondness for Baruch, though Baruch's appeal is broader. He is an American, he is Jewish, he recognizes the menace of an aggressive Germany, and Churchill is indebted to him for an extraordinary act of shrewdness and generosity. Winston was badly hurt in the Wall Street Crash three years ago. Had it not been for Baruch, however, it would have been much worse; he could have spent the rest of his life in debt. He is not a born gambler; he is a born *losing* gambler. In New York at the time, he dropped into Baruch's office and decided to play the market, and as prices tumbled he plunged deeper and deeper, trying to outguess the stock exchange just as he had tried to outguess roulette wheels on the Riviera. In Wall Street, as in Monte Carlo, he failed. At the end of the day, he confronted Baruch in tears. He was, he said, a ruined man. Chartwell and everything else he possessed must be sold; he would have to leave the House of Commons and enter business. The financier gently corrected him. Churchill, he said, had lost nothing. Baruch had left instructions to buy every time Churchill sold and sell whenever Churchill bought. Winston had come out exactly even because, he later learned, Baruch even paid the commissions.